The Joy of Bad Verse

THE JOY
OF BAD VERSE

Nicholas T. Parsons

COLLINS
8 Grafton Street, London W1
1988

William Collins Sons & Co. Ltd,
London · Glasgow · Sydney · Auckland
Toronto · Johannesburg

BRITISH LIBRARY CATALOGUING IN PUBLICATION DATA

The Joy of bad verse.
1. English poetry—18th century
2. English poetry—19th century
I. Parsons, Nicholas T.
821'.008   PR1215

ISBN 0 00 217863 X

First published in Great Britain 1988
Copyright © Nicholas T. Parsons 1988

Phototypeset by Ace Filmsetting Ltd, Frome, Somerset
Made and printed in Great Britain by
T. J. Press (Padstow) Ltd, Padstow, Cornwall

I know that poetry is indispensable,
but to what I could not say

All human race would fain be wits,
And millions miss, for one that hits.
Young's universal passion, pride,
Was never known to spread so wide.
Say, Britain, could you ever boast
Three poets in an age at most?

JONATHAN SWIFT –
On Poetry: A Rhapsody

This book is for Louis

CONTENTS

ACKNOWLEDGEMENTS

I am very grateful to the following, who made suggestions or rendered assistance in tracking down obscure items: Peter Branscombe, Peter Hanàk, Ken Lillington, and Katya Wilson. Leo Clarke, Peta Murray and Helen Swansbourne typed the manuscript with their usual efficiency. Special thanks are due to Paula Breslich and Kate Dunning who offered extended hospitality while I was engaged in research.

The author and publishers are grateful to the following who gave permission to quote from works still in copyright: Associated Book Publishers Ltd for extracts from the following works of the Rev E. E. Bradford: *Sonnets, Songs and Ballads, Passing the Love of Women, In Quest of Love, Lays of Love and Life, The New Chivalry, The Tree of Knowledge* and *The True Aristocracy*; Brown University, reprinted from *American Poetry in the Eighteen Nineties: A Study of American Verse, 1890–99* by Carlin T. Kindilien, by permission of University Press of New England. © 1956 Brown University; Jonathan Cape Ltd, the Hogarth Press, A. D. Peters & Co. Ltd, and the Executors of the Estate of C. Day Lewis for six lines from Part Three of *The Magnetic Mountain* published in *Collected Poems of C. Day Lewis*; the Estate of Jack Loudan and Chatto and Windus for an extract from *O Rare Amanda!*; Mrs Laura Huxley, Chatto and Windus and Harper and Row Inc. for extracts from *Texts and Pretexts* and *On the Margin* by Aldous Huxley; the Estate of Virginia Woolf, the Hogarth Press and Harcourt Brace Jovanovich Inc. for an extract from *The Common Reader* by Virginia Woolf; copyright 1925 by Harcourt Brace Jovanovich Inc.; renewed 1953 by Leonard Woolf. Norton B. Crowell for extracts from his book *Alfred Austin, Victorian* published by the University of New Mexico Press; Curtis Brown Ltd for eight lines from *Jubilee Hymn* and fourteen lines from *Queen Mother's Birthday* by Sir John Betjeman, copyright John Betjeman; Mail Newspapers plc for lines by C. Day Lewis published in the *Daily Mail*, 5 January 1968; J. M. Dent & Sons Ltd for extracts from *The Stuffed Owl* by D, B. Wyndham Lewis and Charles Lee, and extracts from *Everyman's Dictionary of Literary Biography* by D. C. Browning; the Estate of W. H. Auden for an extract from the Introduction to *Tennyson – A Selection* by W. H. Auden published by Phoenix House; Faber and Faber Limited and Random House Inc. for two lines from *City Without Walls* by W. H.

9

Auden, and Faber and Faber Limited and Harcourt Brace Jovanovich Inc. for an extract from 'Tradition and the Individual Talent' in *Selected Essays* by T. S. Eliot; Gale Research Company for an excerpt from 'Martin F. Tupper' by Patrick Scott in the *Dictionary of Literary Biography* Vol. 32, edited by William E. Fredeman and Ira B. Nadel (Copyright © Gale Research, 1984); Hodder and Stoughton and Curtis Brown Ltd for extracts from *The Public School Phenomenon* by Jonathan Gathorne-Hardy, © Jonathan Gathorne-Hardy, 1977; Lorrimer Publishing for extracts from *¡Viva Che!* – *Contributions in Tribute to Ernesto Che Guevara* edited by Marianne Alexandre; Macmillan Publishers and Schocken Books (published by Pantheon Books, a division of Random House Inc.), for an extract from *The Literature of Scotland* by Roderick Watson; Methuen London and Handmade Films for an extract from *The Life of Brian* by Monty Python (four lines from 'All Things Dull And Ugly'); *The Observer* for extracts from reviews by Malcolm Muggeridge and Bernard Levin. Penguin Books Ltd for an extract from *The Penguin Book of Victorian Verse* edited by George Macbeth; A. D. Peters & Co. Ltd for two lines from *Lilibet* by A Loyal Subject of Her Majesty published by Blond and Briggs; Laurence Pollinger Limited for an extract from *Splendid Poseur* by M. M. Marberry published by Frederick Muller Ltd; John Murray Ltd, and Academy Chicago for an extract from the *Lyttleton/Hart-Davis Letters* Vol. 5; Oxford University Press Ltd for an extract from the *Dictionary of National Biography* entry on Martin Farquhar Tupper, for an extract from *The Oxford Book of American Light Verse* edited by William Harman, and for an extract from *Early Victorian England 1830–1865* Vol. 2 by G. M. Young; Pan Books Ltd for an extract from *Extraordinary People* by Derek Wilson (1983); The Society of Authors as the Literary Representative of the Estate of Richard Le Gallienne and Dodd Mead & Co. for extracts from *English Poems* and *R.L.S.: An Elegy* by Richard Le Gallienne; *The Spectator* for extracts from reviews and articles by Marghanita Laski, Peter Levi and A. N. Wilson; Raglan Squire for extracts from *Life At the Mermaid, Books In General,* and *Reflections And Memories* by Sir John Squire; Christopher Tower for extracts from *Victoria The Good* and *A Distant Fluting* published by George Weidenfeld and Nicolson Limited; and Yale University Press for extracts from *William Edmonstoune Aytoun and the Spasmodic Controversy* by Mark A. Weinstein.

Every effort has been made to trace the owners of copyright, but in a few cases it has proved impossible to do so. Any copyright holder who has consequently not been acknowledged may ensure that correct acknowledgement appears in any subsequent editions of this book by contacting the publishers.

INTRODUCTION

Edward L. Burlingame, the renowned editor of *Scribner's Magazine*, once received a letter from an elderly lady that read as follows: 'My husband has always been a successful blacksmith. Now he is old, and his mind is slowly weakening so he has taken to writing poems, several of which I enclose herewith.' The wife's attitude, which will strike a familiar chord with all poetry editors, is dismayingly simple: Scribner's publish poetry, her husband has written some, therefore they should publish it. About her husband's attitude we can only speculate, but we need not necessarily accept her uncharitable assumption that the production of poetry was simply the natural consequence of mental decline. Many persons who appear quite normal in other respects, nevertheless persist in writing poetry, an activity for which they have no discernible talent whatsoever. This book is chiefly about such people, and in particular about the brightest stars in the constellation of inept poets – those who raised the art of bad verse to new heights by plumbing new depths of absurdity. At the same time, my researches are able to offer them the consolation (not that any of them ever looked in need of it) that great poets, too, were capable of scoring the equivalent of the cricketer's 'wide'.

The heyday of the poetaster was from the late eighteenth century to the late nineteenth century, although the species certainly existed before and has not become extinct since. This period is not entirely accidental. The enormous and rapid expansion of reading matter, which in turn reflected the swelling ranks of the middle classes in England and America, meant for a while that almost anyone with a half-baked reflection or a stale platitude to offer could find someone to print it. This phenomenon seems to have been particularly marked in America, where local newspapers would squeeze some simpering verses into the 'Poet's Corner' (after first, perhaps, hacking a few bits off to make it fit the available space).

Even so, many poets were so abysmal that they had to print the stuff themselves, sometimes with the financial assistance of long-suffering friends. A study of the 1890's American poetasters describes the nature of their output very well: 'The guiding principle was clear and rigid: imitate! The novice had only to select a poet whom the audience had received well, reiterate his themes and forms, changing nothing, erasing only the evidences of original expression, and his verse would soon be ready for public display . . . Eccentricities are shadowed in the titles, but even here the effect is of standardization. A title for the representative volume may be selected from a list which includes *Heart Songs* (or *Echoes* or *Effusions* or *Throbs*), *Pansies* (or *Daisies* or *Violets*) and *Other Poems, Choice Poems, Beautiful Thoughts, Dewdrops, Driftwood, Trifles of Twenty Years, Odd Business* and *Sunshine*. (One poet disarmed criticism with the title *My Good Poems*.) One instinct of the representative poet tends to brevity; another urges him to use the title as an index: *Life Thoughts: a book of poems on religion, love, temperance, kindness toward the lower animals, then, now (or past and present), eternal youth, the brighter side of death* [sic], *hidden worth, and various other subjects. It also contains eulogistic poems on lovely Charlevoix and beautiful Petoskey.*'[1]

Among the mass of such poetry a few figures stand out, unique in their unfathomable badness, heroic in their endurance of insult, phenomenal in their complete absence of a sense of the ridiculous. Such were Julia A. Moore, J. Gordon Coogler, Francis Saltus Saltus, Roswell Rice and the Rev. William Cook in America. The joy – for it is a joy – of reading such writers, is partly produced by their unexpected candour or casual insults, these being more the product of a struggle with metre rather than of malice aforethought. The Rev. Cook writes in his famous poem *The Ploughboy* (1854):

> Their grandmother useful, though old,
>   As people used to talk,
> To those children good stories told
>   At home or in a walk.

Lilian Curtis, a contemporary of Julia A. Moore, demonstrates that

---

1. C.T. Kindilien, *American Poetry in the Eighteen-Nineties*, Brown University Press, 1956, pp. 7 and 12.

the habits of bad verse are just as infectious as the measles with her own version of a Moore tear-jerker:

> I loved the gentle girl
> But oh, I heaved a sigh,
> When first she told me she could see
> Out of only one eye.

The British counterparts to these prismatic or naïve writers across the Atlantic are men like William McGonagall and Joseph Gwyer, who shared with the Americans a readiness to add a poetic dimension to terrible disasters, and to rush out an unsolicited elegy before a corpse was cold.

In between the irredeemably bad poetasters, like the Rev. Cornelius Whur, or the apparently unhinged ones, like William Nathan Stedman, and the poets whose justified reputations can easily withstand a few spectacular lapses, lies a grey area occupied by poets such as Thomas Holley Chivers or Joaquin Miller. One or two of their pieces have found their way into the standard anthologies, and have managed to stay there. I suppose Alfred Austin might aspire to this category, but the awfulness of 99 per cent of his work is in no way redeemed by the author's concomitant pretensions. Then there are poets like Ella Wheeler Wilcox and Wilhelmina Stitch, who had a considerable popular following, but whom no critic has taken seriously. These two ladies are more in the business of homily than of poetry, but, of the two, Ella Wheeler has an infinitely greater range and some of her lines have made the quotation books. Their particular style of badness has much in common with 'kitsch' in the visual arts, where human emotions are trivialized and fixed at the level of shop-soiled emblems, while the cathartic experience provided by genuine art is recycled in the form of pastiche. Artistic considerations are, in any case, secondary to such matters as the propagation of a shibboleth or the demonstration of the fact that the poet's heart is in the right place. Ella Wheeler Wilcox neatly sums up this attitude in her poem *Art and Heart*:

> And it is not the poet's song, though sweeter than sweet
>   bell's chiming,
> Which thrills us through and through, but the heart which
>   beats under the rhyming.

13

And therefore I say again, though I am art's one true lover,
That it is not art, but heart, which wins the wide world
    over.

Art and Heart says the same thing in much the same way eight
times in eight stanzas: namely, that however good a performance is,
it is worthless unless the artist is 'sincere'. Unfortunately for this
apparently reasonable point of view, the careers of some very celebrated artists hardly seem to square with it – Salvador Dali comes to
mind, Byron perhaps, D'Annunzio certainly. Ella Wheeler was
absolutely sincere, but then she was not a great artist. She did not
distinguish between the sort of 'sincerity' that gives a work of art its
integrity, and the sort of sincerity that enables you to love your
friends and hate your enemies ('We are the Allies of God to-day/
And the width of the earth is our right of way'), to endorse mother-
hood and condemn loose morals, to praise cheerfulness and
discommend gloom. As a matter of fact, artists can be sincere about
almost anything – one has no reason to suppose, for instance, that
Wagner was insincere in his rancid dislike of Jews, or that Tolstoy
didn't believe he was justified in his savagely inconsiderate treatment of his wife. I have a strong suspicion that both Ella Wheeler
and Wilhelmina Stitch were rather nicer, just judged as ordinary
people, that is, than Wagner or Tolstoy. This, at any rate, is the
impression created by their verses and their *obiter dicta* generally:

Do you wish the world were better?
Let me tell you what to do:
Set a watch upon your actions,
Keep them always straight and true;
Rid your mind of selfish motives;
Let your thoughts be clean and high.
You can make a little Eden
Of the sphere you occupy.

Nicer, certainly; more gifted, perhaps not. The inadequacy of
Ella's treatment of her subject does not so much lie in the sentiments as in their expression. 'Heart' has got the upper hand over

'art' with a vengeance. There is no marriage of the conscious and the unconscious, merely a threadbare lecture. As T.S. Eliot put it: 'the bad poet is usually unconscious where he ought to be conscious, and conscious where he ought to be unconscious.'[1] This is not a notion that would interest, or perhaps even be comprehensible to, the Whurs, the Wilcoxes and the Stitches. Their works exude virtuousness as an Athonite monk exudes the odour of sanctity – the smell is sometimes overpowering, and so is the fragrance of Wilhelmina's 'Fragrant Minutes', which were on offer to readers of the *Daily Sketch* every day. But in the end it is only a smell, the officious incense of a banal piety.

'Sincerity' – and to what level of consciousness? – is also the key to our authors' relationship with their public. The first half of this book attempts to take the reader on a light-hearted tour of justly neglected works where good intentions or dubious honesty, promotion of causes or destruction of enemies, Eros or bathos, ambition or incompetence, have interfered with the poetic process. Sycophancy, didacticism, religiosity, gentility and charlatanism are the ingredients of these poetical pies from which a few exemplary plums have been extracted. It is curious how much more absurd the less pleasant aspects of human nature are when enshrined in the supposed dignity of verse. Brow-beating clerics threaten the reader with tales of sinners who repented too late, or, like Isaac Watts, exhibit a most ungracious attitude towards their fellow authors:

> Meanwhile let Martial's blushless Muse
> Whose wit is poisoned by the stews,
>   Catullus' wanton fire,
> With Ovid's verse, that as it rolls,
> With luscious poison taints our souls,
>   In bogs obscene expire . . .

Left-wing sentimentalists solicit our enthusiasm for unsavoury political thugs. Obsequious laureates eulogize royal blockheads. Doctors tell us in verse what could be told more intelligibly and in a

---

1. T.S. Eliot, *Tradition and the Individual Talent.*

third of the time in prose, or better still, in a consultation. A dentist (Solyman Brown) writes a flowery epic on diseases of the teeth, complete with disgusting details of caries and bleeding gums. Suppressed homosexual schoolmasters supply us with reams of salivary verses celebrating naked small boys. Della Cruscans and Spasmodics pump out their poesy with the imperturbable diligence of British Gas. What makes these poems especially and satisfyingly bad is not their subject matter alone – perfectly respectable poems have been written about most of the topics featured here, with the possible exception of tooth decay – but their authors' peculiar conception of the nature of the art. Some of them plead that their verses are inoffensive, as though that were a justification for printing them; others that they are moral, or reverent, or useful, or encouraging, or that their friends urged them to publish, or simply that the Muse prompted them and they did write. These motives are entirely incidental to the goodness or badness of a poem, as is also whether or not the poet is a good-hearted fellow or the poetess a very kind lady. Yet most of our poetasters seem entirely unaware of this. To misquote Pope, they are quite content to put down: 'What oft was thought but ne'er so ill expressed', and justify it by some criterion quite irrelevant to the art of poetry.

These observations apply to the heroic failures and persistent no-hopers; but I have also leavened their efforts with some contributions of gratuitous and unrepentant infelicity from the great poets. Their innate awareness of the artistic dimension makes their plunges into bathos that much more spectacular – a fall at Beecher's Brook rather than a tumble in the local point-to-point. Of course the results have much in common with those of their less-gifted colleagues, but Tennyson and Wordsworth, when bad, are memorably bad, which cannot generally be said of the competition:

> Dash back that ocean with a pier,
> Strow yonder mountain flat,
> A railway there, a tunnel here
> Mix me this Zone with that![1]

1. Alfred, Lord Tennyson, *Mechanophilus*.

16

Significantly, the more unfortunate examples of a genuine poet operating with his eye not quite on the ball prove to be suitable material for parody. The implication of this is that the original has to be strong enough to make the operation worthwhile. No one bothers to satirize an unknown and incompetent politician, and much the same goes for poets.[1] The memorably bad quality of the original is what makes Swinburne's parody of Tennyson's *The Higher Pantheism* (1870) so delicious. The poem is full of the Laureate's most dubious rhetoric, not least because his, by now, gnawing religious doubt is in conflict with his sense of public responsibility. The hope is that hot air will obscure the unsatisfactory nature of the answers to disagreeable questions.

> Is not the Vision He? tho' He be not that which He seems?
> Dreams are true while they last, and do we not live in dreams?
>
> . . . Speak to Him, for He hears, and Spirit with Spirit can meet –
> Closer is He than breathing, and nearer than hands and feet.
>
> . . . And the ear of man cannot hear, and the eye of man cannot see;
> But if we could see and hear, this Vision – were it not He?

Swinburne's version, *The Higher Pantheism In A Nutshell*, exactly catches the portentous tone of the poem which was very popular with the Victorians, but which exhibits many of Tennyson's absolutely worst traits:

> One who is not, we see; but one, whom we see not, is:
> Surely this is not that: but that is assuredly this.
>
> What, and wherefore, and whence? for under is over and
> under:
> If thunder could be without lightning, lightning could be
> without thunder . . .
>
> Parallels all things are: yet many of these are askew:
> You are certainly I: but certainly I am not you.

1. The exception seems to be McGonagall (*see* Chapter 12). But then he is the exception to everything.

Springs the rock from the plain, shoots the stream from the
                                                    rock:
Cocks exist for the hen: but hens exist for the cock.

God, whom we see not, is: and God, who is not, we see:
Fiddle, we know is diddle: and diddle, we take it, is dee.

There were similarly effective parodies of Southey's sapphics in
The Anti-Jacobin, and most people are familiar with Lewis Carroll's
affectionate burlesques of Wordsworth. But the poetasters, by their
very nature, cannot be parodied, although they are constantly (and
unintentionally) parodying themselves.

A good parodist will echo what is bad in a poem, but he need not
have the last word. Indeed, it is far easier to recognize bad verse
than it is to define it. Usually, one is reduced to listing a few obvious
characteristics such as bathos, unfortunate associations of meaning,
inappropriate vocabulary, metrical incompetence, and so forth. But
lots of poetry may suffer from one or other of these defects without
being classically bad. The connoisseur of bad verse will only wish to
preserve those items that are so spectacularly bad as to constitute
a sort of genre in themselves. Mere tedium, the most ubiquitous
quality in minor authors and the lesser works of great ones, is auto-
matically disqualified as lacking that peculiar power to astonish
which is to be found only in bad verse of the highest quality.
That quality will be instantly apparent, even to the casual reader,
and cannot be faked. Gimmicks, even if they achieve a certain
vogue, are no substitute for the real thing. For instance, a recent
article in *The Spectator* informs us that 'Punk poetry consists
largely of young men shouting insults at their listeners and even
spitting at them', though apparently it does not transfer very successfully to the printed page. Much of the rest of contemporary bad
poetry, it seems, is no more than a branch of agitprop, produced
in rather limited literary environments such as The Black
Women's Writing and Creativity Workshop of the Greenwich
Council for Racial Equality. It is possible that a new incarnation
of the Della Cruscans will arise from these group endeavours,
but I rather doubt it. Where are the Cooglers, the McGona-
galls, the Whurs and the Wilhelmina Stitches of today? I'm in-

clined to think that the best is all behind us. If that is so, this volume becomes more than a mere exercise in nostalgia; it may be seen instead as an act of homage to those gallant literary ladies and gentlemen who believed deeply in the power of words, but could never find the right ones.

PART ONE

Varieties of Badness

One

OUR UNFORTUNATE
ENGLISH HEROES

Patriotism: the last refuge of a bad poet

Than great Eliza none more Umbrage took
Who did on Spain's vast preparations look . . .

Sir Richard Blackmore, *Eliza – An Epick Poem
In Ten Books* (1705)

Even from the chalky bourn of Cantium's shore,
To Alfred's aid the favouring Gillows bore
Bertie, whose daring sires, in search of fame,
To Albion's coast from far Boruscia came,
What time his hardy warriors Hengist led
From Elba's brink to Thames' redundant bed;

Henry James Pye,
Alfred – An Epic Poem in Six Books (1801)

There are no dull subjects. There are only dull writers.

H.L. Mencken

IT MIGHT BE FELT THAT MOST of our English heroes had suffered enough during their lifetimes not to be subjected to the attentions of abysmal poets after their death. Hardly any of them were safe, however, and, as a general rule, the greater the hero, the worse the poet. If patriotism is the last refuge of a scoundrel, poetry sometimes seems to be the last refuge of a patriot. What, one wonders, can have induced Sir Coutts Lindsay, Bt., to try his hand at a poetic drama on *Edward the Black Prince* (1846), or for that matter on *Boadicea* (1857)? Reading these products of ossified history one feels that nothing was more inimical to English literature than a Victorian gentleman with time on his hands and poetry on the brain. Of the two, *Boadicea* at least has some lively moments, such as when the Romans send a herald to parley with the Queen. As the negotiating party enter, she remarks somewhat ungraciously:

> Bloody swine
> That are replete with garbage!

Her reply to the Herald, who had unwisely assumed there would be a swift capitulation, sounds like Mrs Thatcher addressing the Argentinian ambassador in 1982:

> But to your leader, bid him gird his loins!
> By Heaven, I swear the coming war shall be
> Extermination, sword-stroke and firebrand
> To those who are undermost.
> – Get to your horses, redden all your spurs
> Or you may hear my war-hounds on your track.

Like Mrs Thatcher, Boadicea has offspring who are a source of some political embarrassment. Her daughter, Malvina, falls inconveniently in love with a Roman called Julius, who is wounded during

24

the Battle of London. Unfortunately for him, Boadicea happens along as he lies bleeding, and unceremoniously despatches him with her sword. An incensed Malvina calls her mother a gorgon before leaping into the flaming ruins. The tragedy, if it is one, concludes with Boadicea jumping off Dover cliff.

King Arthur has also been subjected to some unsolicited (by the public) poetical attention. The eccentric physician Sir Richard Blackmore (1653–1729) produced 'an heroick poem' in ten books on Prince Arthur (1696) with an index added which helpfully explains the many names of countries, cities and rivers mentioned in the text. He does warn us in the Preface that "tis not true . . . that the Poet's chief business is to please', and seems to have stuck fairly closely to this guiding principle throughout. He also tells us that he wrote the work hastily 'in coffee-houses and in passing up and down the streets', a mode of composition which has not improved the quality of the work. 'Another reason of the Defects that appear in that writing is this, that when I undertook it, I had been long a stranger to the Muses. I had read but little Poetry throughout my whole life . . .' He hints, however, that criticism of the poem was not entirely disinterested, for he was: 'so hardy to venture abroad Naked and Unguarded, when none of the Company [of Covent Garden scribblers] went without a notable Convoy of Criticks and Applauders, who were constantly in their service . . .' And he makes a shrewd hit when he says: 'These Gentlemen pretend to be displeased with *Prince Arthur*, because they have discover'd so many faults in it: but there is good reason to believe they would have been more displeas'd if they had discover'd fewer.'

The work itself is prolix and immensely tedious. Arthur is asked to rescue Gaul from the clutches of Clotar. Before he sets sail, he assembles his army, each cohort of which – its men, its commanders and its geographical origin – is described in excruciating detail. When he lands in France, each cohort of the French army is similarly described. Interested parties can refer to the aforementioned index of places when in doubt. There is a plot at home – it is just possible to disentangle this fact from the verbiage describing the messenger, his station in life, his home town, immediate family, prospects in life, etc. Despite the combined efforts of the Franks, plotters, and the personal intervention of the devil, we find, 10,000 lines later, that Arthur has won at home and abroad. This is a work of stupefying boredom, which only comes alive when Blackmore's chauvinistic instincts are aroused in describing Clotar's court. It is very unlike the home life of our own dear monarch:

[His] dreadful Court, like a Cyclopian Den
Is filled with Rapine and half-eaten Men;
Where lies of mangled limbs an endless store
And wide-mouthed Caldrons flow with Human Gore . . .
For he his Subjects on his Table sets,
And their raw Limbs (a horrid Banquet) eats.

Lord Alfred Tennyson's poem on Arthur (*The Idylls of the King*, 1859) is, of course, rather different. It was immensely popular with the Victorian public, not least because of the picture of moral rectitude presented by the hero. Gladstone was mightily taken with 'this great pillar of the moral order, and the resplendent top of human excellence', and absolutely ecstatic with the closing speeches of Guinevere, where Arthur indulges in an orgy of moral superiority:

Lo! I forgive thee, as Eternal God
Forgives: do thou for thine own soul the rest.

Swinburne contented himself with the observation that these lines represented 'the acme, the apogee, the culmination of all imaginable cant'[1]. W.H. Mallock produced a damaging spoof that purported to be 'the original directions from which the Poet Laureate composed the Arthurian Idylls'. It begins: 'To compose an epic, some writers instruct us first to catch our hero. As, however, Mr Carlyle is the only person on record who has ever performed this feat, it will be best for the rest of mankind to be content with the nearest approach to a hero available, namely a prig. These animals are very plentiful and easy to catch as they delight in being run after.' Having explained the type of prig required from the alternatives available, Mallock continues: 'Take, then, one blameless prig. Set him upright in the middle of a round table, and place beside him

1. Swinburne also remarked irreverently: 'Treated as he treated it, the story is rather a case for the divorce-court than for poetry.' And he used to refer to the poem as 'The Idylls of the Consort' and 'Le Morte d'Albert'.

a beautiful wife, who cannot abide prigs. Add to these one marred goodly man; and tie the three together in a bundle with a link or two of Destiny. Proceed, next, to surround this group with a large number of men and women of the nineteenth century, in fancy-ball costume, flavoured with a great many possible vices, and a few impossible virtues. Stir these briskly for about two volumes, to the great annoyance of the blameless prig, who is, however, to be kept carefully below swearing-point, for the whole time. If he once boils over into any natural action or exclamation, he is forthwith worthless, and you must get another. Next break the wife's good reputation into small pieces; and dust them well over the blameless prig. Then take a few vials of tribulation and wrath, and empty these generally over the whole ingredients of your poem: and, taking the sword of the heathen, cut into small pieces the greater part of your minor characters. Then wound slightly the head of the blameless prig; remove him suddenly from the table, and keep in a cool barge for future use.'

However unappealing the content of *The Idylls of the King* to the modern taste, it at least contains many passages of real poetry and was written by a real poet. In epics on English heroes this is a rarity for which we may be grateful. We have already seen what Sir Richard Blackmore made of Arthur. He also made a stab at Queen Elizabeth I (*Eliza – An Epick Poem in Ten Books*, 1705) and King Alfred. The basic format of *Eliza* bears a striking resemblance to his *Prince Arthur* – there is again a walk-on cast of demons and seraphs, and the line-up of English and Spanish commanders is related at interminable length. The devil seems to be a Catholic – at any rate he conspires with the Pope to get Philip of Spain to marry Elizabeth and invade England at the same time. Elizabeth is not amused:

> . . . Than great Eliza none more Umbrage took
> Who did on Spain's vast Preparations look . . .

Then there is the Armada, and some interesting scenes of the Pope plotting in his study. Of course the ending is a happy one, and we are reassured by a personal visit that the Archangel Gabriel pays to the Queen that the future Protestant succession is secure.

With Blackmore's *Alfred – An Epick Poem in Twelve Books* the first contestant in a crowded field comes into view; for King Alfred has suffered the indignity of being written up by some of the absolutely worst poets in the language, including Martin Tupper, Henry James Pye and Alfred Austin. It is hard to know what the unfortunate Saxon king did to deserve this; perhaps posterity is punishing him for burning the cakes. Of all the epics about him, Blackmore's is the most fantastic. In Book I, Alfred embarks on a sort of Grand Tour 'intending chiefly to improve his mind by the observation he should make on various forms of Government, Laws, Customs, Ceremonies in different Kingdoms etc.'. His adventures, some of them unknown to students of the period, need not detain us, except for the interesting episode in Book IV where the Pope crowns him King of England. He seems to be in no hurry to return, however, and spends some time in Southern Italy where he puts down a rebellion and explains to the King the principles of good government. His next stop is Sicily, where he disapproves of the idleness and vice of the natives. Mount Etna erupts, but ceases to do so when admonished by Alfred. He continues round Europe distributing good advice and bailing out beleaguered kings. Only in Book XII does he return to England, become King, defeat the Danes, convert King Gunter to Christianity and marry his daughter Elsitha. The poem reads like an immense shaggy dog story, and in view of the sprawling acres of irrelevant detail it is a pity the author failed to find a space for the episode of the burning of the cakes.

Henry James Pye (1745–1813), the spectacularly inept laureate, published his *Alfred – An Epic Poem in Six Books* in 1801. In his Prefatory Address to Henry Addington, who was then Chancellor of the Exchequer, the author very properly confesses that he would 'rather be thought a good Englishman than the best poet or the greatest scholar that ever wrote'. He seems to have succeeded in this endeavour, and certainly *Alfred* is a credit to his sense of patriotism. Pye also enlarges on the known biography of Alfred by beginning his poem in the court of Caledonia's King Gregor, where the future English king arrives as a mysterious stranger. The rest of the story is more orthodox, but its principal charm lies in Pye's familiar Della Cruscan diction which is seen to good advantage in descriptive passages. Here, for instance, is a splendid depiction of Gregor's face when he is getting angry:

. . . As when 'the genius of the summer storm'

> Bids midnight-gloom the face of Heaven deform,
> And all the gorgeous tints of Nature shrouds
> In the dun umbrage of electric clouds . . .

Alfred, on the other hand, tends to be lachrymose:

> Across his face his robe he drew, to hide
> Of gushing tears, the involuntary tide;

Battle scenes are encrusted with elaborate similes:

> Not swifter from the sky's empyreal height
> Where his strong eye-balls drink the solar light,
> Stoops the proud eagle on the scatter'd train
> Of crows and choughs that scream along the plain . . .

And there are bizarre moments when Pye reaches for the dramatic image, but it slips inevitably from his grasp:

> Along the hills the foe astonish'd flies,
> And hostile blood the thirsty herbage dyes . . .

As is usual in Pye's work, he does not forget to puff the agricultural interest when the opportunity presents itself:

> 'Tis from the rustic swain's diurnal toil,
> That Commerce draws, with powerful grasp, the stores
> Of every clime from Earth's remotest shores,
> That navies o'er the obedient billow ride . . etc., etc.

These are the very appropriate reflections of Alfred as he approaches the herdsman's hut in which he is to burn the cakes. At least we are given full value in the treatment of this important incident, so unaccountably omitted by Blackmore:

> The objects round him, like the viewless air
> Pass o'er his mind, nor leave an image there;
> Hence oft, with flippant tongue, the busy dame
> The reckless stranger's apathy would blame.
> Who, careless, let the viands waste,
> His ready hunger ne'er refused to taste.

Pye also attended to his duty as Laureate and includes a shameless plug for the Hanoverians:

> . . . At length where Elbe's parental current flows
> Once more her eye insulted England throws;
> Her hopes regard that sacred source once more
> Where Saxon freedom bless'd her happy shore . . .

Nor does he neglect to point out that, under the genial yoke of the new German line, England is getting very, very rich:

> . . . And, as the dewy moisture Sol exhales
> With beam refulgent, from the irriguous vales,
> Descends in favouring showers of genial rain,
> To fertilize the hill and arid plain,
> So wealth, collected by the merchant's hand,
> Spreads wide, in general plenty, o'er the land.

But we (and Pye) are digressing. By Book IV Alfred is receiving help from an unexpected quarter:

> Even from the chalky bourn of Cantium's shore,
> To Alfred's aid, the favouring billows bore
> Bertie, whose daring sires, in search of fame,
> To Albion's coasts from far Boruscia came,
> What time his hardy warriors Hengist led
> From Elba's brink to Thames' redundant bed;

Anticipating that readers may be puzzled by the sudden appearance of Bertie in the story Pye thoughtfully appends a footnote: 'The Berties came from Bertiland, in Prussia . . . and had from one of the first Saxon kings a castle and town in Kent, called Bertlestadt, now Bersted, near Maidstone. Leopold de Bertie was constable of Dover castle in the reign of Ethelred . . .'

In Book V Pye evidently feels the narrative needs a little spicing up lest the reader's attention should be flagging. In a dramatic incident when Ceolph is marching to war, his daughter Emmeline rushes out of a wood having been raped by the Danes:

> 'One only way remains from deep disgrace
> To clear the offspring of a noble race –'
> She ceased – and instant in her struggling breast
> Her fatal poniard sheath'd, and sunk to rest.

30

Ceolph's reaction is spectacular:

> – his maniac eye
> Fix'd on the pale remains that bleeding lie –
> From the pierced heart he drew the reeking blade.
> With frantic look the ensanguined point survey'd,
> While from his eye-balls darts with horrid glare,
> The enfuriate wildness of supreme despair –
> The impulse checking, ere he gave the wound,
> Furious he dash'd the weapon to the ground,
> And, clasping to his breast with frenzied force,
> The mangled bosom of the beauteous corse,
> 'O injured Emmeline! – O, ill-starred maid!
> Sad victim of a father's crimes;' he said . . .

We then proceed to battle, and a nice description of the English bowmen:

> Full in the front the English archers stand.
> The bent bow drawing home with sinewy hand,
> Scarcely the shining barbs the tough yew clear,
> The ductile nerve stretch'd to the bowman's ear.

The result is a victory for Alfred, but not before he has had a narrow escape when Burthred takes a lance-thrust intended for him:

> . . . and life its purple showers,
> Down his white vest and shining armour, pours:

Guthrum is converted and a prophetic druid, whom we previously met in Book I, makes a second appearance. He is even more sententious than before, and takes the opportunity to trace the line of the Brunswicks back to Othbert, Ottoberto or Oberto, a genealogy previously espoused by the Laureate William Whitehead (q.v.) in one of his more eccentric odes.

Pye's effort, long though it is, is a mere hors-d'oeuvre to the main courses of Alfredian epic that followed him. Joseph Cottle (1770–1853), publisher of the Lake Poets, produced his *Alfred – An Epic Poem in Twenty-Four Books* in 1804. He evidently thought highly of it: in a Preface to the Second Edition he defends himself against criticisms at enormous length, even to the extent of showing how he might have written some lines differently had he been a less good poet. Although he rejects the supernatural machinery favoured by Blackmore, there is a vast apparatus of Wagnerian mythology which helps to clog the start of the action. The story of Alfred's life maintains a high level of tedium throughout, and even the burning of the cakes takes twenty-four lines to narrate. It ends with Acca, the neatherd's wife, complaining to her husband:

> When, as the door I opened and look'd around
> There on his wicker chair he sat, his eyes
> Fix'd on the floor, his knife beside, while near
> Lay many a half-form'd bow. But sad to tell!
> My cakes, for thy return, prepared to show
> A wife's affection, lay involved in smoke!
> Now nothing worth! and this great Loon at hand,
> Unmindful. 'Dost thou hear?' she cried,
> And stamp'd her foot, and, with indignant ire,
> Vowed oft and bitterly, no other food
> His lips should touch, till he had eaten all
> The black-burnt cakes.

However, we know from Pye that Alfred, in the best traditions of the British consumer, was quite indifferent to the taste of what he was served, so no doubt he ate them up happily enough.

Cottle's poem may be of punishing length, but John Fitchett's (1766–1838) is a record-book item. It does in fact appear in *The Guinness Book of Records* as the longest poem ever written in the English language. It runs to 129,807 lines and took forty years to write. The author died before his project was complete and his masochistic editor, Robert Roscoe, supplied the last 2,585 lines. *King Alfred – A Poem* appeared in four volumes between 1841 and 1842. The Editor's Preface may be said to mingle vanity with optimism: 'With respect to the different attempts which have hitherto been made to illustrate in verse this favourite topic, it is sufficient to observe that it has had the fortune to be treated only by writers of subordinate powers, and in a manner, and with a success far from commensurate with its scope and dignity.' No one could disagree with this – but is Fitchett's effort any improvement on what has gone before? Even reading a few, a very few, lines of Fitchett causes the eyes to glaze over and the pulse rate to sink ineluctably towards the level of sleep. Beside it *In Memoriam* seems a mere *jeu d'esprit*; and an article in *New Society* is, by comparison with Fitchett, compulsively readable. Roscoe describes how Fitchett devoted his 'labour and his life to the collection of materials for his work', how he visited all the places he described, collected all the books on the period, and investigated all the relevant antiquities. He loyally says that he 'will not enter upon an enquiry whether his object might not have been attained by a less circuitous route', and very prudently refrains from any judgement on the quality of the poem; he confines himself to the observation that it offers 'one of the most remarkable examples of sustained mental energy and unflinching resolution in the pursuit of a great object which the annals of the human intellect can supply'. This is certainly true, but it also implies that a degree of patience is demanded of the reader. The important matter of the burnt cakes does not occur until Book VII, or about 80,000 lines from the beginning:

> The ancient dame bids him with care attend
> Some oaten cakes then baking on the hearth.
> Alas! the cakes forgot soon shew a heap
> All black, memorials of his sad neglect . . . etc.

Alfred gets a beating and is sent to bed foodless, like any Victorian child.

Fitchett's work, a magnificent monument to misplaced effort, was followed by our old friend Sir Coutts Lindsay Bt., whose *Alfred. A Drama* came out in 1845. There is nothing remarkable about it, though the suicide of the defiant pagan Ubbo is charming:

> Odin I come! – I die laughing!

In Lindsay's version also, the cakes are not burnt, which is a great disappointment to students of the genre. This is not a mistake made by Martin F. Tupper (1810–89) in his *Alfred – A Patriotic Play* (1858) which has a lively kitchen scene: 'How now?' [screeches Egga] – 'What amouthing again! How's the manchets? – Whew – they're cinders!' Tupper's five-act play apparently had some success on the stage, no doubt because of its fierce patriotism. The author gives careful stage directions as to how the audience is to be blasted with deafening renditions of 'Rule Britannia' and 'God Save the Queen' at strategic moments.

Alfred, having survived a considerable poetic mauling, finally fell victim to the pen of Alfred Austin (1835–1913) (q.v.), and this seems to have virtually killed him off as a suitable subject for poetry. He was not molested again until G.K. Chesterson wrote a poem about him, which was good enough to cause minimal injury to either party (*Ballad of the White Horse*, 1911). Austin's preface to *England's Darling* (1896) begins confidently: 'The greatest of Englishmen has never been celebrated by an English poet.' This claim, as we have seen, is what Sir Robert Armstrong would call being 'economical with the truth.' No matter; there are, in any case, other justifications for a poem on such a theme at this moment in history: 'It is an interesting, and surely an auspicious, coincidence that the present Heir to the English throne, like Atheling in Alfred's reign, bears the name of Edward, and again, like his mighty namesake, has for consort a lovely Dane.'

As the poem opens, Halfdene is wreaking havoc in the North and forcing freemen to get their hair cut:

> . . . And the long-haired Northumbrian freemen makes
> Harrowers and ploughers to their conquerors,
> Clipped to the nape.

Elsewhere, in the path of Hingvar and Hubta, even a haircut is no guarantee of safety, for they are everywhere:

> . . . wrenching the chalice from the hand of God,
> And tearing from the abbot's tonsured brow
> Alb, stole and chasuble.

It is even worse for women:

> . . . From virgins vowed to Heaven
> Virgins as white as is the Yuletide snow,
> They strip the veil, who straightway die of shame,
> Or, dreader doom, dwell within the sty
> Of wallowing sea-swine.

Only Alfred can reverse this deplorable state of affairs, but first he
has to burn the cakes. At the same time his son Edward is courting
Edgiva. She is not a feminist:

> . . . For a man is masterful, and so should be,
> And I am but a woman; having strength
> To hide my weakness, thus to keep you strong
> But feeble all beside.

By Act II we are in Athelney, and Austin begins to display his
powers as a poet of the agricultural community. Serfs carry loads to
a barn near the King's camp, discoursing the while in an amalgam of
Shakespearian rustic and the language of a Benny Hill sketch:

> Fetch me a hunk of salted flitch
>   And a jug of sweetened ale,
> And off I trudge to bank and ditch
>   Or bang about the flail.
> Who recks of Summer sweat and swink
>   Or winter's icy pang,
> Tilt up the mug, my mates, and drink
>   And let the world go hang
>
> . . . Now youngster, snap the fallen sticks,
>   Now, hearthwife, boil the pot,
> For we have thatched the barley ricks
>   And ploughed the gafol plot.
> The shepherd's star begins to wink,
>   The she-wolf whets her fang;
> Up with the mead-bowl, mates and drink
>   And let the world go hang.

This ditty draws the following comment from a bystander: 'An awry
song for the lambing season, and with the cuckoo a-chuckling over
the foster hedge-sparrow.' To which his companion sagely replies:
'There's more wealth in an old song than in green faggots.'

Meanwhile, back at court, Alfred is distributing scholastic duties
among his clerics – the Bishop of Worcester must revise Pope
Gregory's *Pastoral* and Plegmund has to translate *The Consolation of
Philosophy*. There follows a scene at The Witanagemote where the

freemen enumerate – at great length – Alfred's virtues and talents. After a while he replies, but it is not always easy to follow him:

> What though I had lain within the royal bed,
> Where I had lain with this my cleanly Queen,
> Littered the farrow of a forest sow,
> Should I bemoan the fashion of the world,
> Tonsure the head Pope Leo's very hand
> Anointed kingly, and slink hence to Rome
> A niddering pilgrim?

This speech inspires the English to fight the Danes. We flash back to Edward, and to Edgiva who, as it happens, is a Danish citizen. Alfred has her vetted, however, and she is given full security clearance. She and Alfred begin to get to know each other:

Alfred: Wot you the hour?
Edgiva: It must be past noon,
Because the shepherd's weather-wise hath shut
As doth the goatsbeard in the waning year.

Edgiva is very hot on natural remedies and keeps her skin blooming with preparations from The Body Shop:

> With windflower honey are my tresses smoothed,
> My freckles with the speedwell's juices washed,
> And sleepy breath made sweet with galingale.

There is a long discussion between her and her future father-in-law concerning the names of wild flowers. Alfred has a tendency to show off:

Alfred: Now name me this.
Edgiva: Milkwort or gang-flower.
Alfred: Which the learned call
Rogation-Flower.

This *Mastermind* contest has to be abandoned in favour of throwing the Danes out of Wessex. In a spectacular *coup* worthy of James

Bond, Alfred enters the Danish camp in disguise (the Danes are lying about drinking out of skulls), throws it off after lulling their suspicions, and makes a citizen's arrest on Guthrum. The latter humbly acknowledges him as his overlord, and Alfred magnanimously awards the defeated Dane East Anglia as compensation. Edgiva turns out to be King Sweyne's daughter, much to the relief of the anxious parents who now know that she comes from a good family.

It is hard to decide which is the worst of all these lays of ancient Alfred. The competition is one between tedium and absurdity, but all contain elements of both. The motives of the authors for inflicting these works on the public seem to be more patriotic than literary, but Austin at least probably believed in the literary merit of his poem. And perhaps, subconsciously, there was an attraction in the fact that Shakespeare had never tackled the subject of Alfred (nor, for that matter, of Arthur or Boadicea); there was nothing against which invidious comparisons could be made. Whatever the reason, eulogy of Alfred constitutes a bizarre leitmotiv in the work of English poetasters, an historical mould into which a thin continuous stream of bad poetry could be poured. The persistence of Blackmore, the tenacity of Fitchett, the obsequiousness of Pye – these are matters for wonder, admiration even. The unintentional pleasures they supply are relatively innocent; for just as the eulogies of Stalin have not obscured his essentially criminal nature from posterity, so the incompetence of Alfred's admirers has done little lasting damage to his reputation. Boadicea, Arthur, Elizabeth and Alfred were in no need of being rescued by these poets in the first place, and required only modest first aid after the poets had finished with them.

Two

LIMPING LAUREATES

Effusions of the Servile Muse

Monarchs are always surrounded with refined spirits, so
penetrating that they frequently discover in their mas-
ters great qualities, invisible to vulgar eyes, and which,
did they not publish them to mankind, would be
unobserved for ever.

Dr Johnson, Marmor Norfolciense

What, all this for a song?

William Cecil, Baron Burghley, when importuned
on behalf of the author of The Faerie Queene by Raleigh.

THE OFFICE OF POET LAUREATE was held by three indisputably great poets – Dryden, Wordsworth and Tennyson; a handful of gifted ones, such as Masefield or Betjeman; and a rabble of hacks and nonentities. Since the last named constitute some 50 per cent of the Laureate roll, it is hardly surprising that 'laureatese' became a byword for literary awfulness. Individual production varied in quantity, seldom in quality; a stream of limping eulogies, oleaginous odes and stale epitaphs gushed from the worst of them like a continuous flow of brown Windsor soup into the bowls of royal crested porcelain. The nature of the job made absurdities inevitable – thoroughly unpleasant or even lunatic kings had to be praised to the heavens, English military victories presented as a boon to all mankind, and political controversies systematically misrepresented. All this is thoroughly English, but it has little to do with poetry. The 'occasional' poem, written to order is usually insufferable, even in the hands of a Dryden writing in a genre not wholly unnatural to his genius. For the most part, such works exhibit what D.B. Wyndham Lewis so aptly calls a 'windy splurging and bombinating'.[1]

John Dryden (1631–1700) is generally recognized as the first Laureate, and he was also one of the few occupants of the post able to rescue something for poetry from politics. It was also fortunate for his career that his political and religious views ran parallel to that of the *de facto* or constituted authorities until 1688. In 1658 he was writing *Heroic Stanzas on the Death of Oliver Cromwell*, and in 1660 *Astraea Redux*, which is in praise of the Restoration. By 1687, he was announcing his conversion to the Roman Church in *The Hind and the Panther*. These high profile changes of direction were dictated by conscience rather than self-interest, and in the long run they were his undoing – come the Glorious Revolution he was una-

1. D.B. Wyndham Lewis and Charles Lee, *The Stuffed Owl*, London, 1978, p. xiii.

39

ble or unwilling to perform a further U-turn, was sacked from the Laureateship and deprived of all his pensions and emoluments. He is the only Laureate to have suffered such an indignity, despite the many who deserved it. Worse still, the office was given to Shadwell, the target of Dryden's great satire *MacFlecknoe* (1682) and designated therein as the true heir to the throne of nonsense.

> Shadwell alone my perfect image bears
> Mature in dullness from his tender years;
> Shadwell alone of all my sons is he
> Who stands confirmed in full stupidity.
> The rest to some faint meaning make pretence,
> But Shadwell never deviates into sense.

The honouring of Shadwell must have been an even greater blow to the poet's self-esteem than losing his 'butt of Canary Wyne' when the cheeseparing James II had it stopped.

Dryden's ability to rise to the occasion has seldom been emulated. *Annus Mirabilis* (1667)[1] may be somewhat overripe here and there, but then one has to compare it with other efforts in the genre; before such modern examples as Cecil Day Lewis's *Hail Teesside!* [*sic*] (1968) or Sir John Betjeman's poem on the Queen Mother's 80th Birthday, even the hardened critic is reduced to dumbfounded, if respectful, silence. The ease and fluency of Dryden was both an advantage and a disadvantage, as is often the case with very prolific artists. Macaulay, erupting magnificently in *The Edinburgh Review*, gives us an inimitable portrait of the undisciplined genius: 'His mind was of a slovenly character – fond of splendour, but indifferent to neatness. Hence most of his writings exhibit the sluttish magnificence of a Russian noble, all vermin diamonds, dirty linen and inestimable sables.'

Like most Laureates Dryden lashes his Pegasus till the foam runs off its flanks when praising the great, especially royalty. Of course it is not the business of the courtier poet to make his remarks appropriate to the character of the personage being eulogized; but the

---

1. It has to be admitted that this was written before his appointment to the Laureateship in 1670. In many cases elevation to the post proved to be the kiss of death to a poet. Competent writers slid more rapidly into senility thereafter; incompetent ones sank even deeper into the mire of mediocrity.

consequence of ardent tactfulness, as Sir John Squire has observed[1], that an amusing anthology might be made of 'panegyrics written to undeserving persons'. It would certainly have to include Dryden's description of Charles II's arrival at Dover, when, we are asked to believe, the winds themselves were out of breath with joy and the cliffs of Dover, overcome with impatience while awaiting the monarch's arrival, decided to move out into the channel to meet him:

> The winds that never moderation knew,
> Afraid to blow too much, too faintly blew;
> Or out of breath with joy could not enlarge
> Their straiten'd lungs . . .
>
> . . . And welcome now, great monarch, to your own;
> Behold th' approaching cliffs of Albion!
> It is no longer motion cheats your view,
> As you meet it, the land approacheth you.

In view of this, it is really quite surprising that Dryden had to wait until 1670 before landing the job of court poet, but it should be remembered that he faced stiff competition from some of his colleagues. Their reserves of sycophancy appeared to be unlimited, and far greater than the individuals' store of poetic talent. This was so much an accepted fact of life that absurdities may not always have been noticeable to contemporaries. As Squire remarks, 'Anyone who should address his sovereign today (1927, the reign of George V) in words like those addressed to Charles II by his subjects (e.g. 'Great George, the planets tremble at thy nod') would be suspected of pulling the sovereign's leg.'

Charles did not escape the eulogists, even when he was no longer in a position to enjoy the fruits of their labours. Blasphemy was not considered too extravagant a tribute to his supposed virtues, as we see from the Earl of Halifax's lines on the monarch's death:

> In Charles so good a man and king we see
> A double image of the deity.
> Oh! had he more resembled it! Oh, why
> Was he not still more like, and could not die?

1. In 'Charles II in English verse', *Life at the Mermaid and other essays*, Glasgow, 1927.

This apparent difficulty was actually solved by another poet who pointed out:

> . . . Princes (truly great) can never die,
> They only lay aside Mortality.

Dryden himself despatched the King with a moving account of his last illness in which the doctors manoeuvred like generals conducting a siege:

> But, like a fortress on a rock,
> Th'impregnable disease their vain attempts did mock;
> They min'd it near, they batter'd from afar
> With all the cannon of the medicinal war;
>
> *Threnodia Augustalis* (1685)

This attempt to turn the King's body into a battlefield makes it a moot point as to whether the apoplexy or the doctors were the real cause of his demise.

The advent of William of Orange again brought the panegyrists out in force, though this time Dryden took himself out of the running. Thomas Shadwell (1642?–92), his old enemy, carried off the prize after writing *A congratulatory poem on His Highness the Prince of Orange, his coming into England.* As Kenneth Hopkins remarks in his book on the poets laureate: 'It says something for William's determination that in the face of such a tribute he did not turn tail.' Nor did the Prince's consort escape a blast of hot air from the poet, being celebrated on her arrival with the unfortunate line:

> She comes, she comes, the Fair, the Wise . . .[1]

The appointment of Shadwell introduces the tradition whereby a laureate's talent for versifying was one of the least important considerations for those who selected him. 'I will not pretend to determine how great a poet Shadwell may be, but I am sure that he is an honest man' remarked the Earl of Dorset – meaning, as Mrs

1. Connoisseurs of unfortunate lines may also enjoy the opening one of Part II of Coventry Patmore's *The Angel in the House*, that pious Victorian celebration of female purity. It runs: 'Whene'er I come where ladies are . . .'.

Thatcher might put it, 'he is one of us'. Another tradition that gets off to a good start is that of hostile comment on the poet's appearance and personal habits. In *Absalom and Achitophel* Dryden (or Tate) refers to him as:

> Round as a Globe, and Liquored every chink

and adds for good measure:

> . . . A Monstrous Mass of foul corrupted matter
> As all the Devils had spew'd to make the Batter.
> When wine has given him Courage to Blaspheme,
> He curses God, but God before curst him;

Of course, much of this is no more than the customary exchanges of compliments between literary gentlemen. Shadwell was a popular dramatist of the second rank, a field in which Dryden was more industrious than successful. As a poet, however, Shadwell is uninspiring, managing to rise to heights of absurdity in his ode celebrating the victory at the Battle of the Boyne. The picture of the King enjoying a hail of bullets as if it were a refreshing shower of rain is not convincing; no more so is the attempt to portray a murderous battle as a seductive nymph:

> Not the fierce Lover shows more chearful haste,
> Meeting the beauteous Nymph to be Embrac'd,
> As the Reward of all his Service past;
> Than you to joyn in Battle with a Foe . . .

By the time he starts on the royal shoulder wound, the poet has worked himself into a lather of factitious adulation, and seems neither to know nor care whether he is making any sense at all.

> That *Wound*, at which th'Astonished Muse
> Aid to all Numbers, did refuse.
> A *Wound*, which deeply pierc'd each Gen'rous Heart
> Which your Three *Kingdoms* tenderly did feel;
> A Blow, which made all injur'd Princes start,
> And all the *Great Confederacy* Reel.
> The only *Holy League*, that e'er was made,

A *League* oppress'd *Mankind* to free
From the most Barb'rous Foe did e'er Invade
With Sword, and Fire, and Treachery.
But Heav'n of you took such peculiar Care
That soon the *Royal Breach* it did Repair . . .

Shadwell was succeeded by Nahum Tate (1652–1715), the man who decided that *King Lear* could be improved by the substitution of a happy ending in place of the one supplied by Shakespeare. In his version, Cordelia survives and marries Edgar: 'This monstrosity', writes D.C. Browning[1], 'which was defended by Dr Johnson, held the stage well into the nineteenth century.' Like Dryden, Tate was prepared to have a stab at most genres and subjects. He collaborated on a metrical rendering of the *Psalms* (1696) with the Rev. Nicholas Brady, and is supposed to be the author of 'While shepherds watched their flocks by night'. He also wrote a rambling work entitled *Panacea or a Poem on Tea* (1700) and translated Girolamo Fracastoro's poem about syphilis (q.v.). His poem about *Sliding on skates in very hard frost* (1677) is full of useful information the reader might otherwise have overlooked: he reminds us that frozen water cannot even be made to ripple:

Though hurricanes should rage, they could not now
So much as curl the solid water's brow;
Proud fleets whose stubborn cables scarce withstood
Th'impetuous shock of the unstable flood,
In watry ligaments are restrain'd
More strict than when in binding ooze detain'd.

The amazing thing is that humans, without the assistance of the wind and tide which, apparently, they usually need for propulsion, can get around so well on the ice:

. . . But though their services at present fail,
Ourselves without the aid of tide or gale
On keels of polisht steel securely sail;
From every creek to every point we rove,

1. D.C. Browning, *Everyman's Dictionary of Literary Biography*, London, 1970. In Tate's version the Fool was also dispensed with as a tiresome irrelevance.

And in our lawless passage swifter move
Than fish beneath us, or than fowl above.

Tate is a master of the final couplet which wittily points a moral
not immediately obvious to readers who have not tuned in to his
Weltanschauung. Another poem is a dramatic monologue in which
the captain of a ship sinking in a hurricane addresses his crew. At the
end, all is lost except the opportunity to manufacture a conceit:

> A ring, my Mates: let's join a ring, and so
> Beneath the deep embracing go.
> Now to new worlds we steer, and quickly shall arrive:
> Our spirits shall mount as fast as our dull corpses dive.
>
> *The Hurricane* (1677)

From the same volume of *Poems* comes another irresistible conceit in which Dame Nature wraps herself in a sheet, but the Sun rips
it off and rapes her:

On Snow Fall'n in Autumn, and Dissolved by the Sun

> Nature now stript of all her summer dress,
> And modestly surmising, 'twere unmeet
> For each rude eye to view her nakedness,
> Around her bare limbs wraps this snowy sheet.
> The wanton Sun the slight-wrought shroud removes,
> T'embrace the naked dame, whose fertile womb
> Admits the lusty paramour's warm loves,
> And is made big with the fair spring to come.

Tate did not seem to attract as much abuse as Shadwell or some of
the later laureates. It is true that Pope had a go at him, but an attack
from that quarter was more or less a perennial hazard for contemporary poets. William Oldys, the antiquary, describes him as an
'honest, quiet man with downcast face and somewhat given to "fud-
dling" '. There were even eulogistic poems written about him, but
this may mean that he was not regarded as serious competition by
their authors. Edmund Broadus in his book on *The Laureateship*[1] is

1. Edmund K. Broadus, *The Laureateship*, Oxford, 1921.

severe on him, however. 'Tate's muse was permanently rouged', he writes. 'To the modern reader his verse is singularly irritating. With a rather pretentious elegance of manner, [he] combines a fawning humility, which stamps him, beyond all the other laureates, as the professional sycophant. He is constantly obtruding himself in the act of depreciating himself.' And he concludes 'Tate could write a good poem about tea (it really is a good poem), and when he came to eulogize a great personage or pay tribute to the memory of the august dead, he still wrote in terms of tea.'

Tate's successor was Nicholas Rowe (1674–1718), a successful dramatist whose play *The Fair Penitent* (1703)[1] gave us the term 'Lothario' for a seducer of women. (The part appealed to Garrick who played it frequently.) Although Hazlitt says that 'the genius of Rowe was slow and timid, and loved the ground' he was engaging enough to be friendly with Pope, Swift and Addison. An indication of his lovable character is his reaction to the failure of his first comedy *The Biter* (1704), which flopped completely on the first night. The author enjoyed it, however, and passed the evening laughing uproariously at his own jokes.

Rowe was another Shakespeare enthusiast, the first editor seriously to attempt a careful edition of the plays (*Works of William Shakespeare*, 6 vols., 1709). He included various whimsical additions to Shakespearian biography, thus starting several hares that required a couple of centuries' scholarship to track down and eliminate. Rowe himself wrote what he called a 'she-tragedy' claimed to be in imitation of Shakespeare. This work, which concerned a mistress of Edward IV called Jane Shore, had the following in common with Shakespeare, according to Dr Johnson: the story was English and some of the characters were historical.

Rowe's brief tenure of the laureateship was undistinguished. By the time he had prepared his first ode for George I, the King had left England for Hanover, which he much preferred to his newly-acquired realm. As George spoke no English, it cannot be supposed that he would have taken much interest in the laureate's offerings, however loyal. Nor would he have noticed the delightful 'own goal' in Rowe's first efforts (1716):

1. The play was actually Rowe's adaptation of *The Fatal Dowry* (1632) by Philip Massinger (1583–1640).

Muse, strike the lyre to some immortal strain.
  But oh! what skill, what master hand,
  Shall govern or constrain the wanton band?
Loose like my verse they dance and all without command . . .

But the monarch would certainly have approved the poet's Whig sympathies, which chimed with his own, and no doubt were the main reason for the appointment. 'This Rowe', remarked Thomas Hearne dourly, 'is a great Whig and but a mean poet.'

Rowe was followed by one of the more abused laureates, Laurence Eusden (1688–1730), described by Pope as 'a parson much be-mus'd in beer'. He got the job by writing a flattering poem celebrating the marriage of the Duke of Newcastle, who, as Lord Chamberlain, had the nomination of the laureate in his gift. Newcastle was actually his second choice as patron; he had previously fired off some verses at the influential Lord Halifax, George I's principal minister, but this gentleman very inconveniently died, which is the worst thing a patron can do.

The by now familiar accusations of drunkenness may have had some substance in Eusden's case. Pope describes:

How E— lay inspired beside a sink
And to mere mortals seem'd a Priest in drink.

Certainly it is hard to imagine that some of his spectacularly over-the-top odes could have been composed without the aid of the bottle. George I, whom Lady Mary Wortley Montagu described as 'an honest blockhead', is hymned in terms that even a Tartar despot might consider excessive:

By thee contending nations are ally'd,
To thee *Hesperia* sinks her tow'ring Pride,
Moscovia's Prince begins his Bonds to know,
And roaring Volga silently to flow.
Thee Gallia's Regent with fix'd Eyes admires,
For thee *Germania* feels a Lover's Fires.
From Belgian moles thy praise is heard around,
Thy Albion's cliffs return the pleasing Sound.

47

The shock of surprise at encountering Belgian moles in this context leads one to check the dictionary definitions. 'A massive break-water' doesn't seem particularly appropriate; but nor does 'the small insectivorous animal with very small eyes and soft fur, which burrows in the ground and casts up little heaps of mould'[1]. This is one of a number of *cruxes criticorum* in Eusden's work.

When George II, who detested his father, ascended the throne in his turn, Eusden was ready with another fulsome, if limping, tribute:

> Thy virtues shine particularly nice,
> Ungloomed with a confinity to vice.

When not writing in his official capacity, Eusden was more human, and sometimes even touching. It is almost worth slogging through the preceding 450 lines of his *Hero and Leander* to reach the affecting last couplet:

> But ah! too soon she spy'd him, where he lay
> A Lump of beautiful, tho' breathless Clay.

The next laureate, Colley Cibber (1671–1757) is amongst the most colourful of all. A large part of his twenty-seven years' occupancy of the post was taken up with literary quarrels, in particular a long drawn-out feud with Pope. This was initiated by Cibber's shameless 'borrowing' from a play co-written by Pope and John Gay to beef up his own piece *The Non-Juror*, in which he also took the lead. 'Pope, who was present at an early performance, became so furious he went backstage and picked a quarrel with Cibber. But the actor-manager, almost eighteen years his senior, refused to make any cuts; and the following night he actually punched Gay, when he in turn came round to protest.'[2] He acquired other enemies as a result of his high-handed ways as a theatrical manager and his insolence to dramatists. Fielding accused him of murdering the English language with a goose-quill, and the Jacobite propagandist Nathaniel Mist once announced in his *Journal* that Cibber was dead – a common method of rubbishing the opposition in the eighteenth

1. *Chambers Twentieth Century Dictionary.*
2. *Nick Russell, Poets by Appointment,* Blandford, 1981.

century. Dr Johnson never lost an opportunity for smacking him down although, says Boswell, he allowed that there was 'no reason to believe Cibber's play *The Careless Husband* (which Johnson admired), was not written by himself'. But it was Pope who kept him most continuously in his sights, delivering what would have been a *coup de grâce* to anyone less resilient than Cibber in *The New Dunciad* (1742):

> Round him much Embryo, much Abortion lay,
> Much future Ode, and abdicated Play;
> Nonsense precipitate, like running Lead
> That slip'd through cracks and zig-zags of the Head;
> All that on Folly Frenzy could beget,
> Fruits of dull Heat, and Sooterkins of Wit.
> Next o'er his Books his eyes began to roll,
> In pleasing Memory of all he stole . . .

More simply, if less elegantly, he disposed of Cibber's harmless but not very good verses in praise of Nash with an epigrammatic right hook:

> Cibber! write all thy Verses upon Glasses,
> The only way to save 'em from our A---s.

Like Nahum Tate, Cibber cheerfully 'improved' on Shakespeare, his bastardized version of *Richard III* lasting on the stage until the nineteenth century. Indeed, he made his last appearance as an actor playing in 'his own highly original version of Shakespeare's *King John*. Though seventy-four and without teeth, he insisted on going on; but the performance was not a success, particularly as David Garrick's production of the real King John was playing at a nearby theatre.'[1] More successful were several of his own plays, notably *Love's Last Shift* (1696), which was allegedly translated into French under the title *La Dernière Chemise de L'Amour*[2].

1. Nick Russell, op. cit.
2. The hazards of translation into French remain with us. Auden's '. . . of sites made sacred by something read there/a lunch, a good lay, or sheer lightness of heart' (*City without Walls*) has a French version where 'a good lay' is rendered as *'un bon poème'*.

Although Cibber can be forgiven much for his refusal to take himself too seriously and for his famous *Apology* for his life (1740), it is hard to extenuate the awfulness of his odes. Edmund Broadus makes a gallant effort to do so in his chapter on Cibber[1], but seems to realize it is special pleading: 'No device known to human ingenuity . . . could have saved Cibber from exhausting his stock of compliments to a monarch as colourless as George II, long before the laureate's twenty-seven years of ode-making had expired. Some of these compliments would be taken for irony if another poet had penned them. To say of a king with the soul of a drill-sergeant and a mind incapable of rising above the merest details of business:

> Whose regal state and pomp, we find
> Receive their glory from his mind

is to be either bitterly ironical or hopelessly fulsome, and unfortunately Cibber cannot profit by the alternative.' The same writer adds uncharitably: 'The lull in international strife at the beginning of his laureateship is characterized in language cacophonous enough to frighten the peace-dove from her perch:

> Europe now of bleeding wounds
> Sadly shall no more complain.
> George the jars of jealous crowns
> Heals with halcyon days again.

Most likely the poet is not here lamenting the absence of bleeding wounds, despite the determination of his Pegasus to gallop in that direction. Elsewhere, he struggles to get the intractable German place names of the British army's victories into metre:

> Tho' rough Seligenstadt
> The harmony defeat
> Tho' Klein-Ostein the verse confound;
> Yet, in joyful strain,
> Aschaffenburgh or Dettingen
> Shall charm the ear they seem to wound.
>
> *Birthday Ode* (1743)

1. Edmund K. Broadus, op. cit.

Probably they don't wound the German ear so much as the English. One sympathizes with poor Cibber who had, at that moment, no battles on English soil to celebrate, which might have afforded versifiable English names such as Ashby de la Zouch or Piddletrenthide. It is a relief to turn to the charming picture of domestic bliss that he evokes in his *Birthday Ode* (1732), where we find the monarch at table, together with his Hanoverian brood:

> Around the royal table spread
> See how the beauteous branches shine,
> Sprung from the fertile genial bed
> Of glorious GEORGE and CAROLINE.

This strikes the authentic Cibber note; one hopes it pleased their majesties and that he had his just reward; for, as he very frankly explained in a *Letter to Alexander Pope*, he wrote 'more to be fed than to be famous'.

After Cibber, an opportunity was missed to restore some of the prestige to the laureateship when Thomas Gray refused it. His amusing letter to Mason on the subject encapsulates many of the objections that a serious poet was likely to have on taking on the functions that are better left to the courtiers and sycophants, a ready supply of which is always available.

> Dear Mason,
> Though I very well know the bland emollient saponaceous
> qualities both of sack and silver, yet if any great man would
> say to me, 'I make you ratcatcher to his Majesty, with a
> salary of £300 a year and two butts of the best Malaga; and
> though it has been usual to catch a mouse or two, for
> form's sake, in public once a year, yet to you, Sir, we shall
> not stand upon these things', I cannot say I should jump at
> it; nay, if they would drop the very name of the office, and
> call me Sinecure to the King's Majesty, I should still feel a
> little awkward, and think everybody I saw smelt a rat about
> me . . .

The prize actually went to William Whitehead (1715–85), a scholar and dramatist who was soon embroiled in the customary squabbles – with Goldsmith after Garrick asked Whitehead to alter and improve Goldsmith's first play; with Charles Churchill, the satirist; with Dr Johnson; and with the young Gibbon. The last-named attacked the laureate's Birthday Ode for 1758. In this remarkable production the poet traced the royal line back to one Othbert, or possibly Ottoberto, who flourished in Northern Italy in 963. After various adventures, he proceeded to Germany (according to Whitehead), and founded George's line. Gibbon made short work of this.

Whitehead had to steer a difficult course – it was not easy to write up the glories of the governing class while the king and his ministers were in the process of losing the American colonies. He contents himself with some admonitions addressed to the erring colonists more in sorrow than in anger:

> . . . Enough of slaughter have ye known,
> Ye wayward children of a distant clime,
>   For you we heave the kindred groan,
> We pity your misfortune, and your crime.
>   Stop, parricides, the blow,
>   O find another foe!
> And hear a parent's dear request,
> Who longs to clasp you to her yielding breast.

Unfortunately this didn't seem to cut much ice with the Americans; nor did the much stronger line he took with the French and other European powers, whose failure to direct their affairs in accordance with British interests was so transparently against the expressed wishes of the Almighty. The verses had no effect, or at least not as much as cannon shot – but here the language barrier may be to blame.

Whitehead tried very hard to provide the appropriate verses required of him. Sometimes he succeeded, and sometimes he did not. In the ode for 1761, George III makes his first appearance, not altogether satisfactorily: 'To my way of thinking', writes Kenneth Hopkins, 'the note here is at once incredulous and despairing, but no doubt in this I am at fault'[1]:

1. Kenneth Hopkins, *The Poets Laureate*, London, 1954.

> – And who is he, of regal mien,
>   Reclin'd on Albion's golden fleece,
> Whose polish'd brow, and eye serene
>   Proclaim him elder-born of Peace?
> Another GEORGE! . . .

Later he refers to the new monarch as George II's 'blooming Heir'.

Verses like this may have led Dr Johnson to compare Whitehead unfavourably even with Cibber. 'Cibber's familiar style', he boomed, 'was better than that which Whitehead has assumed. *Grand nonsense is unsupportable.*'

The poet, who was a modest man, made no great claims for his verses and has left us a poignant reminder of the pains to which all laureates are heir in his *Pathetic Apology for all Laureates, Past, Present and to Come*, found among his papers after his death:

> Each morning paper is so kind
> To give his works to every wind.
> Each evening post and magazine,
> *Gratis* adopts the lay *serene*.
> On their frail barks his praise or blame
> Floats for an hour and sinks with them;
> Sure without envy you might see
> Such floundering immortality.

The five years' laureateship following Whitehead was filled by Thomas Warton (1728–90), an amiable scholar and indifferent poet. In the former capacity he published *A Companion to the Guide and a Guide to the Companion* (1760), which satirized antiquarian studies and Oxford guidebooks; it included learned digressions on coffee houses, inns, billiard tables and skittle alleys. This was followed by *The Oxford Sausage* (1764), an anthology of Oxford's wit and wisdom. His *History of English Poetry* (1774–81) was much admired by his fellow scholars. More than any other laureate he seems to exude the fug of the Senior Common Room, his character exhibiting the mixture of deep learning and extreme childishness sometimes to be found in dons. One is not surprised to find him preoccupied with another topic of consuming interest to the heartier type of scholar in his *Panegyric on Oxford Ale*. A modern equivalent of Warton would be the type of learned professor who advertises his enthusiasm for professional football. Love of ease and of ale must have made him popular with the boys of Winchester, where his brother was headmaster. This popularity can only have been increased by his practice of 'ghosting' the boys' exercises for them, with errors adroitly incorporated to allay pedagogical suspicions. He took his clerical duties equally lightly, possessing, it is said, only two sermons, one written by his father and the other printed.

Warton's five-year tenure of the laureateship was uneventful, save for a tricky period in the autumn of 1788 when George III had an attack of insanity. The customary New Year's ode for 1789 had to be cancelled, since Warton could find nothing very suitable to say about a mad sovereign. Fortunately, when it came round to the time for the Birthday Ode, His Majesty had recovered, and the poet was able to refer tactfully to his health, as a 'fair landscape' over which 'the shadow of a great storm' had passed.

The problem became acute – indeed, insoluble – for Warton's successor, Henry James Pye (1745–1813). In the last three years of Pye's tenure, George III had become permanently mad, a state caused, it is said, from worrying over his favourite daughter's illness, though Pye's verses cannot have helped. All traffic in odes was therefore suspended *sine die*, to the relief of the laureate, and the even greater relief of the public.

By common consent Henry Pye is absolutely the worst laureate ever, worse even than Alfred Austin (q.v.) whose productions entertained a whole generation. Pitt gave him the job as compensation for the loss of a parliamentary seat, although Pye's lack of qualities deserving any recognition was outstanding. He had made three speeches in the House during his entire career, the most important of which informed his fellow members that his constituents had not enjoyed a good harvest.

Pye was no more than a slightly bookish country squire whose effusions would have attracted little attention had he not been elevated to the laureateship. Like most country gentlemen he loved the monarchy, the military, and his small estate. This love of the land made him a fitting celebrant of our most agricultural king. Peter Pindar's advice to the new laureate:

> Of Pig-economy exalt the praise;
> Oh flatter Sheep and Bullocks in thy lays;

was not exactly followed, but he did write an astonishing poem on
Shooting (1784):

> Forth from the summer guard of bolt and lock
> Comes the thick guetre, and the fustian frock.
> With curious skill the deathful tube is made,
> Clean as the firelock of the spruce parade:
> Yet let no polish of the sportsman's gun
> Flash like the soldier's weapon to the sun,
> Or the bright steel's refulgent glare presume
> To penetrate the peaceful forest's gloom . . .

Such lines ingeniously combine Pye's affection for country pursuits
with his interest in soldiers[1]. He goes deeper into shooting, and
indeed many other matters, in his *Sportsman's Dictionary*, which has
some interesting advice on how to deal with ailments in animals.
For instance, we find this entry under the letter 'H':

> HEAD, pain in, of goats, often happens through excessive heats
> or colds; also from wet or unwholesome feedings.
>   Take a handful of rosemary tops, an ounce of turmeric
> beaten into powder, and the like quantity of mithridate; boil
> them in water, and put a little vinegar to it, and so let him
> drink half a pint each morning: put vinegar, wherein hyssop
> has been seethed, into his nostrils, and hold up his head, that
> he turn it not out, for six minutes, or thereabout.

Kenneth Hopkins, who quotes the above passage, appends the following extremely uncharitable comment to it: 'Perhaps a future
Laureate, happening to revise this work, will also explain how the
goat makes it understood where the pain is, in the first place.'[2]
   Country life, apart from engendering pains in the head from cold

---

1. Thomas Matthias in *The Pursuits of Literature* (1796) claims that Pye managed to
arrange for his translation of *Tyrtaeus* to be read to five militia regiments on parade.
However, before the reading was halfway through, 'all the front ranks and as many
others as were within verse-shot' dropped their arms and fell asleep. The
unfortunate allied soldiers in the First World War were later to suffer a similar fate
at the hands of Ella Wheeler Wilcox.
2. Kenneth Hopkins, op. cit.

and damp, sometimes breeds a mild form of eccentricity in its adherents. Pye was not entirely free from this, as may be seen from his *Carmen Seculare for the Year 1800* in which he argues passionately that 1800, and not 1801, is the first year of the new century. One or two of his essay titles also evoke his love of the intellectual hobby-horse – e.g. 'The Antiquity of the Round Robin', or 'The Effect of Music on Animals'. As a poet he had certainly mastered the art of bathos, but it is remarkable that he managed to apply his skill equally effectively in prose. Hopkins quotes a Pye aphorism in an essay on the perennially fascinating topic of 'the weather'. Like a damp firework, the punch line resolutely refuses to ignite, despite Pye's vigorous efforts with the blue touchpaper:

> It is a proverbial observation, that, in this country, persons, for want of other topics of conversation, are very apt to introduce the weather, and so to inform the company, as if it were a discovery they had just made, and with which everyone else was unacquainted, that it is a fine or a bad day.

Pye's poetry is not really so entertaining as his prose; his odes are all 'of impeccable loyalty and incredible dullness'[1]. In years of military setbacks he put out suitably cosmetized versions of events that reek more of the Ministry of Information than of the Muses. He did his best to ignore or circumnavigate the King's bouts of insanity. Each year he added to the

> Birthday, torrents from Parnassus
> And New Year's spring-tide of divine molasses

Spring and summer are welcomed again and again in dire Della Cruscan (q.v.) diction:

> . . . and o'er the fertile glade
> In manhood's riper form array'd,
> Bright June appears, and from his bosom throws,
> Blushing with hue divine, his own ambrosial rose.

Over in Europe it is mostly war and desolation:

---

1. *Everyman's Dictionary of Literary Biography*, London, 1970.

Wastes where no hopes of future harvests rise
While floating corses choke th'unpurpled[1] flood,
And ev'ry dewy sod is stain'd with civic blood.

But in Britain, which has sensibly substituted Freedom for wine and
olives, things are every day getting better and better:

No purple vintage though she boast,
No olive shade her ruder coast;
Yet here immortal Freedom reigns,
And law protects what labour gains;
And as her manly sons behold
The cultur'd farm, the teeming fold . . . etc., etc.

Echoes of the complacent tones of country clergymen and the
squirality reverberate through Pye's verses; he was surely much
closer to the spirit of their party, which is still not entirely divorced
from the land, than its modern literary mascot, a manufacturer of
slick thrillers. Nor would Pye have got himself into trouble with
attempted blackmail by ladies unknown to him, for he was, in
Byron's phrase, 'eminently respectable in everything but his
poetry'. Indeed he was a magistrate, first in Berkshire and then in
Westminster, though his performance of these duties was apparently no more assiduous than his efforts on behalf of his parliamentary constituents. Leigh Hunt, in his *Autobiography*, describes Pye
presiding over his court 'in a state of scornful indignation at being
interrupted in the perusal of a manuscript by the monitions of his
police-officers, who were obliged to remind him over and over
again that he was a magistrate, and that the criminal multitude were
in waiting . . .'

With this rather charming cameo of the irascible bard we take
leave of him. Although he was the worst of poets, he was by no
means the worst of men. Perhaps the only really unforgivable thing
he ever did was to commute the laureate's annual butt of canary
wine for cash. Robert Southey, his successor, called it a wicked
decision; and indeed men have been murdered in their beds for less.

With the demise of Pye the calibre of the laureates abruptly
improves, never again to sink as low as George III's blackbird,

1. This should possibly be 'enpurpled'.

57

except perhaps during the tenure of Alfred Austin. Robert Southey (1774–1843) was a turgid poet, but indefatigably industrious (and occasionally sublime) as a prose writer. He had an innocent conceit of himself which is wholly inoffensive, and which protected him both from the ridicule of his enemies and any perception of his own limitations. Byron's great satire on him, *A Vision of Judgement* (1822), has more or less destroyed Southey in the eyes of posterity, but the laureate himself was not much put out. Had not George IV expressed himself well pleased with the poet's long-winded obsequies for his father? Since the new king, as was traditional with the Hanoverians, had intensely disliked his father, Southey could probably assume that the skill of the poem was more admired than its subject.

The tragi-comic elements in Southey's character and career are outlined by Wyndham Lewis and Lee in their introduction to some examples of Southey's uninspiring verse:

> . . . he wrote a History of the Peninsular War without the principal military documents which the Duke refused to lend him, and held they did not matter; he declined Peel's offer of a baronetcy; and having married a second time in 1839, returned from his wedding tour, says the *Dictionary of National Biography* ungallantly, 'in a condition of utter mental exhaustion'. His faults, if they can be so called, were predicting national ruin on small provocation and believing all who differed from him politically to be enemies of God and Society.[1]

In his youth Southey had been a radical, but by the time he took on the laureateship his mind had fixed itself into that rigid mould of paranoia and self-righteousness to which conservative minded persons are prone. Having seen the horrors of recent events in France, he very sensibly decided that reform was preferable to revolution; nobody would have objected to this honest change of heart, had he been able to resist hectoring his audience like a *Pravda* editorial. Thus his Preface to *A Vision of Judgement* (itself a tribute to a monarch who aspired to be a benevolent autocrat) attacked Shelley and Byron in unrestrained language. They were labelled the 'Satanic school' of writers, breathing 'the spirit of Belial in their lascivious

1. D.B. Wyndham Lewis and Charles Lee, op. cit., p. 131.

parts and the spirit of Moloch in those loathsome images of atrocities and horrors which they delight to represent'. This splenetic outburst, reminiscent of Mr Paul Johnson working himself into a frenzy over the BBC, proved to be extremely unwise. Byron's famous response raked through Southey's career in merciless fashion:

> He had written praises of a regicide;
>   He had written praises of all kings whatever;
> He had written for republics far and wide,
>   And then against them bitterer than ever;
> For pantisocracy he once had cried
>   Aloud, a scheme less moral than 'twas clever;
>   Then grew a hearty anti-jacobin –
>   Had turn'd his coat – and would have turned his skin.

Worse still, as the poet is reciting his 'spavin'd dactyls' to the heavenly throng, Byron depicts the late monarch as suddenly jerked into wakefulness; imagining himself to be the victim of a poetical performance by the dreaded Pye, he exclaims:

> What! What!
> *Pye* come again? No more – no more of that!

Nor is the prevalence of quantity over quality in Southey's work neglected:

> He had written much blank verse, and blanker prose,
> And more of both than anybody knows.
>
> He had written Wesley's life – here turning round
>   To Satan, 'Sir, I'm ready to write yours,
> In two octavo volumes, nicely bound,
>   With notes and preface, all that most allures
> The pious purchaser; and there's no ground
>   For fear, for I can choose my own reviewers . . .

The Laureate cannot be prevented from reading his own *Vision of Judgement*, of which he has thoughtfully brought along a copy; but this is too great a torture for the assembled company:

The angels stopped their ears and plied their pinions;
The devils ran howling, deafened, down to hell,
The ghosts fled, gibbering, for their own dominions –

Eventually Saint Peter knocks the unstoppable bard down with his keys, the only way of halting the torrent. Southey falls like Phaeton into the sea and:

. . . first sank to the bottom – like his works,
But soon rose to the surface – like himself;

All satires are unfair – the more effective the satire, the greater the unfairness. Nevertheless, Southey brought this on himself. Nor did he have to write his wretched tribute to George III in the first place, for he had negotiated the abolition of the automatic and obligatory productions of the laureate. He is mostly remembered now for his excellent *Life of Nelson* (1813) and the story of *The Three Bears*. The bulk of his poetry has sunk into oblivion, which makes Thomas Moore's epigrammatic epitaph all the more poignant:

Death, weary of so dull a writer,
Put to his books a *finis* thus:
Oh! may the earth on him lie lighter
Than did his quartos upon us!

The laureateship of William Wordsworth (1770–1850) that began in 1843 was remarkable for its complete and refreshing absence of official poems. The poet was very old and very conservative by the time he went to Buckingham Palace in court dress borrowed from Samuel Rogers, and managed with some difficulty to kneel and kiss Queen Victoria's hand. Like Southey before him and Alfred Austin after him, he had flirted with radicalism at the beginning of his career. As Bertrand Russell irreverently puts it: 'In his youth, Wordsworth sympathized with the French Revolution, went to France, wrote good poetry, and had a natural daughter. At this period he was a "bad" man. Then he became "good", abandoned his daughter, adopted correct principles, and wrote bad poetry.' He wrote not a single line in his official capacity, although he supplied an ode for the inauguration of the Prince Consort as Chancellor of

Cambridge University in 1847. The subject was not promising and the poem was not good, but for that one must blame Wordsworth's son-in-law, Edward Quillinan.

Wordsworth was certainly an ornament to the laureateship, but his successor was probably the most appropriate and most popular choice in the whole history of the office. Alfred, Lord Tennyson (1809–92) was 'the perfect mouthpiece of his age, both in its merits and its shortcomings', states a modern introduction to a selection of his poems; Lady Gregory put it more penetratingly when she remarked that 'Tennyson had the British Empire for God and Queen Victoria for the Virgin Mary'.

Tennyson had been considered for the laureateship after the death of Southey. Since then, he had published his great elegy for Arthur Hallam, *In Memoriam* (1850), which was immediately successful, and more importantly, appealed to Prince Albert. The Prince, who was at the time concerning himself in the search for Wordsworth's replacement, was at once convinced of the necessity of appointing Tennyson. The latter perhaps had heard rumours of the impending honour, for he had a dream the night before the invitation arrived in which: 'Prince Albert came and kissed him on the cheek, and he said in his dream "Very kind, but very German".'[1] The poet was at first undecided as to whether to accept or not, and talked it over with his family and dinner guests that evening. According to Hallam Tennyson, he finally accepted because his friend Venables explained that, if he became Poet Laureate, when he dined out he would always be offered the liver-wing of a fowl.

A fresh and unforeseen hazard of the job immediately manifested itself on the new laureate's assumption of office: seemingly every poetaster in the land hastened to send him their verses for comment, by which they meant approval. Failure to reply merely attracted further letters of an increasingly insulting nature. All self-respecting middle-class Victorians played the piano, painted watercolours and wrote poetry; as products of a romantic age they naturally assumed that the failure of professionals to appreciate their talents was but the common fate of neglected geniuses. Praise of their poems of course stimulated further production of them; but, then, so did depreciation. Tennyson was driven to desperation by these

1. I do not see what is particularly German about this, but possibly manners have changed since Tennyson's day.

poetical bluebottles and once replied to the sender of an unsolicited volume: 'Farewell, yours, A. Tennyson (in the 8th year of my persecution).'

Tennyson took his responsibilities as the oracular voice of his age very seriously. His more controversial effusions were sometimes published anonymously, such as his demand for military volunteers which appeared in *The Times* of 1859 under the single initial T. The fact that this was thought to be the work of the so-called unofficial laureate, Martin Tupper, a talentless and sententious chauvinist, is an indication that it is not in Tennyson's happiest mode. It is the sort of thing that a Home Counties colonel might dash off after reading too many editorials in *The Daily Telegraph*:

> Let your reforms for a moment go!
> Look to your butts, and take good aims!
> Better a rotten borough or so
> Than a rotten fleet and a city in flames!
> Storm, Storm, Riflemen form!
> Ready, be ready against the storm!
> Riflemen, Riflemen, Riflemen form!

As a matter of fact, Tennyson had voted for reform of the franchise, though not without misgivings, which he expressed in a portentous warning to Gladstone:

> Steersman, be not precipitate in thine act
>   Of steering, for the river here, my friend,
>   Parts in two channels, moving to one end –
> This goes straight forward to the cataract:
>   That streams about the bend . . .

In consideration of a promised redistribution between town and country, Tennyson overcame his doubts, but Gladstone's policy towards the navy was too much for him; in a poem published in *The Times* (23 April 1885) he warns that the British will 'kick' Gladstone 'from his place' if he reduced the number of battleships. Characteristically for his age he was fixed in a time warp, and quite unable to appreciate the growing militarism of Germany. France was the great enemy, not least because of the louche behaviour of her inhabitants, and because of her religion. On one occasion he refers to the Catholic church as 'that half-pagan harlot kept by France'[1], but that was also published anonymously and no doubt in a journal not read by Queen Victoria.

The high point – some would say the low point – of Tennyson's laureatese is reached with the *Ode for the Queen's Jubilee* in 1887. It was performed privately at Buckingham Palace for the Queen, whose reaction is not recorded, and then sung at the laying of the foundation stone for the Imperial Institute. Perhaps this was a wise decision as a pleasant tune would certainly help to mask the tone of flatulent boasting:

> Fifty years of ever-broadening Commerce!
> Fifty years of ever-brightening Science!
> Fifty years of ever-widening Empire!
>
> You, the Mighty, the Fortunate.
> You, the lord-territorial –
> You the lord-manufacturer,
> You, the hardy, laborious,
> Patient children of Albion,
> You, Canadian, Indian,
> Australasian, African,
> All your hearts be in harmony,
> All your voices be in unison,
> Singing 'Hail to the glorious
> Golden year of her Jubilee'.

When Tennyson died in 1892, the problem of the succession was not easily solved, since it was hard to find anyone approaching his standing in public esteem. Not that there weren't contenders amongst the ranks of now justly forgotten poets, such as William Watson, Robert Buchanan, and Sir Edwin Arnold. Queen Victoria, discussing the matter with Gladstone, is supposed to have remarked: 'I am told that Mr Swinburne is the best poet in my dominions', and no doubt Gladstone was unwilling to enter into detailed discussions with Her Majesty as to the specific merits of poems like *Dolores*, which celebrated 'our Lady of Pain', or *Faustine*, described as a 'love-machine with clockwork joints of supple gold'.

1. *Suggested by Reading an Article in a Newspaper.*

He contented himself with the observation that Swinburne's political views were 'impossible'[1]. Certainly Swinburne would have provided a startling contrast to his moralistic and imperial-minded predecessor; even though he had by now been delivered into the semi-house-arrest of Watts Dunton in Putney, he was still given to the occasional outburst of republican fervour; nor had his interest in lesbianism and flagellation abated. Watts Dunton, hearing the poet pacing the floor above him at The Pines, fondly imagined another great epic was on the way; but often the great man's Muse was supplying him with quite other material, of which Queen Victoria would definitely not have approved. In any case, Swinburne himself was not interested in the laureateship; the only candidate with the right qualifications, he informed a circle of admirers, was Canon Dixon, the author of *Mano* (1833) and a *History of the Church of England* (1878–1902). (It was sometimes a little hard to tell whether Swinburne was joking or not.)[2]

In the event, Gladstone could not make up his mind, and Lord Rosebery, who briefly succeeded him as Prime Minister, also put the problem on one side. It fell to Lord Salisbury to make an appointment which was to become resoundingly popular with all who enjoy the richer absurdities of the British establishment in solemn mood, but which very nearly sank the laureateship for good. Like Pitt before him, Salisbury saw no reason why a political failure (in this case, twice rejected by the electorate), should not make a very good laureate, providing his opinions were sound. Accordingly, he offered the job to Alfred Austin (1835–1913), a conservative leader writer on *The Standard* and the author of some outstandingly bad poems. In some quarters the bestowing of any poetical honour on such a man aroused a mixture of hilarity and derision; this did not trouble Austin, whose armour-plating of self-satisfaction was almost impossible to pierce. Sydney Carlyle Cockerell recorded in a letter that 'Austin himself used to say that his appointment was a very simple matter, the recognition of his being at the head of English literature'. That certainly puts Swinburne, Kipling, William Morris and Coventry Patmore in their place.

1. *The Critic* even claimed that the appointment of Swinburne would 'hasten the death of the Queen'.
2. If Canon Dixon's candidature failed, he recommended Lord De Tabley.

Many of the attacks unleashed on Austin were aimed at the man as much as at the poet; he invited obloquy with his egotism, his posturing chauvinism both of the male kind and the other variety, his lack of humour, and his dreary servility to right-wing shibboleths. As for his work, some of the lyrics are harmless enough in the sentimental Victorian manner; but his ambitious dramatic poems are mostly farragos of witless pomp and improbable circumstance.[1] All the same, one should begin by dispelling two calumnies which seem to have arisen because almost any line of verse, however implausibly bad, was potentially a line by the laureate in the eyes of his enemies. But he never wrote of Dr Jameson's raiding party that:

> They rode across the veldt
> As fast as they could pelt . . .[2]

which is more likely to have come from one of the many parodies of Austin's febrile outburst on the subject. Nor is there any hard evidence that he penned the celebrated lines on the illness of the Prince of Wales:

> Along the wires the electric message came
> He is no better; he is much the same,[3]

which do not have the authentic ring of Austinian bathos. The matter has been gone into more thoroughly than perhaps it warrants by J. Lewis May in *The Dublin Review* (July, 1937) and he concludes that 'however lamentably some of Austin's verse may trail on broken wing', he could never have written anything as tragically feeble as this. It was probably the production of some wag as a commentary on Oxford's Newdigate Prize Poem; for which the set subject in 1871 was 'The Prince of Wales's Illness'. The Newdigate has cer-

---

1. The various prefaces to these, in which Austin trumpeted his claims to greatness in baroque effusions of pretended modesty, do not make them any easier to stomach.
2. Even so painstaking a scholar as John Gross in *The Rise and Fall of the Man of Letters* (London, 1969, footnote, p. 81) quotes these lines as if they were Austin's own.
3. Norton Crowell, in his biography of Austin, quotes a contemporary as saying that Austin wrote these lines about the dying Tennyson; but I can find no evidence for this claim either.

tainly been a mortuary for the Muses in its day, but that is no reason to drag Austin into the matter.

Austin's poem on the Jameson raid is quite as bad as the lines misquoted above would suggest, but somewhat different. It immediately delivered him over to his enemies, but what was far worse, annoyed Queen Victoria, who wrote indignantly to the Prime Minister about it. As is well known, Dr Jameson led an unsanctioned raid into the Transvaal from Rhodesia in defence of the 'Uitlanders', whom he regarded as oppressed by the Boers. This was a spectacular flop; Jameson surrendered and was politely handed over to the British by the Boers for trial. Austin's rollicking defence of this undistinguished episode appeared in *The Times* some nine days after the surrender, on 11 January 1896. The poem bears a superficial resemblance to Kipling, but the content is pure Austin:

> Let lawyers and statesmen addle
> Their pates over points of law:
> If sound be our sword and saddle,
> And gun-gear, who cares a straw?
> When men of our own blood pray us
> To ride to their kinfolk's aid,
> Not Heaven itself shall stay us
> From the rescue they call a raid.

Unfortunately, the Uitlanders failed to rise in support of Jameson, so perhaps they were less keen to be 'rescued' than had previously been thought. Austin's picture of foolish lawyers and statesmen 'addling their pates' over points of law instead of getting on with invading those who had annoyed them, would certainly have appealed to Adolf Hitler. As in the Sudetenland, there were 'girls and mothers' (so the poet darkly hints) in imminent danger of a fate worse than death:

> So we forded and galloped forward,
> As hard as our beasts could pelt,
> First eastward, then trending norward,
> Right over the rolling veldt:

The poem may have displeased the Queen and the Government,

but it delighted such journals as *Punch* which immediately rushed
out what are known in the world of pop music as cover versions:

> Let lawyers and statesmen addle
> Their pates over points of law;
> Of pegasus I'm in the saddle,
> But why does he cough 'Hee-haw'?
> Eight stanzas! Inspired! Mad ones!
> Sound well if sung to a band!
> There! dash it! some good, some bad ones,
> To finish with 'crushings' and 'Rand'.

And on the stages of the music-halls, too, the laureate's effort did
not go uncelebrated. Arthur Waugh, who was a friend of Austin,
wrote mournfully in his *London Letter* that: 'As poetry, it is true [the
lines] could scarce be worse; . . . they are being recited at the
Alhambra every evening by Mr E.H. Vanderfelt, and seem to please
a section of the gallery.'

The laureate himself attributed all this to jealousy. In his *Autobiography* he is careful to avoid all mention of the actual poem, a
curious omission in view of his incessant quotation from his other
works. In an indirect reference to the fall-out from it, he serenely
compares himself to Petrarch, for whom, as he points out, the Bays
also brought no peace of mind, but only the slings and arrows of
envious scribblers. Probably he had no regrets. One feels that he
would have enjoyed the opportunities for propagandist verse in our
own age. Who better than Austin could have hymned the patriotism
of businessmen who bust the Rhodesian oil sanctions, or of statesmen who lied to Parliament at the time of Suez?

It has often been remarked that it was the most unfortunate day
of Austin's life when he was appointed Poet Laureate, but this cannot have been his own view. Apart from his image of himself as
being 'at the head of English literature', he clearly relished his contribution as an upholder of official virtues and as a political seer. As
a correspondent for *The Standard*, he covered the 1869 Vatican
Council for a while, and assured his readers that there was absolutely no possibility the Council would agree to the proposed
dogma of papal infallibility. The Council, less well informed about
itself than Austin, at once proceeded to endorse the doctrine, but by

then he was covering the Franco–Prussian war. Here, his predictions were rather more successful. Like Tennyson before him, he was extremely pro-German; more particularly, he was absolutely besotted with Bismarck. The latter unwisely asked the poet for a copy of his Gallophobic poem *The Challenge Answered*, and Austin's cup overflowed. Thereafter he regarded himself as being in the Chancellor's confidence, though it is doubtful whether Bismarck took the same view. T.H.S. Escott, writing in *The Contemporary Review* of July 1913, describes an incident which illustrates Austin's conviction of his own importance and influence: 'During this time *The Standard* correspondent at Versailles [i.e. at the Franco–Prussian peace negotiations] was Alfred Austin, while Laurence Oliphant represented *The Times*. The two men were the best of friends; but as an instance of Austin's tendency to magnify his apostleship, Oliphant used to tell how, on a certain morning, Austin expressed misgivings about the relations between the Courts of St James and Berlin. "I have not", rejoined Oliphant, "heard of any hitch." "Nevertheless", replied Austin, "I fear there must be because only an hour or two ago I met Bismarck and saw great coldness in his bow to me." ' Norton Crowell, who quotes this in his biography of Austin[1], adds a waspish comment: 'The break-down of international relations he might discern in a distant greeting; he could never suspect a personal dislike.' On home ground, the poet was no less determined to establish an aura of gravitas about his person: 'Dinner guests at Swinford Old Manor [Austin's country house] were both amused and startled by the dramatic bearing of the servant, who announced the entrance of their hosts with the impressive words, "The Poet Laureate and Mrs Austin".'[2]

When not adding his three ha'p'orth to the political debate, Austin set himself up as a critical sage. His literary essays of 1869 disposed of various contemporaries in the manner of a bloated flea feeding on a great man's ear. Of the then laureate he wrote grandly: 'The age of Tennyson! The notion is, of course, preposterous.' His remarks about Browning are no less ill-judged, and seem to be more a description of himself than of his target: 'It is bad enough that there should be people, pretending to authority among us, who call

1. Norton B. Crowell, *Alfred Austin: Victorian*, Albuquerque, 1953, p. 28.
2. Crowell, op. cit., p. 27.

a man a great poet when, though unquestionably a poet, he has no marks of greatness about him. But that is a venial error, and a trifling misfortune compared to what would be the misery in an age which gibbeted itself beforehand for the pity of posterity by deliberately calling a man a poet who – however remarkable his mental attributes and powers – is not specifically a poet at all. I hope we shall be spared this humiliation. At any rate, I must protest against being supposed willingly to participate in it.' Who cared, one wonders, whether Austin participated in anything, least of all a 'humiliation' of his own fabrication? Nevertheless, the fatuous comment provoked Browning to some ill-tempered remarks about 'the filthy little snob' Alfred Austin; more amusingly, he satirized the literary pretensions of the tiny laureate by constantly referring to him as a 'Banjo Byron'.

Perhaps Austin nurtured a secret hope that English literature was about to embark on 'the age of Austin', and that his critical task was to clear the dead wood and lumber from the path of the advancing juggernaut. In such a case he had a clear duty to save the nation from such a catastrophe as the 'gibbeting of itself beforehand for the pity of posterity'. If persistence were the criterion for poetic stature, Austin would no doubt earn pride of place in the poetic Pantheon. If other, more usual, criteria are applied, his claim is not so strong. His astonishing verse dramas and his idiosyncratic love poems are dealt with elsewhere in this volume, but a few remarks about his political and laureate productions are relevant here.

In his youth, Austin had the briefest of flirtations with liberal ideas, but he soon settled into a comfortable groove of uncritical imperialism. Surveying the world from his Kentish fastness, he approved of the Americans, whom he graciously invited to participate in the acquisition of the spoils of colonialism, and violently disapproved of the Tsar and the French. His poem against the last-named is a good example of his alliterative declamatory style, by means of which the readers, if not the opposition, are beaten half-senseless:

> O thou nation, base besotted, whose ambition
> cannon shotted,
> And huge mounds of corpses clotted with cold
> gore alone can sate!

> May the God of Battles shiver every arrow
> in thy quiver,
> And the nobly-flowing river thou dost covet[1]
> drown thy hate.

Bismarck is said to have been so delighted with the poem that he memorized all nine stanzas, and the thought of them being recited in a thick Prussian accent is indeed daunting.

Apart from admiring Prussians, especially when they were slaughtering Frenchmen, Austin supported the Polish insurrection and, with qualifications[2], the movement that culminated in Italian independence. Indeed, Italy inspired a romantic verse tale entitled *Rome or Death!* (1873), at the beginning of which the hero, Godfrid, is discovered wintering on Capri with Miriam. Miriam is one of Austin's more bewildering heroines. Her lineage seems to go back to an ancient mésalliance between the Gods and man:

> Her body was of glorious make; her limbs
> Vaunted the strain of that Olympian line,
> Reared upon earth as sung in deathless hymns
> When mortal mould was filled with juice divine.

On the other hand, she seems to have become a sort of female Bacchus, perhaps as a consequence of being exposed to the notoriously corrupting Capri sunshine:

> . . . as she came anear, the juicy bells
> She merrily held and dangled in his face.

With the invasion of Garibaldi, Godfrid, Miriam and another admirer of Miriam's named Gilbert, set out for the mainland. Their disembarcation at Naples is memorably recorded:

> Then out they sprang, – first Miriam, Gilbert next,
> Last Godfrid, – and the eager host pressed round;
> Rude fishermen, hoarse women half unsexed
> And rude sea-urchins frisking o'er the ground . . .

1. i.e. the Rhine.
2. The qualifications were that he hastened to disclaim any intended criticism of the papacy. Austin himself was a Catholic.

Ignoring the rude sea-urchins, the little band makes for Rome. On the way, they encounter babies acting as traffic-policemen:

> The very babes in arms with gesture droll
> Held out their little dimpled fists, and showed
> The line that looked the straightest to the goal.

They arrive at Rome and besiege it, together with Garibaldi. Miriam loves Gilbert, but will only marry him when Rome is freed. When the garrison counterattacks, Gilbert is mortally wounded, and Miriam relents sufficiently to wed him just before he expires.

Rome or Death! is written in strains of unbelievable bombast, and does not illustrate the author's contention in his Preface that political subjects can be well managed in poetry. Nor, alas, does Austin's other Risorgimento poem on the reported wounding and capturing of Garibaldi. *Aspromonte* is a fine specimen of the higher doggerel, which bangs along merrily like a patter song from the Savoy operas:

> Well, then, know we would not barter this our never-
> flinching martyr
> For the very largest charter we could coax from 'Right
> Divine',
> That his blood upon your ermine only makes us more
> determine
> To exterminate the vermin who have baulked his grand
> design.
>
> And you think a wounded hero may hereafter count as zero
> And that every desperate Nero rules the cities which he
> burns;
> That a wild steed caught and snaffled means a nation
> wholly baffled
> And its future may be raffled in your diplomatic urns!

Despite the violence of this, Austin is careful to state in an appended note that he 'should be sorry if any one supposed that his sympathies are not, and have not always been with constitutional monarchy in Italy'.

The Tsar, of course, was not a constitutional monarch. Austin felt he could safely let himself go when writing about such a tyrant, and his sympathy for the unfortunate Poles does him credit. Alas! the verses which he penned on their behalf do not; moreover, they show the disastrous influence of Swinburne:

> Shrink! England! What! Shrink when intoxicate Tartar,
>   Deriding your wrath, rides in blood to the waist?
> When the flesh of the virgin, the bones of the martyr,
>   The breast of the matron, are bared and defaced?
> Do you deem diplomatic frivolities ample
>   To save you your title of moral and just
> When a horde of ensanguined barbarians trample
>   Mankind and remonstrance alike in the dust?

This kind of thing lends substance to his biographer's melancholy comment that 'far too often [Austin] apparently misdiagnosed as the stirrings of the Muse the more mundane phenomena of metabolism'[1]. At least his chauvinistic view of Britain ('Men deemed thee fallen, did they?') is less percussively, if no less ridiculously, expressed:

> The dupes! Thou dost but stand erect, and lo!
> The nations cluster round; and while the horde
> Of wolfish backs slouch home-ward to their snow,
> Thou, mid thy sheaves in peaceful seasons stored, –
> Towerest supreme, victor without a blow,
> Smilingly leaning on thy undrawn sword!

With this image of Britannia leaning casually on her sword while the opposition retreat with their tails between their legs, it is appropriate to take leave of Austin. It is very much the pose he struggled to adopt, not only with regard to the pack of jackals over the water, but also towards his noisy critics. It is a pose of studied serenity and effortless superiority – a natural one for a man 'at the head of English literature'. It followed that no attention need be paid to the minor blemishes (if any) in his work. Edward Marsh in his memoirs recalls the laureate's reaction when someone had the temerity to

---

1. Norton Crowell, op. cit., p. 53.

point out to him a few of his grammatical errors. 'I dare not alter these things', he said, 'they come to me from above.'

Austin's successor, Robert Bridges (1844–1930) was extremely low-key compared to his bustling and self-important predecessor. He was also a gifted minor poet and scholar whose greatest achievement on behalf of English literature was to edit the first edition of the work of Gerard Manley Hopkins. Although he was jeered at by the unpleasant Horatio Bottomley (who called him 'the dumb laureate'), he surprised everybody by producing, at the very end of his life, his long meditative poem *The Testament of Beauty* (1929). He had the satisfaction of enjoying a major success at the age of eighty-five, and the poem itself ran through fourteen impressions in the first year of publication. The revival of the laureateship that began with Bridges continued with John Masefield (1878–1967), who had a far wider public for his poetry. Since his work struck a sympathetic chord with readers, and was full of vitality and narrative interest, it was often attacked by the toping adherents of literary cliques. His niche in the Pantheon is secure, however, and the general level of competence of Masefield and Bridges has made it difficult to demean the laureateship subsequently by appointing a modern equivalent of Austin or Pye. Cecil Day Lewis (1904–72), who followed Masefield, was probably the most daring appointment ever in political terms. As a member of 'The Auden generation' he had held Marxist views in the 1930s, although he was safely pinkish by 1968. In his case, it was impossible for hostile elements to dig out a youthful indiscretion like Southey's *Wat Tyler*, since his early poetry is mostly his best. All the same, there were one or two works which would have been better left in the bottom drawer, such as his play *Noah and the Waters*, written shortly after he joined the Communist Party. This affiliation had had a predictably dire impact on his work. The play even displeased the *Daily Worker* – though perhaps that means it was not so absolutely bad after all.

To the general public, Day Lewis was best known as a popular detective story writer under the *nom de plume* of Nicholas Blake. (The leading character of his novels, Nigel Strangeways, is supposedly based on W.H. Auden.) His output of these stories (he wrote twenty in all) far exceeded his yield of poetry; nevertheless, he gallantly attempted to fulfil the responsibilities of the laureateship by producing some tepid, if well-intentioned, occasional pieces.

The first of these celebrated the 'I'm backing Britain' campaign of 1968, and was published on the front page of the *Daily Mail*. The campaign sprang from a New Year resolution of five typists at a Surbiton factory, who proposed that everyone in the country should work an extra thirty minutes a day for no additional money. Support for this Stakhanovite notion came from an alliance of persons that united under one banner such unlikely fellow toilers as the Duke of Edinburgh and Mr Robert Maxwell. The Duke, who was already famous for instructing Britons to pull their fingers out, would no doubt have overlooked the laureate's slighting reference to the rentiers in their cells padded with banknotes. The faint echo of the poet's ideological past was more than compensated for by the prevailing tone of headmasterly exhortation:

> . . . Be as you were then, tough and gentle islanders –
> Steel in the fibre, charity in the veins –
> When few stood on their dignity or lines of demarcation,
> And few sat back in the padded cells of profit.
> . . . To work then islanders, as men and women etc., etc.

Also in 1968, Day Lewis made his contribution to the reorganization of local government with his ode entitled *Hail Teesside!* The attempt to flatter whole regions and their inhabitants had been made by earlier laureates, but it cannot be said that the precedents were encouraging. Kenneth Hopkins remarks of the wretched Pye that his 'few lines on Millbrook will surprise readers who know that unattractive suburb of Southampton today, and serve at the same time to show that Pye's talents had reached no final perfection in the forty-odd years of his practice'[1]:

> O Millbrook! shall my devious feet no more
> Pace the smooth margin of thy pebbly shore? . . . etc., etc.

One doesn't know whether Day Lewis ever directed his 'devious feet' to Teesside, but his picture of 'Old ironmasters and their iron men' is vivid enough. Sensitive souls may rebel, however, at the

---

1. Kenneth Hopkins, op. cit., p. 115. It is tempting to think that Pye's 'devious feet' is a light-hearted reference to his handling of metre. Tempting, but not sustainable.

notion of poets, of all people, lending support to the destruction of ancient identities for the sake of 'administrative reform'. 'Teesside', one feels, should not be 'hailed' – no more should 'Cumbria' or 'Cleveland'.

The last Poet Laureate before the present one was the much-loved Sir John Betjeman (1906–84). He was one of the most popular choices ever, a household name since becoming an eccentric television performer. His amiable oblong visage had appeared on our screens suffused with melancholy, as he evoked the undervalued glories of his favourite age – Gothic revival, Victorian railway architecture, gas lights and suburbs. Interviewed by *The Times*, he remarked that he was 'pleased to be the successor of Tennyson, Wordsworth and Bridges but not quite so pleased to be the successor of Alfred Austin. [He was] sure he wrote some good poetry. [He had] been reading his work looking for it.' He immediately struck an important blow for the dignity of the laureateship by reversing the odious Pye's 'wicked' decision to take £27 per annum in lieu of wine. The laureate now gets a few bottles from the Queen's wine merchant equivalent in value to £27. This is a far cry from the 126 gallons originally bestowed on the thirsty poets of the Restoration, but better than nothing at all.

The new laureate's official productions were, like those of most of his predecessors, the subject of hostile comment in the press. It was so widespread when he published his *Jubilee Hymn* (1977) that he was provoked into remarking plaintively: 'The words were meant for singing, not reading.' Of his poem on the wedding of Princess Anne and Captain Mark Phillips, he said: 'I wanted it to be quite clear, very simple, and not like a Christmas card.' These admirable intentions produced a poem that begins:

> Hundreds of birds in the air
>   And millions of leaves on the pavement,
> And Westminster bells ringing on
>   To palace and people outside –
> And all for the words 'I will'
>   To love's most willing enslavement.
> All of our people rejoice
>   With venturous bridegroom and bride.

The 'hundreds of birds in the air' are presumably the flocks of feral pigeons which are such an unwholesome nuisance in London, unless, of course, other birds had specially come up from the country for the occasion.

The *Jubilee Hymn* has a certain charm and reminds one of such innocent effusions as *All Things Bright and Beautiful*. It would certainly pass muster in a collection of verses for children. But perhaps his most heartfelt tribute was written for the Queen Mother on her 80th birthday[1]. This gracious lady has charmed several generations of loyal Englishmen with her irrepressible smiling and radiant hats. It was potentially the laureate's finest hour when he sought to express the nation's and the racing fraternity's undying affection for her in appropriate verses. Alas! The result is pure E. Jarvis Thribb, and even the reference to 'Our Faithful friend' seems more appropriate to one of the royal labradors than to a Queen Mother:

> We are your people;
> Millions of us greet you
> On this your birthday
> Mother of our Queen.
> Waves of goodwill go
> Racing out to meet you,
> You who in peace and war
> Our Faithful friend have been.
> You who have known the sadness of bereavement,
> The joyfulness of family jokes
> And times when trust is tried.
> Great was the day for our United Kingdoms
> And God Bless the Duke of York
> Who chose you as his bride.

This only goes to show that Wordsworth was quite right to avoid writing anything in his capacity as laureate.

Sir John was among our most gifted laureates when he stuck to his lathe, and his gentle satires of suburbia and middle-class proprieties will live on when his *Jubilee Hymn* and wedding odes, like so many before them, have been consigned to the literary dust-

---

1. 4 August 1980.

bin. When Tennyson died, the whole nation mourned the passing of a national hero; when Betjeman lay dying 'waves' of very personal affection went 'racing out to meet' him. The news was received with relief that his favourite teddy bear, Archibald, who was rushed across the country, arrived in time to be with him at the end. As for Sir John's successor, Ted Hughes (born 1930), if he is prudent he will keep his laureate productions to the absolute minimum that loyalty and propriety permit.

Three

OLEAGINOUS ODES
AND ECCENTRIC ELEGIES

*Egregious eulogy;
elegy as an additional hazard of mortality*

And is there one Fanatique left, in whose
  Degenerate Soul a thought can stray,
And by the witchcraft of a cloud oppose
  This Bright, so long expected Day?
    Whence are these wild effects of Light,
    Emergent from our tedious night?
Oh! Can it be, those life-creating beams
  That warm the Earth, and gild our streams,
Purging th'infected air, our eyes, and mind
Making even Moles themselves to see, should strike
  these poor men blind?

> from: James Shirley's panegyric on Charles II,
> the King who betrayed his country to the French
> with The Treaty of Dover, 1670.

Hark! She bids all her friends adieu;
  Some angel calls her to the spheres,
Our eyes the radiant saint pursue
  Through liquid telescopes of tears.

> Dr Watts, *On The Sudden Death of
> Mrs. Mary Peacock*

Death in the Palace; Death in the Cot;
Death in all Ranks! 'Tis but the common lot.
Death writes the fearful legend up 'No More'
Over the mantelpiece, and on the floor.

> John Stanyan Bigg (A Spasmodic poet,
> author of *Night and the Soul*)

'IT IS MELANCHOLY TO THINK', writes Macaulay, 'how many of the highest and most exquisitely formed of human intellects have been condemned to the ignominious labour of disposing of common-places of adulation in new forms and brightening them into new splendour.'[1] It is even more melancholy to think how many of the least exquisitely formed of human intellects have enthusiastically submitted themselves to the same indignity. Macaulay's examples – Tasso 'extolling the heroic virtues of the wretched creature who locked him up in a madhouse', 'Statius flattering a tyrant, and the minion of a tyrant, for a morsel of bread' – at least had plenty of excuse. They were hungry, and often at the mercy of capricious patrons. The modern sycophant is more likely to have his eye on a knighthood, or the laureateship, or both. William Watson (1858–1935) actually got his knighthood in 1917, but the laureateship eluded his grasp.[2] The immediate cause of his elevation was a grovelling ode to Lloyd George, who was then Prime Minister, in which he is compared to the Merlin of Arthurian legend:

> A man with something of the cragginess
> Of his own mountains, something of the force
> That goads to their loud leap the mountain streams.
>
> . . . the man of Celtic blood
> Whom Powers Unknown in a divine caprice,
> Chose and did make their instrument, wherewith

1. Thomas Babington Macaulay,' Mr Robert Montgomery', *Edinburgh Review*, April 1830.
2. It went to Alfred Austin instead. Watson wrote the Introduction to Austin's *English Lyrics* (1890) – a fine example of a louse puffing a flea; but he was most put out by the appointment. He wrote grandly to his mother that Austin 'was far more acceptable to my mind than if any real rival of mine, like Henley or Bridges, men of genius, had been selected.'

To save the Saxon; the man all eye and hand,
The man who saw, and grasped, and gripped and held.

It is a moot point whether writing this sort of thing is less disrep-
utable than buying a knighthood from Maundy Gregory, Lloyd
George's Honours salesman, but it is obviously cheaper. 'This must
certainly be the most eulogistic poem ever written about a British
politician,' observes Sir John Squire grimly, and adds: 'There is
nothing about Mr W.M. Hughes[1], Lord Milner, Lord Curzon or
Lord Devonport in the [present] volume; these, perhaps, will be
dealt with in Sir William's next book, which, I do not doubt, will be
ready before long. But Sir Edward Carson gets his meed in a sonnet
To The Rt. Hon. Sir Edward Carson, on leaving Antrim, June 30, 1916.'[2]
However, there is no gratitude amongst poets, just as there is none
in politics, and by 1921 Watson was writing indignant sonnets
against the Prime Minister's Irish policy. No longer a Welsh Wizard, he is now described as a superannuated St George.

The original eulogy, *The Man Who Saw*, was accompanied in the
same volume by an even more astonishing poem entitled *The Three
Alfreds*. This celebrates three gentlemen of that name, each of whom
saved England in one way or another: King Alfred, Alfred, Lord
Tennyson, and Alfred, Lord Northcliffe. (This form of portman-
teau eulogy surely has potential for development by the patriotic
poets of today; could not a passable sonnet be made from *The Three
Roberts*, praising the combined talents of Robert the Bruce, Robert
Southey, and Robert Maxwell?) The content of Watson's poem is
not quite as interesting as its general idea. King Alfred is lauded as
the victor of Ethandune, Alfred, Lord Tennyson is described as
'Victoria's golden warbler', and Northcliffe comes before us as the
man:

Who, in the very whirlwind of our woe,
From midnight till the laggard dawn began,
Cried ceaseless, 'Give us shells – more shells,' and so
Saved England.

In a note attached to the poem when it appeared in book form, Wat-

1. The Australian Prime Minister.
2. Sir John Squire, *Books in General*, Martin Secker, 1918, p. 235.

son says: 'Friends have asked the author not to re-publish this son-net. He does so because he believes it to be the truth.'

Although the elephantine flattery favoured by Watson is not now fashionable, hagiographical versifying is still with us. The death of President Kennedy brought the songbirds out in force, and a vol-ume[1] was published expressly to include the most excruciating trib-utes to him in verse; the general level of the poems may be judged from the following:

> He sort
> of embodied
> the air he sort
> of embodied the
> air where democracy
> stood tall, Jefferson
> and Robert Frost were
> his advisers, he sort
> of clearly gave evidence
> of wit and democracy . . .

This sort of treatment is reserved exclusively for rulers whose image is favourably received by the public and has little to do with statesmanship or administrative ability. Hard-working, dull and honest politicians must expect the usual abuse, but crooks and tyrants who take trouble over their media packaging, may expect the odd lyrical tribute. In a volume entitled ¡Viva Che!², for instance, we find Fidel Castro described as 'Fiery prophet of the dawn'. The book, as the title suggests, is actually an anthology of tributes to Ernesto 'Che' Guevara published in 1968. In the Acknowledgements, the Cuban Embassy in London is enthusiasti-cally thanked for its co-operation with the project; and: 'Finally we wish to thank all those who wrote in or sent contributions that we were unable to publish for lack of space.' In view of what does get in, this may be considered a lucky escape for the reader. 'In such a

1. *Of Poetry and Power*. This volume does not appear to have been published in the United Kingdom. There are some amusing observations on it and similar works in Malcolm Muggeridge's *Tread Softly For You Tread On My Jokes*, Collins, 1966.
2. *¡Viva Che! Contributions in tribute to Ernesto 'Che' Guevara* edited by Marianne Alexandre, Lorimer Publishing, 1968.

compendium of contemporary cant', wrote Malcolm Muggeridge in his review of the book, 'it is difficult to pick out the highlights, but if I were to make an award for the outstanding fatuity, it would go to the late Sir Herbert Read for his comparison of "Che" with Tolstoy. One can quite see the scarcity value of "Che" to those on the look-out for heroes of the Left. The wartime resistance movements, which might have been expected to yield a good crop, have been bedevilled with retrospective controversy. Stalin enormously depleted the hagiographic resources of the Left when he turned nearly all the Marxist Elect into traitors and criminals . . . who but Che could have attracted so wide a range of admirers as the ones assembled by Marianne Alexandre [Editor of the book]? They include such diverse figures as Lord Ted Willis, and Graham Greene; the poets Logue, and Sontag, and Jean-Paul Sartre, Monk Merton, All Souls Caute and Allan Sillitoe.'[1] In between the romantic pictures featuring 'Che' as the saviour of mankind are the poems – rambling, self-conscious and exhibitionistic. A Mario Benedetti from Uruguay contributes some lines reeking of ill-digested propaganda; an ideological E. Jarvis Thribb writes from Hanoi demanding more Vietnams. Light relief is provided by Don Collis (England) with his vision of 'Che' as a sort of woodland sprite:

> Fleet through the forest trees
> Ran Che Guevara
> Moccasined were his feet
> Round his cigar a
> Beard curled in devil's horns
> Brushed by the clutching thorns
> Soundless he rushed, a breeze
> Shaking the mighty seat
> Of McNamara. [sic]

'A legend,' writes Graham Greene in his piece, 'is impervious to bullets' – he might have added, so is bad poetry. There is an offering from Robert Lowell that appears to have been written when drunk, a miserable 'Haiku' from Christopher Logue and a characteristically whimsical poem by Adrian Mitchell (reprinted by permission

1. Review in *The Observer*, Sunday, 18 August 1968.

of *Peace News*): Dan Schechter of the USA gives us a piece of prose which is for some reason divided into verses on the page:

> Was his death vain?
> The inevitable outcome for a romantic
> adventurer whose vision substituted
> the impatient clatter of machine-gun
> bullets for the inevitable unfolding
> of the dialectic?

Then more pictures, and – Oh wonder! Oh joy! – a *close-up* of the saint's hands, pen in one, cigar in the other: a subject worthy of Dürer. After Andrew Sinclair of England has compared 'Che' to other unpleasant cult figures such as Zapata and Lumumba, we reach a crescendo of bathos in Ted Willis' poem which contains the immortal lines:

> Your body did not arise on the Third Day.
> In practical terms
> You are quite dead.

This, it would seem, is the only significant difference between 'Che' and Jesus Christ.

An opportunity for poetasters such as the death of a 'Che' Guevara comes only rarely, but the Queen – or at any rate the monarchy – is always with us. Laureates are more circumspect than they used to be, of course, and nowadays there is little to be gained from laying it on with a trowel as was done for Charles II and the early Hanoverians. There are, however, a few eccentrics around who are obsessed with monarchy in the same way that some otherwise apparently adult men are obsessed with stamp collecting or model railways. One of these, who half-wished to remain anonymous, added to the perennial spate of books on royalty his own very individual contribution: *Lilibet* by 'a loyal subject of Her Majesty'.[1] I say 'half-wished' to remain anonymous because the publishers included with review copies a gossip-column item claiming to identify the

---

1. Blond and Briggs, 1984. The full title is: *Lilibet: an account in verse of the early years of the Queen until the time of her accession.*

poet as A.N. Wilson. This ploy attracted adverse comment from Bernard Levin who reviewed the book in *The Observer*; he admitted, however, that 'some rather more likely candidates' for authorship 'must be ruled out. The Great McGonagall is dead; Beerbohm's Savonarola Brown is fictitious; the leading contemporary candidate, Mr Clive James, could well have written it, but is not much given to hiding his thingummy under a whatsit.' After quoting a few choice couplets such as:

> Delay and disappointment could not flatten
> The ardour of Lieutenant P. Mountbatten,

Levin wondered aloud as to the intentions of the author in giving his doggerel to the world. '. . . where in [the] spectrum is our anonymous poetaster supposed to fit? Where does he want to fit? His ghastly lines will not appeal to the multitude; if they are supposed to be satire they are so blunted with incompetence that they altogether fail of effect; and if they are designed to please the Queen it must be obvious that unless she has recently taken leave of her senses she is very likely, on dipping into her presentation copy, to be sick all over her breakfast.

'If the author would care to reveal his intentions along with his name, he may make a small contribution to sociology; certainly he has made none to biography, history, royalty or poetry.'[1]

An even more bizarre tribute to our present Queen's great forebear appeared in 1982 and was reviewed by the aforementioned A.N. Wilson in *The Spectator*. Christopher Tower's *Victoria the Good* (a title reminiscent of Alfred Austin, whose *Victoria the Wise* appeared in 1901) was something of a publishing curiosity. 'Over 600 pages', lyricizes Wilson, 'bound in cloth: over a dozen handsome coloured plates, depicting eras of the monarch's life. How could Lord Weidenfeld, one asks oneself, sell such a book for £9.95. Viewed merely as an object (paper, cloth) at twice the price, the volume would be cheap. And no review could fail to sing the praise of Mr Tower's patient plodding task: 600 pages, all of them in verse!' In blank verse, actually, and none too hot blank verse in the extracts quoted by Wilson:

1. Quotations from a review by Bernard Levin in *The Observer*.

> But here where liberal attitudes prevail
> And authority is tolerant of
> Manifestations of ill discipline
> To the extent that people are aware
> That however insupportable . . .

At the end of the poem there is a touching scene where fairies dance around the dying Queen, and the verse is relieved with a little rhyming:

> Since never once was spurned or broken
> Never denied nor once forgot
> That elemental vow once spoken
> Here in this gladsome island grot.

Nevertheless, the reviewer feels compelled to praise all concerned for their heroic, if eccentric, labours: 'Lord Weidenfeld, for publishing a book which hardly anyone will want to read; Arthur Barbosa, whose accomplished brush supplied delightful plates recapturing the wallpaper, the carpets and the trees, the soldiers' uniforms, the tablecloths, each tiny detail of Victoria's life.

'To publisher and illustrator, then, all praise is due for work superbly done. But Mr Tower deserves the higher praise. How many months or years it took to write, one hates to contemplate: but with what joy the poet probably fulfilled his task. Its very pointlessness inspires respect, like those who build cathedral replicas with used Swan Vestas and a tube of glue . . .'

Mr Tower is the author of other volumes also issued by the noble house of Weidenfeld. In one of them (*A Distant Fluting* – 1977, 800 pages) there are other notable poetical salutes to persons or institutions. 'Professor Sir Max and Lady Mallowan' are the recipients of a witty tribute:

> Between them both there is not much to choose:
> One follows clues until he finds the end,
> One knows the end whence she fashions clues.

Particularly graceful are the *Thoughts After The Author's Design For The Libyan Coat of Arms Had Been Approved By The King And The National Assembly*. (Those were the days!)

> May it as an emblem stand
> Through the ages proud and firm,
> For a race which – if not grand
> In today's accepted term –
> Is more gentle, quiet and wise
> Than most ones of vaster size.

No doubt the National Assembly were delighted with this benevolent pat on the head from the Old Etonian poet.

It is, of course, gallant of Lord Weidenfeld to risk his company's capital on works such as *Victoria the Good*, *A Distant Fluting*, *Oultre Jourdain* (1980 – 327 pages, illustrated) and *Firuz of Isfahan* (1973 – 392 pages, illustrated), especially as the firm is not known for its poetry list. Perhaps the works of Tower are considered as 'loss leaders', and in the future other equally distinguished poets will be expected to take note and flock to the Weidenfeld banner.

One ingredient lacking in Tower's work is the exchange of compliments with other poets. This has almost as long a tradition as the mutual abuse of literary rivals. Most of such eulogies are more conscientious than entertaining, but Edward Edwin Foot's tribute to Shakespeare has some unexpected pleasures:

> O thou bright charmer of the inmost spark!
> Why revell'd thou so soon in death's grim holiday –

he complains; and the last stanza contains some characteristic Footisms:

> 'Will's' cloudy days nigh spent, his sun arose!
> (God with him, tickling his fair brow and sparkling eye)
> With wisdom wrote he'n majesty [*sic*]
> On high-born kings and lowly peasantry
> In rhyme's sweet readings; lines of quaint sarcastic prose:
> Perhaps offendingly to some; whilst others sigh,
> Or laugh, or cry, and timidly
> Enjoy the witty man's bright pleasantry . . .

More recently, Auden attracted much idolatry from the poets of his generation, some of which is enjoyably over the top. To Charles Madge he seems to have appeared as 'The Hound of Heaven':

But there waited for me in the summer morning
Auden, fiercely. I read, shuddered and knew.[1]

And C. Day Lewis adulated the poet in lines that might have embar-
rassed a lesser man:

Look West, Wystan, lone flyer, birdman, my bully boy!
Plague of locusts, creeping barrage, has left earth bare:
Suckling and centenarian are up in the air,
No wing-room for Wystan, no joke for kestrel joy . . .

. . . Gain altitude, Auden, then let the base beware!
Migrate, chaste my kestrel, you need a change of air.[2]

If this is the sort of thing written about a person still living, one
wonders what is in store for us when they die. It helps, of course, if
death comes at an opportune moment, before the fashion for the
idol's work has evaporated or, in the case of statesmen, before his
past misdeeds have caught up with him. All the same, few of the bad
poets are prepared to spit on a grave. They do not do it well, and it is
not what they feel their public wants. Joseph Gwyer (q.v.), for
instance, was ready with an ode for the not entirely admirable
Napoleon III when he died in England in 1873:

Oh, death, thy venom poison'd dart
Has struck the Emperor[3] to the heart,
Thou heedest not the rich, the poor
When'er thou callst they're here no more.

Napoleon's gone, his spirit fled
Soon o'er the world the tidings spread,
And nearly all the papers spoke
Of him in grief, 'twas such a stroke.

'*Nearly* all the papers spoke'? This is an unexpected touch of
frankness in a eulogy, but it may have been dictated more by the
necessities of metre than by Gwyer's desire to reveal the presence of

1. *Letter to Intelligentsia* in 'New Country'.
2. C. Day Lewis, *Collected Poems,* Jonathan Cape, 1954, p. 97. From *The Magnetic
Mountain* (1933) Part Three.
3. Ex-Emperor by then.

87

dissenting voices. Equally charming is the anonymous tribute to George V, which mingles respect with a keen sense of value for money in royalty:

> Greatest sorrow England ever had
> When death took away our Dear Dad,
> A king was he from head to sole
> Loved by his people one and all.
>
> His mighty work for the Nation
> Making peace and strengthening union –
> Always at it since on the throne:
> Saved the country more than a billion.

Elegies of a more private nature are stock items for unknown and struggling poets; their imaginations do not supply sufficient materials to satisfy what Juvenal called *'cacoethes scribendi'*[1] and deaths therefore provide a steady stream of subject matter. Dramatic or sudden death is, of course, the ideal grist to the Muse's mill. A Mr Francis, writing in 1760, gives us an elegy on *Colonel Robert Montgomery Written on the Fatal Spot where a Lamentable Duel Transpired.* It concludes with the lines:

> Soon has obdurate Balls prepost'rous roar'd
> And horrors envelop'd his martial sound,
> Shot through the Soul immerg'd his fabric Hoard
> And him supine, submerg'd in frigid Ground.
> Submerg'd he lies, co-wretched am I now.

Another example, taken from the same inestimable volume,[2] concerns a bride who died on the day of the wedding, enabling the Rev. Henry More to point out, with hideous appropriateness:

> The grave, cold bridegroom! clasp'd her in his arms
> And kindred worms destroyed her pleasing charms.

---

1. 'The incurable itch for writing'.
2. Christopher Adams, *The Worst English Poets*, Allan Wingate, 1958.

There is a distinct echo of Marvell's *To His Coy Mistress* in the Reverend's poem, though it does not gain by the comparison:

> Then worms shall try
> That long preserved virginity
>
> . . . The grave's a fine and private place,
> But none, I think, do there embrace.

The eighteenth century, as we note from the productions of the Graveyard Poets, was really rather keen on death, so long as the treatment of it was suitably sententious. In the hands of a poetaster, this stylized and mannered approach usually means that even the most dramatic fatalities fail to ignite the reader's sympathy as one feels they should. A case in point is Samuel Bently's *The River Dove: A Lyric Pastoral* (1768). The author tells us in a note that the poem concerns an actual occurrence, the victims being the Rev. Dean Langton and Miss La Roache, who met with an unfortunate accident. 'On a visit to Wenman Cokes Esq. at Longford, [they] went to entertain themselves with a sight of Dovedale, where the Dean was unfortunately killed while attempting to reach the top of one of the rocks, with the lady on the same horse. The lady was saved by the hair of her head being entangled in some bushes.' The tragic circumstances having been explained, there is very little for the poem to add – but Bently soldiers on gamely. The actual demise of the Dean is one of the least moving in literature:

> The lady by lace-braided Hair
> Entangled in Brambles was found
> Suspended unhurt in mid-air,
> The Dean met his Death with the ground.

One has only to compare the deaths recorded by nineteenth-century poets to see how the reader is getting poor value for money from Bently. George Meredith has a cliff death which is justly famous, though in this case the victim, a sacrifice to save the town from the plague, was pushed over the edge:

> He cancelled the ravaging Plague
> With the roll of his fat off the cliff.

Indeed, the nineteenth-century public were enthusiastic consumers of violent death, both in prose and poetry. Dr Erasmus Darwin was merely setting the trend when he wrote his tear-jerking poem about *Eliza*, who unwisely took her two children to spectate at the Battle of Minden. At the moment when their father, who was a participant, appears to have survived the struggle, Death strikes Eliza down:

> A ball now hisses through the airy tides
> (Some Fury wings it, and some Demon guides),
> Parts the fine locks her graceful head that deck,
> Wounds her fair ear, and sinks into her neck;
> The red stream issuing from her azure veins
> Dyes her white veil, her ivory bosom stains.
> 'Ah me!' she cried, and sinking on the ground,
> Kiss'd her dear babes, regardless of the wound:
> 'Oh cease not yet to beat, thou vital urn,
> Wait, gushing life, Oh! Wait my love's return!'

After this there was no stopping the corpse mongers, and for a hundred years the bodies thudded satisfyingly from the poetry presses. Brave children went down with the ship, or heroically expired after spending several stanzas staggering along a railway line to stop an oncoming train from plunging to destruction. Brides dropped dead at the altar, and mothers died in snowstorms. Men were liable to be mashed to pieces in railway accidents, like Conductor Bradley in John Greenleaf Whittier's poem:

> Conductor Bradley (always may his name
> Be said with reverence!) as the swift doom came,
> Smitten to death, a crushed and mangled frame . . .

If they survived these everyday catastrophes, they would probably suffer a more conventional male death in battle.[1] Parallel to the drama came a continuous stream of flat-footed elegy, the tone of which can be gauged from the Editor's Preface to *The Northern Harp*

1. Readers interested in this remarkable taste for ghoulishness should consult Michael Turner's amusing *Parlour Poetry* (Michael Joseph, 1967), where all the old favourites will be found.

by Marion Albina Bigelow (New York, 1853): 'So large a number of elegies have been selected, for the reason that such compositions are more popular among the masses than any other species of *serious* literature. The author is wholly incapable of levity and the reader will find nothing of it in any of her productions.' This is indeed a daunting prospect, but the editor evidently regards it as a strong selling point. Nor was he short of material, having been 'permitted to examine more than a thousand manuscripts'. He does say he would have attempted some emendations 'did not the author prefer her original form of expression' – a restrained remark that speaks volumes about his negotiations with the poetess. Her pervasive melancholy he attributes to the fact that all her brothers died of consumption. Her natural bent, however, was not so different from dozens like her, who treated the same themes in the same way; her titles could be duplicated in innumerable parallel volumes – 'Passing Away', 'The Consumptive', 'The Graveyard', 'A Burial at Sea', or 'Two Smothered Children'. This prevailing popularity of the death theme is summed up by C.T. Kindilien[1] in his description of American poetasters: 'Although there has been a steady flow of friends and relatives to "the other shore" whom the poet can immortalize, he does not neglect the traditional graveyard tour. With uncles, grandparents, fathers, schoolmates, and the corner policeman suitably eulogized, there is still the inspiration to be derived from a visit to an "old cemetery" ':

> There is a greater charm to me
> The wondrous chiseled diction
> That on the moss-grown slab we see,
> Than reading modern fiction.

This poet speaks for many! The daily newspaper, a job, every trip (*Lines suggested by a coffin standing in the baggage-room at the Grand Central Station*), anything may turn into an opportunity for a poem dealing with death. There are poems for dying actors (just 'waiting my cue'), dying miners ('rugged men weep'), dying lovers ('I'm sitting by your side, Mary' or 'I'm standing by your grave, Mary'); and if the poet is stymied, he merely imagines his own death:

1. C.T. Kindilien, *American Poetry in the Eighteen-Nineties*, Brown University Press, 1956, p. 16.

> Shovel it on to me lightly
>   Shovel it gently and slow,
> Nor ever once think of me slightly
>   As you cover me up down below.

For these nineteenth-century scribblers in America and England the sales potential of poetry saturated with death was as great as that of novels saturated with sex today. Nor should one consider each collation of diseased platitude as necessarily insincere. In 1822 Wordsworth wrote an epitaph[1] for his daughter's grave in Grasmere church which cannot have been anything other than the product of deep grief; its opening lines exhibit all the appalling sincerity of his very worst productions:

> These vales were saddened with no common gloom
> When good Jemima perished in her bloom;
> When (such the awful will of heaven) she died
> By flames breathed on her from her own fireside . . .

The rest of the poem is more dignified, although its pious and bland invocation of 'God's will' at the end echoes the complacent religiosity of the poetasters. Perhaps the effect of these lines would be more moving if Harry Graham had never written 'Billy in his bright new sashes/Fell in the fire, and was burnt to ashes', but even then one feels that the unfortunate Jemima has been ill-served by her husband and her father. If the reader is brought to the edge of tears by such writings, they are more likely to be tears of laughter than of sympathetic pity. Tennyson produces much the same unintended results with his famously bathetic conclusion to *Enoch Arden*:

> So past the strong heroic soul away.
> And when they buried him, the little port
> Had seldom seen a costlier funeral.

---

1. John Hayden, Editor of the Penguin *Collected Poems of Wordsworth* is unable to excuse Wordsworth the responsibility for this exercise in bathos – he states that the poet 'most likely wrote the whole from a draft written by Edward Quillinan, husband of the deceased, Jemima Anne Deborah Quillinan'. (Note to the poem, p. 1017.)

The recognized expert in this field was Dr Watts, whose *Elegiac Thought on Mrs Anne Warner* affords a tantalizing glimpse of the accommodation arrangements in Paradise:

> Behold her ancestors (a pious race),
> Rang'd in fair order, at her sight rejoice,
> And sing her welcome. She along their seats
> Gliding salutes them all with honours due,
> Such as are paid in Heaven: and last she finds
> A mansion fashion'd of distinguish'd light,
> But vacant; 'This,' with sure presage she cried,
> 'Awaits my father; when will he arrive?
> How long, alas, how long!' Then calls her mate:
> 'Die, thou dear partner of my mortal cares,
> Die, and partake my bliss; we are for ever one.'

Such elegies as Wordsworth's and Watts' are at least spontaneous tributes, whether or not their protagonists would have been better off without them. There have been writers, however, who exploited hatches and dispatches for commercial gain by sending a few hastily conceived verses to the rapturous parents or the distraught relicts. Such a one was Elkanah Settle (1648–1724), of whom it was complained that no one could arrive in, or depart from, this world without his attempting to levy a small charge in the form of unsolicited verses, and that he had added 'a new hazard' to mortality. This must have been the nadir of the genre, only available to us now in the work of *Private Eye's* E. Jarvis Thribb, who lets nobody pass over without a burst of threnody in the best traditions of Marion Albina Bigelow. His leaden elegies are an eloquent reminder of the dying tradition of the verse tombstone, and have the added attraction that you can fabricate as many as you like in the same manner without anyone noticing the difference:

> So, farewell then
> Liberace!
> You played the piano with nimble
> Fingers, and were good at winning
> Libel actions. Keith's Mum says
> We shall not see your like
> Again.

Four

THE DIDACTIC MUSE

Metrical approaches to disease,
drink and political discussion

Eley, unknown to me, thy name I prize.
For oft thro' thee a basket's changed in size,
And many a head therein lain latent
That else had lived but for thy patent.

Alexander Webber, op. cit.
'Eley' still survives as a brand name
for shotgun cartridges.

Thy mangled corpse upon the rails in frightful shape was
found,
The ponderous train had killed thee as its heavy wheels
went round,
And thus in dreadful form thou met'st a drunkard's
awful death
And I, thy brother, mourn thy fate, and breathe a purer
breath.

James Henry Powell, *Lines Written to a Friend on the
Death of His Brother, Caused by a Railway Train Running over Him
Whilst He was in a State of Inebriation*

Often and oftener with his breath
Mixes the steam of moral death,
From which his home in horror shrinks –
Rumour mutters low, 'he drinks'.

M'Donald Clarke,
Death in Disguise (1833)

THOSE LITERARY WORKS WHICH SURVIVE the test of time can usually be said to have successfully combined instruction with pleasure. The fanatical and humourless mind, which regards art forms simply as sledgehammers to be used for battering the public into conformity, has seldom produced enduring works. The shelves of the British Library groan under the weight of unread tomes by seventeenth-century divines and nineteenth-century sermonizers. In the Soviet bloc, the literary sewage of officially accepted 'socialist' writers pours off the presses – and straight into oblivion.[1] Literary good manners might be thought a prerequisite for gaining the reader's ear, but this is not a consideration for the state or church-supported ideologue; his mission is to close minds rather than open them, to bully rather than persuade, and to threaten rather than to reason.

In open societies the didacticist is, of necessity, in competition with purveyors of more appealing products, which often renders his work a good deal more nutritious than, for instance, the congealed verbal porridge of Marxist–Leninist rectitude. Usually he has found it more profitable to concentrate on those single issues which come under the general heading of sin. Thus we find that, as far back as the reign of James I, the poets and the pamphleteers were hurling abuse at tobacco. The King himself not only wrote a famous tract against the weed, but collected some of the best pamphlets together and had them issued for the edification of the reading and smoking public. It was natural that verse should play its part, as it does in so many advertising campaigns, and one of the most combative efforts was written by Joshua Sylvester. His 1620 tract is entitled *Tobacco Battered and the Pipes Shattered (About their Ears, that idl'y Idolize so base and barbarous a Weed or at least-wise over-love so loathsome Vanity)*. In his 'three Puffs' – that is, argumentative blasts – he demonstrates,

1. There are signs that '*glasnost*' is beginning to limit the output, to the great indignation of talentless writers and the old guard at *Pravda*.

95

firstly, that smoking helps the opposition (tobacco mostly grows in Philip of Spain's empire); secondly, that the practice is generally an accompaniment to other immoralities, being favoured by tosspots in the pubs, and lechers in the stews, etc.; and, thirdly, that smoking ruins body and soul, as well as wasting money. A further objection is the undesirability of trafficking with the New World at all; for have not Europeans taken to it all their vices and brought back from it all its diseases? Sylvester makes a number of points which most non-smokers would be inclined to agree with; moreover, he broadens his attack to include other smoke-producing horrors, such as guns. In an ingenious passage he shows that pipes, appearances to the contrary notwithstanding, are actually greater evils than pistols:

> Two smoky Engins in this latter Age
> . . . Have been invented by too-wanton wit,
> Guns and Tobacco-Pipes, with fire and smoke
> (At least) a third part of Mankind to choke
> . . . Yet of the two, we may (think I) be bold
> In some respect, to think the last the worst,
> (However, both in their effects accurst),
> For Guns shoot from-ward, only at their foes
> Tobacco-Pipes home-ward, into their own,
> (When for the touch-hole firing the wrong end
> Into ourselves the Poysons force we send;)

Not long after Sylvester warned the nation against tobacco, Nahum Tate rendered an important service to Public Health by translating Girolamo Fracastoro's poem on syphilis from Latin into English. The disease may have been, like tobacco, another gift from the New World to the Old – at any rate, one theory holds that Columbus' men brought it back from Haiti in 1493. However that may be, it was Fracastoro who gave the disease the name by which subsequent generations have known it. In the third book of his poem he tells the story of King Alcithöus and his shepherd 'Syphilus', who was struck down by the 'syphilis' for neglecting to worship Apollo. After he confessed his impiety and repented, he was cured by a decoction of the sacred tree called Guaiacum. The attraction of Fracastor's new name for the affliction was that it cast no aspersions on anyone: the English had formerly called it the

French Pox, the French called it the Neapolitan Disease, the Italians called it the French or Spanish Disease and the Turks called it the Disease of the Franks or Christians. Since it was usually carried by invading armies, this attempt to pin responsibility for it on one's enemies was understandable; but disease is no respecter of politics, and by 1497, we are told, syphilis had made an unwelcome début in Aberdeen. Doubtless the Aberdonians called it the Sassenach Disease.

'Fracastor' was an interesting man: a poet, a physician, and a philosopher, who lived from 1483 to 1553. He wrote his poem in Latin hexameters during a period of exile on Lake Garda, and in 1525 sent the first two books to Cardinal Bembo for criticism. Bembo admired the graceful Latin, but objected that mercury was not the best cure; he recommended Guaiacum (the worldly prelates of those days were of course well up in such matters). This resulted in the addition of the poem's third book and the aforementioned story of 'Syphilus'. Alternative cures are exhaustively discussed by Fracastor, while his prophylactic advice follows Galen's principles of rectifying disharmony in the humours.

'To the modern reader', writes Mr Heneage Wynne-Finch, a recent translator of Fracastor, 'a poem on syphilis, even though the gloom of its central theme is heightened, as here, by digressions, seems to carry with it a suggestion of the grotesque. But no such thought would have troubled the minds of Fracastor and his contemporaries.'[1]

Nahum Tate's version for Jacob Tonson in 1686 also gives a picturesque account of Fracastor's life, character and appearance: 'He was low of stature but of good bulk, his shoulders broad, his hair black and long, his face round, his eyes black, his nose short and turning upwards by his continual contemplation of the stars' (Fracastor was also an astrologer). The poet's demise is described with a good deal of pathos: 'He was above 70 years old when he dyed, which was by an Aploplexy that seized him while he was at dinner at his country seat. He was sensible of his malady, though speechless, often putting his hand upon the top of his head by which sign he would have had his servants administer a cupping glass to the

1. *Fracastor – Syphilis or the French Disease – A Poem in Latin Hexameters by Girolamo Fracastoro*, with Translation, Notes and Appendix by Heneage Wynne-Finch, Heinemann Medical Books Ltd, 1935.

part affected, by which he had formerly cured a nun in Verona, labouring under the same distemper. But his domesticks, not conceiving his meaning, apply'd first one thing and then another, till in the evening he gently expired.'

Tate prefaces his translation with some entirely superfluous, and, indeed, offensive verses, in which he has the gall to lay all blame for the spread of the disease on women:

> Whence should that foul infectious torment flow
> But from the baneful source of all our wo?
> That wheedling, charming sex, that draws us in
> To ev'ry punishment and ev'ry sin.

In the poem itself, we are spared no details of the progress of the disease:

> While Flesh divides, and shows the Bones below,
> Dire ulcers (can the Gods permit them) prey
> On his fair Eye balls, and devour their day.

The suggested means for avoiding the disease echo the advice of school chaplains down the years, consisting chiefly in fresh air, exercise and no love-making. The cures, as often seems to be the case in early medicine, sound just as bad as the disease, although Fracastor tries to persuade us otherwise:

> With these Ingredients mix'd, you must not fear
> Your suffering limbs and Body to besmear,
> Nor let the foulness of the course displease,
> Obscene indeed, but less than your Disease.

The 'ingredients' referred to include pig fat, larch and cedar gum, turpentine, myrrh, sulphur, black Hellebore – to name but a few. Covered in this hideous mixture, the patient is told to retire to bed and sweat for five days. Assuming he is still alive after this period, he should notice a marked improvement:

> The Mass of Humours now dissolv'd within,
> To purge themselves by Spittle shall begin,

Till you with Wonder at your feet shall see,
A tide of Filth, and bless the Remedy.

Wynne-Finch complains that *Syphilis* has been regarded 'solely as a landmark in the history of medicine' and praises the beauty of the poet's diction and his 'singular felicity of style'. He even puts in a word for Fracastor's excellent sense of humour, which is not immediately evident to the casual reader, though apparently he does exclaim at one point: '. . . *porcae heu terga fuge'* – a remark which 'suggests that his views on roast pork were sound'.

A later medical poet was also interested in syphilis, though he wisely confined himself to prose for his *Synopsis of the History and Cure of Venereal Diseases* (1737). John Armstrong MD (1709–79) is drily described in Anderson's *Poets of Great Britain* as 'more successful an author than a physician'. This does not augur well for his patients, since he is spectacularly ungifted as a poet. Anderson attributes his failure as a doctor to his inability 'to intrigue with nurses, nor associate with the various knots of pert, insipid, well-bred, impertinent, good-humoured malicious gossips, that are often found so useful to introduce a young physician into practice'. This view of him is reinforced by the poet James Beattie's crisp observation that he had 'a rooted aversion against the whole human race, except a few Friends, which it seems are dead'. Armstrong himself seems aware that his personality was less than magnetic and that he had done little to overcome this, when he attributes the failure of his play *The Forced Marriage* to his refusal to 'dangle after managers'.

In his work his saturnine Scotch disposition is everywhere evident. His didactic poem *The Art of Preserving Health* (1774) follows the familiar precepts of the Edinburgh University medical school (where he studied) and contains much that is dispiriting for the hedonist. '. . . The poet's advice to those of "jovial make",' write D.B. Wyndham Lewis and Charles Lee, 'is perceptibly tinged with gloomy pleasure at their sufferings. He advises washing, in moderation. The Age of Reason, indeed, had no passion for the bath. As to feather-beds, he permits them chiefly – if one may translate correctly from the text – to company promoters and drunkards.'[1]

---

1. D.B. Wyndham Lewis and Charles Lee, *The Stuffed Owl*, J.M. Dent and Sons, 1930, p. 60.

In his Preface to his *Collected Miscellanies*, we get a hint of what Armstrong's bedside manner must have been like. He contrives to deliver a stinging insult that magnanimously includes not only any potential readers among his contemporaries, but the readers of future generations as well: 'If the best judges of this age honour [me] with their approbation, all the worst too of the next will favour [me] with theirs; when by Heaven's grace [I] will be too far beyond the reach of their unmeaning praises to receive any disgust from them.' He also says he 'always most heartily despised the opinion of the Mobility [*sic*] from the lowest to the highest' – a contempt that cannot have served him too well in his capacity as physician to the British Army in Germany.

The Art of Preserving Health is certainly not eccentric from the medical point of view. Armstrong advises a retreat to the country as a relaxation and tonic – somewhere like Richmond, Windsor, or even Ham:

> O! wrap me in the friendly gloom that hides
> Umbrageous Ham!

Essex is not recommended, because of her 'baneful fogs' which result in 'cold tremors',

> . . . and mighty love of rest,
> Convulsive yawnings, lassitude and pains
> That sting the burden'd brows, fatigue the loins, etc. . . .

And marshes are always unhealthy, particularly hot ones, which produce such symptoms as:

> Skin ill-perspiring, and the purple flood
> In languid eddies loitering into phlegm.

Book II brings us to one of Armstrong's central preoccupations, namely diet. The fit and active person can manage to absorb salts and fats:

> . . . His daily labour thaws,
> To friendly chyle, the most rebellious mass

That salt can harden, or smoke of years;
Nor does his gorge the luscious bacon rue,
Nor that which Cestria sends, tenacious paste
Of solid milk.[1]

But the weaker brethren and sluggards should take care what they eat:

> . . . But ye of softer clay,
> Infirm and delicate! and ye who waste
> With pale and bloated sloth the tedious day!
> Avoid the stubborn aliment, avoid
> The full repast; and let sagacious age
> Grow wiser, lesson'd by the dropping teeth.

Armstrong is ahead of his time in taking a firm stand against choles-terol and over-indulgence. He refers decorously to diarrhoea:

> . . . aliments too thin,
> By violent powers too easily subdued
> Too soon expelled . . .

and reminds us that all beasts instinctively seek out the food that is most natural to them, and therefore most nutritious, with the pos-sible exception of the man-eating horses of Thrace. He is in favour of regular vigorous exercise, such as the chase, but those who are anti-bloodsports should take up forestry and woodchopping; (one wonders if Gladstone ever perused the works of Armstrong). Cold baths after heavy exercise are to be avoided. Tepid baths (not too often) are acceptable, being good for health and also, as the poet delicately hints, good for the sex-life by making people less sweaty and smelly. Having dealt very thoroughly with the soma, he turns to the psyche, which he sensibly treats as an aspect of general physical health. Patients are advised not to dwell morbidly on love or death, and to avoid hangovers and excessive drinking (it only inflames the passions and unbalances the judgement). Virtue is not only desirable but sensible; don't be a skirt-chaser, and don't lose your temper;

1. This is a reference to Cheshire cheese.

above all, listen to plenty of good music. All this is unexceptionable, the only question being whether it might not have been explained better in prose than poetry.

Such a question is posed even more urgently by the only laureate of the dental profession I have been able to discover. This was the remarkably energetic Solyman Brown (1790–1876), the son of Nathaniel and Thankful Brown of Litchfield, Connecticut, who managed to be active, if not eminent, in such diverse fields of endeavour as poetry, Congregationalism, Swedenborgism and dentistry. In 1833 he published his great work *The Dentologia – A Poem on the Diseases of the Teeth*, which did much to elevate the profession of dentistry from the low esteem in which, perhaps justifiably, it was then held. Footnotes compiled by the author's friend and mentor Eleazar Parmly, Dentist, gave sensible advice on dental hygiene; and an appendix supplied a list of 300 qualified dental practitioners in America. An idea of Brown's method may be gleaned from the 'Argument' that prefaces the First Canto, and which runs as follows: 'Invocation to living beauty as seen in the human countenance – Importance of personal charms to the female sex – Man a natural physiognomist – Mental and moral qualities mirrored in the features – Original beauty of the human race – Beauty of angelic natures when purified from the stains of mortality – Subject of dentistry proposed – Universal law of nature in regard to human teeth – Importance of good dental practitioners.' We soon see that the poet is alive to the difficulties of the task he has set himself:

> Full well I know 'tis difficult to chime
> The laws of science with the rules of rhyme;
> Plain vulgar prose, my subject seems to claim,
> Did not ambition prompt the higher aim . . .

The reader can only be delighted that ambition so prompted him, for the *Dentologia* contains many passages of exceptionally vivid dental verse. Here, for example, he discourses on the first crop of teeth in childhood:

> One common destiny awaits our kind; –
> 'Tis this, that long before the infant mind,
> Attains maturity – and ere the sun
> Has through the first septennial circle run,

> The teeth, deciduous, totter and decay,
> And prompt successors hurry them away.

(One of Parmly's notes at this point explains for the benefit of the scientifically minded, which teeth fall out and why.) The Second Canto descends abruptly from the somewhat ethereal tone of the first and discusses such grim matters as the 'operation of lancing the gums; fatal consequences of neglect, or of inefficient remedies'. The Third Canto deals, *inter alia*, with poor discipline in regard to teeth-cleaning. In a moving passage the poet hymns the beauty of a certain Urilla, whose celestial blue eyes and vermilion cheeks make him yearn to hear her speak:

> For sure such language from those lips must flow
> As none but pure and seraph natures know.
>
> . . . 'Twas said, – 'twas done – the fit occasion came,
> As if to quench betimes the kindling flame
> Of love and admiration: – for she spoke
> And lo, the heavenly spell for ever broke
> The fancied angel vanished into air,
> And left unfortunate Urilla there:
> For when her lips disclosed to view,
> Those ruined arches, veiled in ebon hue,
> Where love had thought to feast the ravished sight
> On orient gems reflecting snowy light,
> Hope, disappointed, silently retired,
> Disgust triumphant came, and love expired!

The Fourth Canto is perhaps of most direct relevance to students of dentistry, dealing as it does with such matters as the onset of caries, how to stop cavities with gold foil, and how to fit false teeth. It contains some of Solyman's most vivid flights, in particular a description of disease prowling about on the enamel seeking whom he may devour:

> Whene'er along the ivory disks, are seen,
> The filthy footsteps of the dark gangrene;
> When caries come, with stealthy pace to throw
> Corrosive ink spots on those banks of snow –

103

> Brook no delay, ye trembling, suffering fair,
> But fly for refuge to the dentist's care . . .

The Fifth and last Canto returns to the philosophical vein of the beginning and includes such profound topics as the 'importance of the teeth to the arts of eloquence and vocal music'. In the affecting conclusion, we read of the trials of one Seraphina, who used to sing in the village choir, but has had to give it up:

> For, lo, the heavenly music of her lip –
> So sweet, the labouring bees might stop to sip,
> Has passed away; discordant notes succeed,
> And Seraphina's bosom lives to bleed.
>
> Ye ask the cause: – by premature decay,
> Two of her dental pearls have passed away;
> The two essential to those perfect strains,
> That charm the soul when heavenly music reigns

Help is at hand however, for:

> . . . the dental art
> Can every varying tone with ease restore
> And give thee music sweeter than before! –

The Dentologia is a remarkable poem, and there is no doubt that Solyman Brown was a remarkable man. He was one of the founders of the American Society of Dental Surgeons in 1840, opened his own dental supply depot, published the semi-annual *Dental Expositor* (1852–4), and was involved with the New York Teeth Manufacturing Company. *Dentologia* was not his only poem on teeth – he published *Dental Hygeia: a poem* in 1838 – but it is his most famous contribution to literature, and possibly dentistry. Part of it appeared, perhaps to the surprise of readers, in *The American Journal of Dental Science*, where it was also enthusiastically reviewed. 'The author,' said the reviewer, 'not only evinces a thorough and scientific knowledge of all the principles of the art, but also a mind highly cultivated and richly imbued with poetic fancy.' It is true that both Brown and Parmly were at that moment on the Journal's Editorial Committee, and that Brown was actually joint-editor with the reviewer, Chapin Harris; but there is no reason to suppose that other literary critics amongst the ranks of the dental profession would have taken a different view. Perhaps emboldened by the popular response to *Dentologia*, the editors published another poem some issues later by Giles McQuiggin. In *The Aching Tooth*, he addresses the assembled top and bottom sets as if they were recalcitrant and rowdy schoolboys:

> . . . Why should Cuspidatus ask a right
> That to Incisor he'd refuse to grant?
> Or why Incisor, seek a place of pow'r
> To which his friend Molar might not aspire?

But this is poor stuff compared with Brown's purple passages of sententiousness and bloodcurdling descriptions. In a thinly populated field of endeavour he stands supreme, and one has only to compare an anonymous contemporary poetaster's handling of the dental theme to recognize Brown's individual claim to immortality:

> You have gone, old tooth,
> Though hard to yield,
> You have long stood alone,
> Like a stub in a field.
>
> Farewell, old tooth . . .
> That tainted my breath,
> And tasted as smells
> A woodpecker's nest.

Not all didactic poetry is concerned with pushing a morality, a way of life, a remedy, or a profession. James Grainger's (1721–66) *The Sugar Cane* (1764) pushes a product, and does so at awesome length. Dr Johnson, who had admired the same author's *Translation of Tibullus*, was not impressed by so much labour on such a subject. 'What,' he enquired 'could Grainger make of a sugar-cane? One might as well write *"The Parsley Bed – A Poem"* or, *"The Cabbage Garden – A Poem."* ' These are thoughts which also occur to the modern reader as he hacks his way through the dense foliage of Grainger's agronomic poem. In his Preface, the author candidly confesses that 'though I may not be able to please, I shall stand some

chance of instructing the reader . . . which should be the principal
aim of every writer who wishes to be thought a good man'. Certainly, nobody could complain that the poem is not stuffed with
information, some of which is rather incongruous. Boswell relates
that *The Sugar Cane*, when read at Sir Joshua Reynolds' house, made
the assembled wits burst out laughing when, after much blank verse
pomp, the poet began a new paragraph with the words:

'Now, Muse, let's sing of rats . . .'

'And what increased the ridicule was, that one of the company, who
slily overlooked the reader, perceived that the word had originally
been *mice*, and had been altered to rats as more dignified.'

Nevertheless, Grainger's indefatigableness has earned him a
niche in English literature. Anderson includes the poem in his collection of the English poets, though apparently more out of gener-
osity than conviction. '*The Sugar Cane*,' he observes, 'is one of those
performances in which the exertion of a poet's genius may be very
great, and yet his success but moderate.' After pointing out the
drawbacks of the subject, he very conscientiously adds: 'Much
praise is due to him for the liberal and diffusive pains he has taken in
his *Notes* to enlarge the knowledge of West-Indian botany. They
may indeed be considered, both in their medical and botanical
capacity, as a very valuable part of the work; and possibly there are
few parts of it more entertaining . . .' Indeed, a mere rivulet of
verse runs through dense acres of notes in all four books of the
work. 'Entertaining' is not quite the word that springs to mind to
describe them, but entertainment hardly seems to have been the
author's aim. 'I have often been astonished,' he writes, 'that so little
has been published on the cultivation of the sugar cane, while the
press has groaned under folios on every other branch of rural economy.' This lamentable omission he proceeds to remedy, pausing
only for the obligatory royal salute:

Imperial George, the monarch of the main,
Hath given to wield the sceptre of those isles,
Where first the muse beheld the spiry cane,
Supreme of plants, rich subject of my song.

That done, we are at once plunged into the sun-soaked landscape of the West Indies. The list of botanical curiosities is rather formidable, but each of them is further explicated at interminable length in the notes. Nevertheless, there are passages of charming observations, some of which are quite easy to understand:

> Of composts shall the Muse disdain to sing?
> Nor soil her heavenly plumes? The sacred Muse
> Nought sordid deems, but what is base; nought fair,
> Unless true Virtue stamp it with her seal.
> Then, planter, wouldst thou double thine estate,
> Never, ah! never, be asham'd to tread
> Thy dung-heaps.

Grainger's rhetorical enquiries have a delightful way of accumulating other and more substantial questions, like a snowball being pushed slowly down a slope:

> Say shall the experienc'd muse that art recite
> How sand will fertilize stiff barren clay?
> How clay unites the light, the porous mold,
> Sport of each breeze? And how the torpid nymph
> Of the rank pool, so noisome to the smell,
> May be solicited by wily ways
> To draw her humid train, and, prattling, run
> Down the reviving slopes?

Tricky questions of technique, however, demand more concrete treatment, and here Grainger occasionally offers the reader the cheery, but firm, brush-off sometimes to be heard on *Gardeners' Question Time.*

> Whether the fattening compost in each hole
> 'Tis best to throw, or on the surface spread
> Is undeterm'd: trials must decide.

And Grainger, like the BBC presenter, then hurries us on to the next question:

> Enough of composts, muse; of soils enough:
> When best to dig and when inhume the cane;
> A task how arduous! next demands thy song.

Book II of the poem deals with the vermin that attack the cane (this is where the rats and mice come in), and ends with a love story, evidently tacked on in case the reader's interest in agronomy was flagging. Book III contains a McGonagallesque account of the mysteries and technicalities of sugar-making. Book IV contains advice on the selection of slaves, which does not quite square with Dr Percy's depiction of the poet as one of the most generous and benevolent men he knew:

> Must thou from Afric reinforce thy gang? –
> Let health and youth their every sinew firm;
> Clear roll their ample eye; their tongue be red;
> Broad swell their chest; their shoulders wide expand;
> Not prominent their belly; clean and strong
> Their thighs and legs, in just proportion rise.
> Such soon will brave the fervours of the clime;
> And free from ails that kill thy Negro-train,
> An useful servitude will long support.

There is advice also on deworming these useful black creatures and preventing them from 'bloating' by means of bleeding.

The poem ends with another fine patriotic flourish ('Britain shall ever triumph o'er the main'), leaving the reader with the distinct impression that the sugar cane was created for the Hanoverians, and vice versa; certainly it was never intended for

> False Gallia's sons, that hoe the ocean isles,
> Mix with their sugar loads of worthless sand,
> Fraudful, their weight of sugar to increase.

This is the sort of behaviour that prompted the otherwise tightly corsetted poetess Anna Seward to write:

> My inmost soul abhors the bloody French.

Dr Grainger also tried his hand at a ballad, which may be noticed in passing, as it also has a West Indian setting. It concerns a lover called Bryan who is returning to the region, perhaps to administer sugar cane production. As the ship comes in sight of the shore, the headstrong youth leaps overboard, the sooner to reach his sweetheart, who is standing at the water's edge waving his handkerchief. This proves to be foolhardy:

> Then through the white surf did she haste
> To clasp her lovely swain,
> When ah! a shark bit through his waist
> His heart's blood dy'd the main!
>
> He shrieked! his half sprung from the wave,
> Streaming with purple gore,
> And soon it found a living grave
> And ah! was seen no more.

Grainger, we see, is certainly a poet of surprises, not all of them pleasant ones.

The temptation to deliver a lecture in verse has overcome even greater poets than Dr Grainger. There were times when Wordsworth could not resist it, almost always with dire consequences. Aldous Huxley described his elaborate *Ode on the Power of Sound* as 'one of the worst poems ever written by a great man'[1]; and he remarks on Wordsworth's 'complete and absolute failure to render in poetical terms either the quality of music, or its significance, or its value'. The ode is prefaced by a dense 'Argument' that seems designed to deter all but the most masochistic of readers: 'The Ear addressed, as occupied by a spiritual functionary in communion with sounds, individual, or combined in studied harmony . . . etc.' This Spirit, to the dismay of the reader, is the mediator for practically every sound that Wordsworth can think of:

> The headlong streams and fountains
> Serve thee, invisible Spirit, with untired powers;
> Cheering the wakeful tent on Syrian mountains,
> They lull perchance ten thousand thousand flowers.

1. Aldous Huxley, *Music and Poetry in Texts and Pretexts*, Chatto and Windus, 1959, p. 244.

That roar, the prowling lion's *Here I am*,
How fearful to the desert wide!
That bleat, how tender! of the dam
Calling a straggler to her side.
Shout, cuckoo! – let the vernal soul
Go with thee to the frozen zone;
Toll from thy loftiest perch, lone bell-bird, toll!
At the still hour of Mercy dear,
Mercy from her twilight throne
Listening to nun's faint throb of holy fear,
To sailor's prayer breathed from a darkening sea,
Or widow's cottage-lullaby.

'I cannot call to mind,' wrote Wordsworth indignantly to Alexander Dyce, 'why you should not think some passages in "The Power of Sound" equal to anything I have produced; when first printed in "Yarrow Revisited", I placed it at the end of the Volume, and in the last edition of my poems, at the close of the Poems of Imagination, indicating thereby my *own* opinion of it.' It is a matter for some wonder that Wordsworth thought so highly of verses in which the reader is expected to swallow such images as shouting cuckoos that toll from perches and faintly throbbing nuns. We are reminded that the co-author of *Lyrical Ballads* lacked a sense of the ridiculous to a heroic degree: who else could have begun a poem about Furness Abbey with the lines:

Well have yon Railway Labourers to THIS ground
Withdrawn for noontide rest. They sit, they walk
Among the Ruins, but no idle talk
Is heard; to grave demeanour all are bound;
And from one voice a Hymn with tuneful sound
Hallows once more the long-deserted choir . . .

The picture of even evangelical railway labourers abandoning their beer and sandwiches for a burst of community hymn-singing stretches the reader's credulity to breaking point, but Wordsworth's sincerity is unimpeachable. His feelings about railways themselves were ambivalent: although he invested in railway stock and approved of the benefits of easier transport, the announcement

110

of a projected Kendal and Windermere Railway provoked him to write a poem of protest in the *Morning Post*. And as the railway mania gathered momentum, so his doubts increased, until he was heard to complain that we had 'too much hurrying about in these islands'. Perhaps for these reasons we have been spared an 'Ode to Steam' by Wordsworth, but this deficiency has been supplied by other poets. Anna Seward wrote a characteristically impenetrable protest about the effects of the railway in Colebrook Dale, though she also seems fascinated by the

> . . . vast engine, whose extended arms,
> Heavy and huge, on the soft-seeming breath
> Of the hot steam, rise slowly; – till by the cold
> Condens'd, it leaves them soon, with clanging roar,
> Down, down to fall precipitant . . .

Erasmus Darwin, a friend of Anna's, who unfortunately encouraged her to write poetry, celebrated steam in his bizarre poem *The Economy of Vegetation* (published as early as 1792 when steam power was in its infancy). He looks forward to the day when not only 'the slow barge' and 'rapid car' will be steam-driven, but also the 'wide-waving wings expanded' for the 'flying chariot' will be seen clanking through the skies. Nor was the opportunity missed to reinforce sound religion with imagery drawn from the new invention; a tombstone in the cloister of Ely Cathedral commemorates the victims of a railway mishap most appropriately with an epitaph that begins:

> The Line to heaven by Christ was made
> With heavenly truth the Rails are laid,
> From Earth to Heaven the line extends
> To Life Eternal where it ends.

This, of course, was before Dr Beeching wielded his axe. After exhibiting Jesus as 'the way' and God's word as the 'first Engineer', the poet ingeniously compares First, Second and Third Class carriages to Repentance, Faith and Holiness; and he concludes with a thinly veiled threat that those who miss the train will rue the day:

You must the way to Glory gain
Or you with Christ will not remain.
Come then poor sinners, now's the time
At any Station on the Line.
If you'll repent and turn from sin
The Train will stop and take you in.

The inducement offered to travel on this line, which must have
given it the edge over competitors, was that there was no fare pay-
able.

The true Laureate of Steam was Thomas Baker, who flourished
between 1837 and 1857. A civil engineer by trade he was besotted
with the wonders of steam power, which he celebrated in *The
Steam-Engine; or, The Power of Flame, an Original Poem in Ten Cantos*
(1857). 'He was among the first to observe,' write D.B. Wyndham
Lewis and Charles Lee, 'that the Great Western track is so planned
that two engines running on separate parallel rails may meet and
pass, but never crash into each other.'[1] The same authors preface
their extract from Baker's poem – a passage which deals with Lord
Stanhope's projected design for a paddle steamer – with the following necessary caution: 'The lines in [this] extract [which run]:

His frame was made to emulate the duck
Webb'd feet had he, in Ocean's brine to play,

refer not to Lord Stanhope (as might appear from a hasty first reading) but to the paddle steamer of his Lordship's patronage.'[2]

Lord Stanhope hit upon a novel plan
Of bringing forth this vast Leviathan
(This notion first Genevois' genius struck;)
His frame was made to emulate a duck,
Webb'd feet had he, in Ocean's brine to play;
With whale-like might he whirl'd aloft the spray;
But made with all this splash but little speed;
Alas! the duck was doom'd not to succeed!

1. D.B. Wyndham Lewis and Charles Lee, op. cit., p. 192.
2. Op. cit., p. 193.

Thomas Baker's poem is not really aimed at the layman, though there are incidental passages of great human interest, such as the account of Huskisson being run over. For the most part, however, it deals with matters of engineering that are not ideally suited to verse, although the roll call of inventors is charmingly done:

> . . . But Paucton's snake-like screw behind the car,
> The best propellor for the CHIEFS OF WAR,
> Is safely placed beneath the rolling sea,
> And thus preserved from scaith of gun-shot free;
> Rennie's conoidal triple-bladed screw
> Displaced the last, and full attention drew;
> Ericsson, of aerial-engine fame,
> For his six-bladed one advanced his claim;
> . . . But MAUDSLAY'S FEATHERING SCREW of double blade
> Threw these, and all the rest, into the shade . . .

Perhaps the most ambitious attempt to encompass scientific information in the verse form was made by Erasmus Darwin (1731–1802), the grandfather of Charles, whose discovery of evolution he to some extent anticipates: his great work *The Loves of the Plants* (1789) was originally to have been a collaborative effort between him and Anna Seward, he supplying the science, she the poetry. However, Lichfield's Swan could progress no further than the Introduction, because she soon discovered that the subject matter was 'not only vegetal but sexual' and involved the use of words 'which only learned persons were freely permitted to use'.[1] One can see what she meant when one reads Darwin's frank description of the spinster truffle and the enceinte oyster:

> So the lone Truffle, lodged beneath the earth,
> Shoots from paternal roots the tuberous birth.
> No stamen-males ascend, and breathe above,
> No seed-born offspring lives by female love . . .[2]
> . . . Unknown to sex the pregnant oyster swells
> And coral-insects build their radiate shells.

1. Lafcadio Hearn, *Some strange literary figures of the eighteenth and nineteenth centuries*, Hokuseido Press, Japan, 1927.
2. It is interesting to compare these lines with Mrs Hemans' handling of a similar

These lines are actually from Darwin's posthumously published *The Temple of Nature*, from which comes also the following information-packed passage:

> Allied to fish, the Lizard cleaves the flood,
> With one-celled heart, and dark irrigescent blood;
> Half-reasoning Beavers long-unbreathing dart
> Through Eirie's waves with perforated heart;
> With gills and lungs respiring Lampreys steer,
> Kiss the rude rocks, and suck till they adhere;
> With gills pulmonic breathes th' enormous whale,
> And spouts aquatic columns to the gale.

Erasmus Darwin joins Armstrong and Grainger in the pantheon of persistent physician poets (he was offered, but declined, the post of doctor to George III). It is astonishing that these gentlemen found the time to write so much and so superfluously – one tends to assume that they neglected their patients. But Darwin was in fact highly regarded as a doctor (unlike Armstrong) and even more fêted as a scientist. He was less highly regarded as a poet, and it certainly didn't help that his intellectual circle in Lichfield was in direct competition to Dr Johnson's. Nonetheless, the eccentricity of his poetry was not allowed to detract from his dignity as an academic. From the point of view of posterity, the only really serious charge that can be levelled against him is that he assiduously encouraged Anna Seward to write poetry, with the inevitable consequence that she did so.

With the onset of the nineteenth century and its concomitant urban squalor, one other form of didactic verse comes into fashion. The temperance writers were especially strong in America and

---

theme. The phrasing of the last line would probably have dismayed Anna Seward:

> How awful the thought
>   Of the wonders underground,
> Of the mystic changes wrought
>   In the silent, dark profound.
> How each thing upwards tends
>   By necessity decreed,
> And a world's support depends
>   On the shooting of a seed!

included in their ranks a lively mixture of professional moralists and amateur poets. One splendid attack on the booze manufacturers begins:

> The Distillers came down like a wolf on the fold,
> And their pockets were bulging with shekels of gold, –
> And the sheen of their silver was gorgeous to see,
> As they shelled out their ducats in fair Peoree!

Ella Wheeler Wilcox began her incredibly successful career as a purveyor of kitsch verse with a little volume on abstinence entitled *Drops of Water* (1872). And before her, Roswell Rice (1850?–76), 'The American Orator and Poet' (a sort of American McGonagall), exploited the temperance theme among others:

> 'O father! mother! I must die!
> Delirium tremens fires my brain!'

begins one of his efforts; and it ends:

> Beware! ye blood-bought youth beware!
> And shun this most besetting sin!
> Strive hard in brighter world to share
> A crown that Drunkards never win.

McGonagall himself wrote a memorable poem on *The Demon Drink*:

> Oh, thou demon Drink, thou fell destroyer;
> Thou curse of society, and its greatest annoyer.
> What has thou done to society, let me think?
> I answer thou hast caused the most of ills, thou demon Drink.

These verses are justly famous, not least for the shrewd way in which the poet links a weakness for drink with unsound judgement:

> The man that gets drunk is little else than a fool.
> And is in the habit, no doubt, of advocating for Home Rule;
> But the best Home Rule for him, as far as I can understand,
> Is the abolition of strong drink from the land.

115

He has several other poems on the same theme, the most moving of which is *The Poet's Dream of the Destroying Angel*, who comes to raze the public houses in Dundee. The poet follows the angel around the town, and at one point sees the Devil spectating from the roof of the town hall:

> And while the Angel was thus addressing the people,
> The Devil seemed to be standing on the Townhouse
>   Steeple,
> Foaming at the mouth with rage, and seemingly much
>   annoyed,
> And kicking the Steeple, because the public houses were
>   going to be destroyed.

Although the evils of drink were a favourite Victorian theme, by Edwardian times the earnestness seems largely to have gone out of the issue; perhaps this was due to the ambivalent stance of mass market entertainment, such as the music-halls, where drink, sex and sin are generally considered as disastrous but enjoyable. It comes as something of a surprise, therefore, to find the eccentric clergyman E.E. Bradford (q.v.) resurrecting the theme in his *Sonnets, Songs and Ballads* of 1908. One of these is entitled 'His Mother Drinks', and concerns a boy recovering in hospital. The last stanza admirably recaptures the Victorian ballad's atmosphere of drama and pathos:

> A kindly nurse who sees his wistful smile
>   To cheer him cries:
> 'The doctor says that in a little while
>   He'll let you rise,
> And send you home again!' His eyes grow dim.
>   She little thinks
> What since his father died home means to him –
>   His mother drinks!

In the twentieth century moral and scientific didacticism is rarely to be found in English verse, not least because poetry is no longer a mass medium of communication. The spirit of the genre lingers on in political verses, most of which are too dreary to quote. We should not leave the theme, however, without a brief immersion in an inimitable example that combines the sleeve-tugging intimacy of the Ancient Mariner with the sterile argumentation of the students' union. As Sir John Squire, who rescued it from oblivion, generously remarks, it might have gone quite well in prose[1]: but in verse, this tale of a man who falls in love with a girl and has long discussions with her about politics has all the romance of a *Guardian* leader article:

> . . . I ceased and somewhat eagerly she asked:
> 'Then you would justify the socialist,
> Or Anarchist, the brute assassin, masked
> As a reformer, him who has dismissed
> All scruples and himself or others tasked
> To murder innocence? Can there exist
> A reason to excuse Luccheni's[2] action
> Of life's great rights most dastardly infraction?'
> 'Excuse it, no!' I said; 'nor justify it;
> But understand it, yes! – I find confusion
> In both your questions; and your words imply it,
> They have their base in popular illusion.
> In Socialism and Anarchism, deny it
> Who will, there's no imperative inclusion
> Of violence. Each aiming at reform
> Would lay life's ever-raging life and storm.'

Deny it who will, didactic poetry is not what it used to be.

---

1. It is quoted in his essay 'The Beauties of Badness', in *Life at the Mermaid and Other Essays*, Collins, 1927, pp. 61–70.
2. Luigi Luccheni was the anarchist who murdered the Empress Elizabeth of Austria in Geneva, on 10 September 1898.

Five

RHYMING RELIGION
AND HUMOROUS HYMNOLOGY

Threats and consolations from the pious poets

. . . May to them our spight
Be like our love to *Christ*, both infinite . . .

> Joseph Beaumont D.D.,
> *Unreasonable Reason*

He knows our frame, and with parental love,
He chides our follies while His bowels move.

> J. Pickering, *Providence*, from
> *Pathetical and Consolatory Poems*, 1830

O Lord, Thy people know full well
That all who eat flesh and fell,
Who cannot rightly speak or spell
    Thy various names,
Shall be for ever broiled in hell
    Among the flames

> A.C. Swinburne,
> *The Cannibal Catechism*

THE MOST DELIGHTFUL VERSE OF ANY HYMN must surely be that of an anonymous Boston divine, who produced these lines redolent of Protestant vigour:

> Ye monsters of the bubbling deep
> Your Maker's praises shout;
> Up from the sand, ye codlings, leap
> And wag your tails about.[1]

This tendency to involve the natural world in enthusiastic worship is a recurrent phenomenon in religious writing, and it often results in memorable feats performed by fishes, birds, sheep – and even worms:

> Earth from afar has heard thy fame
> And worms have learnt to lisp thy name . . .

claims one hymnodist. And Dr Watts[2] has also noted the piety and obedience of fishes:

> Amidst thy watry kingdoms, Lord,
> The finny nations play,
> And scaly monsters, at thy word
> Rush through the northern sea.

---

1. Compare the lines of Joseph Gwyer (q.v.) on *A visit to Beddington Park*:

> The insects humming round my ear,
> To me said then begone dull care,
> The trout did from the brook arise
> And splash their thanks up to the skies

2. Isaac Watts (1674–1748).

119

He also justly reminds us that God, not the Water Board, is the only begetter of H_2O:

> On the thin air, without a prop
> Hang fruitful showers around:
> At thy command they sink, and drop
> Their fatness on the ground.

Despite the conspicuous exertions of the natural world to obey the divine command, Watts admits that God is often hard to please, and sometimes impossible. He pictures him riding:

> . . . on a cloud disdainful by
> A Sultan or a Czar;
> Laughs at the worms that rise so high
> Or frowns them from afar;

But on the whole, Dr Watts' Calvinism is sensibly diluted for English consumption. He is fundamentally of the school which considers that everything agreeable in the world redounds to the credit of Our Maker. About the responsibility for everything disagreeable he remains, for the most part, tactfully silent, but hints that the Devil most likely has something to do with it. The apotheosis of this view may be seen in the work of Cecil Francis Alexander (1818–95), who even cosmetized poverty as an entirely proper part of the divine dispensation:

> The rich man in his castle
> The poor man at his gate,
> God made them, high or lowly,
> And ordered their estate.

This came from Alexander's celebrated hymn much sung in infant schools:

> All things bright and beautiful
> All creatures great and small,
> All things wise and wonderful
> The Lord God made them all.

This, of course, is an attractive notion, but is it theologically sound? Since the pious are constantly referring to 'Almighty God', can he really, like some totalitarian hero-figure, be allowed to preside over nothing but spectacular successes in the realms over which he holds sway? The Monty Python team evidently think not:

> All things dull and ugly
> All creatures short and squat
> All things rude and nasty
> The Lord God made the lot.

The problem of how far we should take the notion of divine responsibility by no means impinged on everybody. The average clerical mind was quite happy to put on one side such evidence as didn't fit the comfortable, orthodox picture, while maintaining, with the Rev. Patrick Brontë, that 'the grand First Cause of this and every other phenomenon is God'. The father of Charlotte, Emily and Anne wrote several poems based on this premise, though they cannot be said to exhibit the literary talent of his daughters. One of them was printed as a Reward Book for Sunday Schools (1824) and stands out as an engaging exercise in didacticism. *The Phenomenon* or *An Account in Verse of the Extraordinary Disruption of a Bog*, which took place in the Moors of Haworth on 12 September 1824, commendably attempts to combine useful scientific information with religious rectitude. Expanding on his contention that God was ultimately responsible for the happening, he allows that there may also have been meteorological and geological causes, all of which he enumerates. The poem begins unaccountably in the Garden of Eden, after the author has warned his readers in the Preface that he had taken care to intersperse throughout such observations as might be profitable as well as pleasing. Pupils are also advised that they may need to have a dictionary at their elbow.

His method may be illustrated by the passage in which a tide of mud rolls across the moor and threatens to engulf the adjacent plain. Natural phenomena, or rather, Satan, had started it, but it is God who calls a halt:

> . . . had not God, who stills the ocean's roar,
> And hems it in with one eternal shore

Said to the wide, the deep disparting hill –
'Restrain thy foaming fury – peace be still . . .'

. . . Thus Power Infinite and Love Divine,
The utmost bounds of Satan's rage define;
Even when he seems to roam without a rein
God counts the links of his eternal chain.

Although this may not have been so reassuring for any animals or
their owners engulfed in the mud, it is certainly an ingenious way of
frightening schoolchildren into obedience. Rev. Brontë cannot, of
course, resist comparing the Haworth bog flood to the one Noah
survived; and his picture of the unsuspecting animals, like foolish
children at play, is done with a certain relish:

The finny tribe to 'scape these horrors try,
And sunk in muddy suffocation die.
The snowy geese, that crop the grassy brim,
The motley ducks, that gabbling, featly swim
With unsuspecting joy await the roar
Of that thick flood, that tangling, whelms them o'er . . .

The Rev. Brontë's poems were actually printed alongside those
of his daughters in an edition of their works, an act of filial piety
which can only shame children more jealous of their literary reputation. G.K. Chesterton, in one of his essays, quotes a not untypical
stanza:

Religion makes beauty enchanting;
And even where beauty is wanting,
    The temper and mind
    Religion-refined
Will shine through the veil with sweet lustre.

'If you read much of it,' remarks Chesterton, 'you will reach a state
of mind in which, even though you know the jolt is coming, you can
hardly forbear to scream. We have read much of the gloomy life of
the Brontë sisters in their dark and narrow house, on their sombre
and savage moorlands. We have heard a great deal of how their
souls were attuned to the storm, whether of wild winds or stern

words. But I can imagine no storm so paralysing as the noise of a reverend gentleman reading that poem; no torture so savage as the ruthless repetition of that metre; no inhuman cry so awful or so freezing to the blood, even out of the very heart of the hell of *Wuthering Heights*.'[1]

The Rev. Brontë's poetry is unlikely to have reached a wide public, but it is scarcely worse than the pious offerings of one of the most spectacularly successful bad poets ever. Robert Montgomery (1807–55) was the author of *The Omnipresence of the Deity* (1828) which ran through eight editions in as many months. Like Southey's *A Vision of Judgement*, it is chiefly remembered for the demolition job that it provoked, in this case by Macaulay in the *Edinburgh Review*. The poem is completely devoid of any interest or merit, but a successful sales campaign passed it off on the gullible evangelical market as a work of deep religious significance. Macaulay begins his piece by exposing the publishers' practice of shameless 'puffing', a means by which, then as now, inferior goods were offloaded on readers anxious to improve their education and their image. He continues by demonstrating that Montgomery's verse consists substantially of other persons' verses recycled: 'The poem . . . commences with a description of the creation, in which we can find only one thought which has the least pretension to ingenuity, and that one thought is stolen from Dryden, and marred in the stealing:

> 'Last, softly beautiful, as music's close
> Angelic woman into being rose.'

The all-pervading influence of the Supreme Being is then described in a few tolerable lines borrowed from Pope, and a great many intolerable lines of Mr Robert Montgomery's own.' Warming to his theme, Macaulay begins systematically to bulldoze the author's pretensions and expose his dubious methods: 'There is a very pretty Eastern tale of which the fate of plagiarists often reminds us. The slave of a magician saw his master wave his wand, and heard him give orders to the spirits who arose at the summons. The slave stole the wand, and waved it himself in the air; but he had not observed that his master used the left hand for that purpose. The spirits thus

1. G.K. Chesterton, 'On Bad Poetry', in *All I Survey*, Methuen, 1933, p. 61.

irregularly summoned tore the thief to pieces instead of obeying his orders. There are very few who can safely venture to conjure with the rod of Sir Walter [Scott]; and Mr Robert Montgomery is not one of them.'

If Montgomery's brazen plagiarism were not sufficient offence, there was always his grammar and syntax to be considered. A couplet castigated by Macaulay has become quite famous:

> The soul, aspiring, pants its source to mount
> As streams meander level with their fount.

And a splendidly portentous muddle occurs in the lines:

> And here let Memory turn her tearful glance
> On the dark horrors of tumultuous France,
> When blood and blasphemy defiled her land,
> And fierce Rebellion shook her savage hand.

'Whether,' writes Macaulay, 'Rebellion shakes her own hand, shakes the hand of Memory, or shakes the hand of France, or what any one of these three metaphors would mean, we have no means of knowing. Elsewhere Montgomery supplies us with: "a shipwrecked sailor, who "visions a viewless temple in the air" '; a murderer who stands on a heath, with ashy lips, in cold convulsion spread; a pious man, to whom, as he lies in bed at night,

> The panorama of past life appears,
> Warms his pure mind, and melts it into tears;

a traveller, who loses his way, owing to the thickness of the "cloud-batallion", and the want of "heaven-lamps", to beam their holy light. We have a description of a convicted felon, stolen from that incomparable passage in Crabbe's *Borough*, which has made many a rough and cynical reader cry like a child. We can, however, conscientiously declare that persons of the most excitable sensibility may safely venture upon Mr Robert Montgomery's version . . ."[1]

1. Thomas Babington Macaulay, 'Mr Robert Montgomery', *The Edinburgh Review*, April 1830.

Although Macaulay spoiled the market for Montgomery's next efforts (*A Universal Prayer* and *Satan, or Intellect without God*), *The Omnipresence* rolled onwards, an unstoppable juggernaut of cant and pretentiousness. By 1858 it had reached twenty-eight editions. As D.B. Wyndham Lewis and Charles Lee put it: 'The poem was sufficiently divorced from all the lovely Graces, rich in elementary bathos and bombast, and steeped in the suburban religiosity of the period to find instant success with the British public.'[1] No wonder that Montgomery, although he contemplated bringing a libel action against Macaulay, soon abandoned the idea and settled down to enjoy the huge income from his sanctimonious compilation.

Montgomery's windy, and often nonsensical, formulations tap a vein of religious sentimentality that prefers the numinous to the concrete. The latter has its own body of literature, a striking characteristic of which is the absence of Christian mercy in dealing with the opposition:

> Those treach'rous plots my foe conceiv'd
>   Abortive are and vain;
> The pit he digg'd has prov'd a grave
>   His ruins to contain.
>
> On his malicious head returns
>   The mischief he contriv'd;
> The violence, for me design'd
>   Is to himself arriv'd.[2]

This satisfying state of affairs is described by Nicholas Brady and Nahum Tate in their lively rendering of Psalm VII. Psalm XVII is even more uncompromising:

> Through Him the necks of prostrate Foes
> My conqu'ring feet in triumph press:
> Aided by Him I root out those
> Who hate and envy my success.

1. D.B. Wyndham Lewis and Charles Lee, *The Stuffed Owl*, J.M. Dent and Sons, 1930, p. 173.
2. Nicholas Brady and Nahum Tate, *An Essay of a New Version of the Psalms*, London, 1696.

It has to be admitted that a perceptible note of intolerance, vindictiveness even, is a feature of Protestant literature when sinners and triflers are under consideration. The fate of children who 'scoff and call names' should, of course, be a harsh one, but some might feel that Dr Watts is slightly overreacting when he describes what they may expect:

> But lips that dare be so profane
> To mock, and jeer, and scoff
> At holy things or holy men
> The Lord shall cut them off.
>
> When children in their wanton play
> Serv'd old Elisha so;
> And bid the prophet go his way,
> 'Go up, thou bald-head, go:'
>
> God quickly stopp'd their wicked breath,
> And sent two raging bears,
> That tore them limb from limb to death
> With blood, and groans, and tears.

Sometimes the violence of these pious writings may be the result of oversight or even poor copying. Sir John Squire maintains that a metrical version of the Psalms allowed by the Authority of the General Assembly of the Kirk of Scotland renders the closing lines of *By the Waters of Babylon* as follows:

> Yea, happy shall he be,
> Thy tender little ones,
> Who shall lay hold upon and them
> Shall dash against the stones

This is not really the spirit even of extreme Presbyterianism, and one can't help feeling there is some mistake. Squire also quotes a couple of lines from Dr Watts that exhibit that very moral gentleman's tastes in a curious light:

> Not all the gay pageants that breathe
> Can with a dead body compare.

126

There can be absolutely no doubt, however, that the Rev. Joseph Beaumont D.D. (1616–99) means exactly what he says in his *Unreasonable Reason*. If he seems conspicuously lacking in charity in his remarks, we must understand that he lived through difficult times. The Roundheads turned him out of Peterhouse – perhaps not very surprisingly as he publicly referred to them as 'apostate scum of vassals'; (and he described the politically acceptable dons who succeeded him and his colleagues as 'intruding drones'). However, at the Restoration he returned, and, says Squire[1], 'became one of the fattest pluralists of his day, and lived to a very advanced age in full possession of his faculties and emoluments.' Whether the acidulated quality of his poem may be attributed to hunger or to indigestion after overeating, the effect on the reader is electrifying. Subtle-minded theologians and thinkers, such as Arius and Plotinus, whom he regards as undermining the faith, are summarily dealt with. In particular, Socinus and his followers are given a terrible drubbing:

> May all thy damned Brood, where'r it creep
> Feel their own viper's stings, which now they keep
> Close in their studies. May Confusion's Blast
> Dared so long, come thundering downe at last.
> May their fowle Names prevent ye Destinie
> Of their vile Corps, and rot before they die.
> Be hate their Portion: May to them our Spight
> Be like our love to *Christ*, both infinite,
> Unlesse they'l not be too wise to imbrace
> For horrid Monsters, Truth's all-beauteous face.
> Be toads more fair; be Adders hisses sweet;
> Be Dragons comely; May these rather meet
> In my poor Bosome, then my Heart should drink
> But ye least Drop of ye *Socinian* sink.

This liveliness of language is evident in much evangelical literature as well, but usually in a less sophisticated form. Few of the earlier Protestant hymnodists could resist the arresting – even bloodcurdling – image. In the hands of a William Cowper the effects are undeniably powerful, if rather repulsive:

1. J.C. Squire, *Life at the Mermaid and Other Essays*, Collins, 1927, p. 48.

There is a fountain fill'd with blood
Drawn from Immanuel's veins;
And sinners plunged beneath that flood
Lose all their guilty stains.

Dr Watts, however, somehow misses this medieval crucifixion effect:

Believing we rejoice
To see the curse remove;
We bless the Lamb with cheerful voice
And sing his bleeding love.

Straightforward colloquial language has much to commend it, but there are pitfalls nonetheless; these the Rev. A. Freston, A.M., failed to avoid in his poem on *The Formation of the World* (1787):

Let us make Man, said now th'Eternal One . . .
Before his Maker the new creature stood
Naked, forlorn, and destitute of food.

And Mrs Hamilton-King, dealing with a slightly earlier phase of the Creator's activity, speaks of the moment when:

. . . God formed in the hollow of his hand
This ball of Earth among His other Balls . . .

Dr Watts excels himself in his portrait of the backsliding believer who 'blushes to lie grovelling on the ground' and longs to soar into the empyrean:

. . . Beyond those crystal vaults
And all their sparkling balls;
They're but the porches to thy courts,
And paintings on thy walls.

It is difficult for the hymnmaker to combine simple language with sound doctrine, since the former is concerned with honest and practical communication, while the latter is the product of centuries of opaque theological bickering. Perhaps the best solution is to let yourself go as a poet and blandly claim that the images you use, despite any appearances to the contrary, are symbolic representations of Christianity. This was the technique adopted by George Wither (1588–1667), who was described as 'fanatical rhymer and intemperate Puritan' by Swift, but whose *Hymns and Songs of the Church* contain some energetic and readable verse. His version of *The Song of Songs* is extremely erotic, but the author goes to considerable lengths to explain that the poem is actually about Christ's relationship with his church – which is that of bridegroom to bride. Remarks about breasts are, we are told, obvious references to the Gospel. Of the Fifth Canticle he does say guardedly: '. . . the explanation of each several metaphor will be too large for this place. Nor will every capacity reach unto the particular application of them. It may suffice, therefore, if such do (by implicit faith) sing these mysteries with a general application of them to Christ and his Church, believing themselves members of that spouse; and that Jesus Christ is he who in this song professeth an entire affection, not only for the whole mystical body of the faithful but even to every member of it in particular.' This instruction prepares us for dealing with Canto Eight, which runs:

> Sister and espoused peer,
> Those thy breasts, how fair they are!
> Better be those dugs of thine
> Than the most delicious wine;
> And thine ointments are
> Sweeter than all spices far.

Some people think that the Puritans were simply disagreeable and their writings dull. A perusal of the works of George Wither does not confirm this; like many a poet and hymnodist who came after him, he wasn't about to let a little religion cramp his style.

Six

EROS AND BATHOS

A bad dream of fair women

. . . But in vague ways I most insanely yearn
  To meet some lean, dwarfed, fetid, hairy thing
With loathsome skin and bulging eyes of rheum,
Then with wild sighs to make the monster burn
  With Love's delight and bid his hot arms cling
Around my beauty in the perfumed gloom.

Francis Saltus Saltus, *The Courtesan's Whim*
(which might also have been entitled *'nostalgie de la boue'*)

Kiss in the bower,
  Tit on the tree!
Bird mustn't tell,
  Whoop! he can see.

Alfred, Lord Tennyson

Many mellow Cydonian suckets,
  Sweet apples, anthosmial, divine,
From the ruby-rimmed beryline buckets,
  Star-gemmed, lily-shaped, hyaline:
Like the sweet golden goblet found growing
  On the wild emerald cucumber-tree,
Rich, brilliant, like chrysoprase glowing
  Was my beautiful Rosalie Lee.

Thomas Holley Chivers (1809–58)

WHEN FIRST CONFRONTED WITH THE EXCITEMENTS of physical sex, absolute beginners rapidly make a disconcerting discovery: unbridled enthusiasm is all very well in its way, but a minimum of expertise makes matters progress more satisfactorily. This is a discovery which the aspirant erotic poet often never makes; all too frequently, the poetaster's public love-making tends only to provoke a certain sympathy for the object of his affections. If, nowadays, the problem is more evident (and the embarrassment correspondingly greater) that is because the uninhibited vocabulary favoured by many of our contemporaries is no better camouflage for the poet's inadequacies than was the coyness of a previous age. The 200-year transition from the latter to the former is as complete a cycle as the one that begins with the Restoration and ends with Dr Bowdler's *Family Shakespeare*. Now we have Mr Craig Raine's poem on his friend's '*Arsehole*'[1], then we had Edward Jerningham's (1727–1812) poem '*Il Latte*'.

The title of Jerningham's poem means 'milk' in English, but such bluntness of language was deemed inappropriate by the polite eighteenth-century poet; for the milk referred to turns out to be human, and the whole poem is no less than a hymn to the breasts. Moreover, it emerges that Jerningham has a cause to advance, namely the desirability of breast-feeding, upon which subject he is as dogmatic and progressive as a Dr Spock. In order to inspire in his readers the right sense of respectable enthusiasm for these useful and attractive adjuncts to the female anatomy, Jerningham paints a

1. *The Spectator* (16 April 1983) had this to say about it: 'Bees cluttered round the infant Pindar's lips; but they have left the middle-aged Mr Raine alone, and he has had to start looking up other people's bottoms. He has looked long and hard. Readers of his poem "*Arsehole*" . . . will feel that Mr Raine has really had the last word on the subject.'

131

delightful picture of them as the revered shrine around which flutter infatuated Cupids, who spend their time bathing in milk. The overall effect is of a Rubens picture in words.

> That shrine! Where Nature with presaging aim
> What time her friendly aid Lucina brings,
> The snowy nectar pours, delightful stream!
> Where fluttering Cupids dip their purple wings.

Regrettably, feckless parents farm out their babies to wet-nurses:

> To venal hands, alas! can you resign
> The Parent's task, the Mother's pleasing care?
> To venal hands the smiling babe consign?
> While Hymen starts, and Nature drops a tear.

Instead of gadding about in society ('When mid the polish'd circle ye rejoice/Or roving join fantastic Pleasure's train') mothers should stay at home and suckle their offspring:

> Unswayed by Fashion's dull unseemly jest
> Still to the bosom let your infant cling,
> There banquet off an ever-welcome guest,
> Unblam'd inebriate at that healthful spring.

The poet adroitly navigates his way around all the verbal hazards inherent in his subject (what supreme tact he shows in not rhyming 'breast' with 'jest'), and leaves the reader not only convinced by his main argument, but revelling in a pleasing vision of babies completely hooked on 'snowy nectar'.

Although the advent of the romantic poets freed poetic diction from the ice-pack of eighteenth-century politeness, unreal and frequently absurd treatments of the physical side of things persisted. A 'romantic' formula simply replaced a 'classical' one. The poetaster took Byron, Shelley, or Keats as his model; but since he or she was unable to master the matter of such strongly individual geniuses, we are left only with the manner. In 1891 Stanley Savill is still muddling together an astonishing mixture of conventional pathos and stale images, producing not so much poetry as a sort of verbal slurry left over from poetic traditions:

> Her fevered little hands she wrung
> > In bitterness of heart,
> Anon, to soothe the smart,
> Her arms about her bosom clung
> > The while she tapped her grieving lips
> > With rosy finger tips.
>
> Now with her tender palms she pressed
> > The aching temples of her pain;
> Anon she beat her virgin breast
> > Impatient of her pain,
> Until her heart rebellious rose
> And stained the billowy breadth of snows
> > With blushes for her wanton blows.

Such verses remind us rather forcibly that, in poetry as in life, breasts should be handled with a great deal of care. The nineteenth century sometimes seems to be obsessed with them. The descriptions, which are a far cry from Jerningham's elaborate reticence, tell us a good deal about the poet's sexual tastes, sometimes in rather startling language. In *The Marvel of Arabia*, Thomas Holley Chivers provides an example of versified voyeurism typical of the extravagance of his style:

> Her white breasts hang on her bosom
> > Like Magnolias in the bud
> Side by side, about to blossom,
> > Fairest ones in all the wood –
> Like Angel's fruit, upon some Heavenly Tree,
> Growing in Eden, not to touch, but see.

Tennyson, describing Rose, the gardener's daughter, is undecided about how much he and the reader should be allowed to contemplate of her exceptional bosom; this uncertainty produces lines of characteristic coyness:

> An unforgotten vision! The clear heat
> Bathing the ripe anemones, that kissed
> Each other in her lips, deepened the blush
> Below her violet eyes and underneath

Glowed on one polished shoulder – basking warm
Between the half-seen swell of maiden breasts,
Moulded in smoothest curves . . .

Tennyson later thought better of this and produced a sanitized version in which the ardent sunshine is portrayed as:

. . . . doubling his own warmth against her lips
And on the bounteous wave of such a breast
As pencil never drew . . .

But this reads like the sort of change the Lord Chamberlain used to
insist on in plays. Alfred Austin (q.v.) was perhaps the most whole-
hearted breasts enthusiast of them all. The acres of his poetry
devoted to the subject might be described as the metrical equivalent
of what are known as 'breastscapes' in the work of J. Russell Flint.
In his effusion on the city of Florence (which he describes somewhat alarmingly as a 'hot ferocious dam whose womb outheaves/
More whelps than she can suckle, yet for all/Will not relax from any
she conceives/Her savage-looking grip, but fiercely hugs/All to her
overtasked dugs'), he waxes indignant against anti-mammalian
prudes:

In that same palace, the Uffizi, I
    Remember to have marked a virgin lift
Upon a silver salver up on high
    The offering of her breasts – no trivial gift.
'Tis Lippo Lippi's picture; and hard by,
    A painter, not by instinct, but by shift
The venal lacquey of this age of ours
    Had for her bosom substituted flowers.[1]

'No trivial gift' indeed, but perhaps one a little too generous for
the 'venal lacquey's' customers. They were the same customers who
rebelled at being asked to endorse the Aphrodite figure in George
Meredith's poem *With the Persuader*. At any rate, he wrote to a
friend that the work was 'too much for the magazines, and may be

1. Alfred Austin, *The Human Tragedy – A Poem*, 1862.

for you', adding disingenuously 'yet it is innocent as statuary.' He also asks her to apply to him if she finds any obscurities in it, but she would probably have found the following passage clear enough:

> A simple nymph it is, inclined to muse
> Before the leader foot shall dip in stream:
> One arm at curve along a rounded thigh;
> Her firm new breasts each pointing its own way;
> A knee half bent to shade its fellow shy,
> Where innocence, not nature, signals nay.
> The bud of fresh virginity awaits
> The wooer, and all roseate will she burst:

'Unfortunately,' remarks F.L. Lucas, 'I feel Meredith lacked a Greek sense of restraint; as might be expected from one who had the somewhat simple faith that the "core of style" is "fervidness" and would even rebuke young ladies because their nostrils were not lively, nervous and dilated . . .'[1] One wonders if he also required their breasts to point in different directions.

It is a short step from the frankness to be found in Meredith to the exaggeration evident in many lesser poets who flourished in the 1890s. Just as it is the fate of revolutionaries to found new orthodoxies, so it is the fate of the taboo-destroying writer to inspire a line of imitators who fall victim to stale convention. The worst offerings of the so-called decadents in the 1890s degenerated into tame posturing, or a sort of punk propriety, in which *femmes fatales* and various *grand guignol* props are seasoned with sadism, masochism, perversion, spleen, morbidity and madness. The best of these poets managed some languorous and exotic lyrics in a minor key – Ernest Dowson is the outstanding example of effective theatricality; and others, such as John Davidson or Francis Thompson, widened their scope beyond the mannerisms of the lesser lights, and beyond the decadent preoccupations of their French hero Baudelaire, to include passionate (and erotic) religious invocation, and appeals to a social conscience. The same cannot be said for the American Francis Saltus Saltus, who wrote over 5000 poems before he died aged thirty-nine. His work is an *olla podrida* of decadent themes with the pathetic fallacy thrown in as a dream topping:

1. F.L. Lucas, *Style*, Cassell and Co., 1955.

To a Scrap of Seaweed

Tossed by the tempest and fluctuant tide
The vulgar plaything of the slimy eel;
Crushed by the vessel's keel or cast aside,
What bitterness thy injured heart must feel!

'Although he idealized cigarette-smoking women, looked for pornography in the Bible, and honoured Baudelaire, Gérard de Nerval, and Le Marquis de Sade,' writes C.T. Kindilien, 'he never escaped the tone of the boy who expected any moment to be caught smoking behind the barn.'[1] He works his way conscientiously through the characters and situations of 'decadence' – indeed he sometimes seems to be ticking them off on a mental list:

Oh! such a past can not be mute
Such bliss can not be crushed in sorrow,
Although thou art a prostitute
And I am to be hanged tomorrow.

A poem like this effectively supplies the *nostalgie de la boue* element. Another, *Puella Erotica*, treats the vice-ridden world of ancient Rome like a painting by Franz von Stuck (with a little help from Alma Tadema), after it has been put through the Hollywood mangle and emerged as a scene in *I, Claudius*:

Effeminate Caesars with a satyr leer
Sigh to her ear
Their brutal whims and maddening desires
No gleam of pleasure lingers in her glance
Fixed on the wanton dance,
Turned by the torment of a hundred lyres.

. . . Nude slaves drag hampers of rich food and spice
Perfumes and ice,
Unto the reeking, gold-crushed board in haste,
With monster lampreys from Pompeii caught fresh
Fed upon human flesh,
To tempt her morbid delicacy of taste.

1. C.T. Kindilien, *American Poetry in the Eighteen-Nineties*, Brown University Press, 1956, pp. 188–9.

One aspect of Saltus that is particularly engaging is his tendency to introduce modern naturalistic effects into his period fantasies. The action of his dramatic fragment *Dolce Far Niente* (which is nevertheless set in Seville) takes place in Dona Serafina's room ('furnished in the modern Spanish style' – which apparently means 'flowers, birdcages, a piano, guitars'). Don Alonzo and Serafina are alone, and the topic of conversation is the heat; or rather that is what Serafina wants to talk about:

Alonzo:	'Tis very hot.
Serafina:	Yes, very.
Alonzo:	. . . My soul ne'er sleeps
	Since first my dazzled eyes beheld thy charms,
	Thy pearly teeth, the Paros of thine arms,
	Thy fragrant hair . . .
Serafina:	Hush, hush, it is too warm,
	To lavish praises on my face and form:
	Had you not better smoke a cigarette . . .
	And sip this sherbet which is frozen yet.

The sherbet fails to cool Alonzo's ardour, and Serafina has to take a strongly practical line with him:

> Charming indeed; considering the heat,
> Your graceful Muse with Vega's could compete.
> But pray lie still, and calm such ardent fire,
> Love is not pretty when we both perspire . . .

This indeed is a problem for many honeymooners; but the unfortunate Alonzo has not even reached first base, despite the astonishing lengths to which he has gone to set up a seduction:

> Your *duena*, gagged, lies cursing us down stairs,
> Your *madre* in the church is at her prayers;
> A forged letter, *hem*! but as you bid,
> Now sends your noble *padre* to Madrid . . .

But Serafina is in no hurry:

> I fear your transports will disturb my lace
> And ardent kisses *always* mark my face.

Alonzo realizes that patience is the only policy likely to yield results:

> And by the way, before I do forget
> Allow my offering you a cigarette.

Serafina asks him to play the guitar – evidently she is determined to get her money's worth out of the situation. But it *is* rather hot:

> Really my love, the weather warmer grows
> 'Tis *very* hot, but I will not oppose
> Your gracious wish.

After one verse of a song Alonzo faints from the heat and Serafina seizes the opportunity to tax him with the attention he is paying to Inez (we are not told, but presumably Alonzo comes round in time to hear this). He responds with some angled insinuations about her and Juan. Serafina has an answer:

> Juan, my dear, is but a family friend
> And to my love would never dare pretend.
> I do not see what you are jealous at.
> *Dios*! a man who wears a green cravat.

The green cravat is sufficiently damning to convince Alonzo, and the action starts to warm up, despite the heat:

Serafina:	Come to my arms, thou best beloved of all.
Alonzo:	. . . I cannot stir,
	Rest on my lips thy lips' hot sensuous fur . . .
	Come Serafina, come.
Serafina:	. . . It is too hot
	For me to move; come *you* to *me*;
Alonzo:	Light of my soul, to *me* you should approach.

At this point Serafina, voicing a thought that has already occurred to the reader, says:

> I never thought your love would come to this.

In one of those abrupt changes of genre which Saltus managed so
adroitly, we now find ourselves in a French farce:

Serafina: Come!
Alonzo: Come yourself.
Serafina: I will not.
Alonzo: Indeed?
          Well *stay*, and take the siesta you need.

to which Serafina retorts:

          As your boiling passions grow to tame,
          I think that you had better do the same.

So they both decide to take a nap:

Alonzo: May your repose be sweet, my dearest love.
Serafina: My hope!
Alonzo: My faith!
Serafina: My bird!
Alonzo: My heart
Serafina: My dove
Alonzo: How sweet it is to slumber, cool and free,
          I love you –
Serafina: I adore you.
Both: Dream of me!
          Both sleep. (The fragment ends.)

This perceptive study of the effect of heat on human relationships cries out for a performance, perhaps at the National with
Rowan Atkinson as Alonzo and Penelope Keith as Serafina. The
programme note could draw interesting parallels between Saltus'
use of the dramatic hiatus and the same phenomenon in the work of
Samuel Beckett.

Space does not permit further exploration of the hidden shallows
of Francis Saltus Saltus, so we leave him with one last example of his
erotic and exotic language put to magnificently inappropriate use in
The Spider, which inspires in the poet rather different emotions
from those it inspires in the housewife:

          Then all thy feculent majesty recalls
          The nauseous mustiness of forsaken bowers,

The leprous nudity of deserted halls –
The positive nastiness of sullied flowers.

And I mark the colours yellow and black
That fresco thy lithe, dictatorial thighs,
I dream and wonder on my drunken back
How God could possibly have created flies!

Of the English decadents there were few such persistent offenders against taste and sense as Saltus, but the attempts to excite and shock sometimes betray the desperation of the exhibitionist who feels he is being ignored. The last refuge of the nineties for a number of 'decadent' poets proved to be a place where a love of self-display and glittering ornament could be gratified, namely the Catholic Church. The male-oriented ambience was an added bonus for the homosexuals among them; the frocks were appealing, the ritual was ancient and exotic and the audience was largely captive – that is, if you became a priest like John Gray. Indeed, the priestly role seems to have amply satisfied his aesthetic cravings, formerly so louche. The 'before' and 'after' effect is startling. For example, his poem *The Barber*, written 'before', is a steamy erotic fantasy:

The dream grew vague. I moulded with my hands
The mobile breasts, the valleys; and the waist
I touched; and pigments reverently placed
Upon their thighs in sapient spots and stains,
Beryls and crysolites and diaphanes,
And gems whose hot harsh names are never said.
I was a masseur; and my fingers bled
With wonder as I touched their awful limbs.
Suddenly, in the marble trough, there seems
O, last of my pale mistresses, Sweetness!
A twy-lipped scarlet pansy. My caress
Tinges thy steel-gray eyes to violet.
Adown thy body skips the pit-a-pat
Of treatment once heard in a hospital
For plagues that fascinate, but half appal.

So, at the sound, the blood of one stood cold.
The chaste hair ripened into sudden gold.
The throat, the shoulders, swelled and were uncouth;

140

The breasts rose up and offered each a mouth.
And on the belly pallid blushes crept.
That maddened me, until I laughed and wept.

That the same man who wrote this should end his days writing
verses like the following is rather a disappointment for his readers,
though no doubt it was a relief for the church:

The holy night that Christ was born
The ox stood reverently apart,
Both ruminating eaten corn,
And pondering within his heart.

It can be seen that the Gray of the earlier poem collects many of the
standard ingredients of the decadent's recipe including cosmetics,
blood, the Fatal Woman, disease and hot flushes. Of these, the most
recurrent image was the Fatal Woman, '*La Belle Dame Sans Merci*',
the '*Puella Erotica*' – to name but a few of her various guises. The *ne
plus ultra* of the type is celebrated by Richard Le Gallienne in his
Beauty Accurst, a satisfyingly overripe poem that illustrates a perennial truth of bad verse studies: if you try and pump more 'poetry'
into an overworked image than it can bear, it bursts like a bicycle
tyre. It is hard not to believe that this piece was intended as a parody
of nineties' affectation, but since so assiduous an expert on the
period as Mario Praz[1] regards it as seriously intended, it must be
taken as such in the absence of evidence to the contrary. We join
this remarkable and electrifying female at the point where she goes
for a stroll in the woods:

Lo! when I walk along the woodland way
    Strange creatures leer at me with uncouth love,
And from the grass reach upward to my breast,
    And to my mouth lean from the boughs above.

The sleepy kine move round me in desire
    And press their oozy lips upon my hair,
Toads kiss my feet and creatures of the mire,
    The snails will leave their shells to watch me there.

1. *See* Mario Praz, *The Romantic Agony*, OUP, 1970, p. 281.

But all this worship, what is it to me?
   I smite the ox and crush the toad in death:
I only know I am so very fair,
   And that the world was made to give me breath.

I only wait the hour when God shall rise
   Up from the star where he so long hath sat,
And bow before the wonder of my eyes
   And set *me* there – I am so fair as that.[1]

Le Gallienne also works anthropomorphism and the pathetic fallacy for all they're worth, which produces results not unlike the hilariously eroticized natural world of *Cold Comfort Farm*:

The floating call of the cuckoo
Soft little globes of bosom-shaped sound,
Came and went at the window;
And, out in the great green world,
Those maidens each morn the flowers
Opened their white little bodices wide to the sun:
And the man – sighed – in his sleep,
And the woman smiled.

Then a lark staggered singing by
Up his shining ladder of dew,
And the airs of dawn walked softly about the room
Filling the morning sky with the scent of woman's hair,
And giving, in sweet exchange, its hawthorn and daisy breath:
And the man awoke with a sob –
But the woman dreamed.[2]

'Bosom-shaped sounds', flowers with little bodices and staggering larks on ladders of dew are a formidable tax on the reader's tolerance. One sees why a contemporary unkindly described his work as 'Wilde and water'. In stark opposition to the decadents' obsession with woman as an erotic and frigid-hearted sadist, burning with lustful and often perverted desires but devoid of feeling, was the view of poetical and moral orthodoxy. Woman was a temptress, but

1. Richard Le Gallienne, *English Poems*, London, 1900.
2. Richard Le Gallienne, R.L.S., *An Elegy*, London, 1895.

this aspect of her nature had to be rigorously suppressed in favour of an image of pure, virginal, maidenhood. The exception, of course, was the woman deliberately portrayed as bad, such as Vivien in Tennyson's *Idylls of the King*, who displays many of the characteristics the Victorians most feared in the female sex – seductive cunning, plausibility, and an ability to manipulate the male concept of woman's moral superiority as compensation for her sexual inferiority. Vivien takes the wizard, Merlin, on an excursion to the woods, and with her feminine wiles she all but seduces him. (Tennyson's sex scenes tend to fade out at the crucial moment, and of course Merlin *was* very old.) This book of the *Idylls* ends with some lines that have dismayed even Tennyson's most ardent admirers:

> . . . And shrieking out 'O fool!' the harlot leapt
> Adown the forest, and the thicket closed
> Behind her, and the forest echo'd 'fool'.

The starting point for the traditionalists is, of course, Eve. As Adam Lindsay Gordon charmingly reminds us, she was the first sinner:

> Our common descent we may each recall
> To a lady of old caught tripping,
> The fair one in fig leaves who damned us all
> For a bite at a golden pippin.

Alfred Austin is the most outspoken custodian of the party line and develops the ideology a little further in the dedication (to Burne-Jones) at the beginning of his *Narrative Poems*: 'In Art, as in life, and whether the art be painting, poetry or music, there is the masculine element, and there is the feminine element. Both are good, but surely only on condition that the masculine element predominates . . .'[1]

1. In a letter to *The Times* in 1909 protesting against the proposed emancipation of women Austin wrote: 'Will anyone deny that in great emergencies, men are, as a rule and collectively, calmer and more submissive to sound judgement than women, whose virtues reside rather in another direction?

'Give women the franchise – and I cannot doubt it is a minority of them who wish to have it, and only the more emotionally combative of that minority who would exercise it – it is conceivable that war might be brought about by women

But if Austin was in some measure the official spokesman for this point of view, its high priest was Coventry Patmore, whose long-winded celebration of the idealized and submissive Victorian wife bore the title *The Angel in the House*. As a poem, it has not fared well with subsequent generations, though the contemporary public loved it. Edmund Gosse described Patmore as 'the Laureate of the tea-table with his hum-drum stories of girls that smell of bread and butter', and Virginia Woolf, lecturing on 'Professions for Women', incited women writers to 'kill the Angel in the House'. The poem is perhaps not as bad as the opposition would suggest, but a faintly sanctimonious air hangs over it that is repellent to the modern reader. Swinburne dealt it a mortal blow when he produced his parody *The Person of the House*; he was particularly devastating with the childbirth scene, over which a prudish Patmore had been inclined to drool:

> I covered either little foot
>   I drew the strings about its waist;
> Pink as the unshell'd inner fruit,
>   But barely decent, hardly chaste,
> Its nudity had startled me;
>   But when the petticoats were on,
> 'I know,' I said, 'its name shall be
>   Paul Cyril Athanasius John.'
> 'Why,' said my wife, 'the child's a girl.'
>   My brain swooned, sick with failing sense;
> With all perception in a whirl
>   How could I tell the difference?
> 'Nay,' smiled the nurse, 'the child's a boy.'
>   And all my soul was soothed to hear
> That so it was: . . .

Swinburne indeed was a merciless exposer of orthodoxy. The women of his poems are unreal abstract incarnations of sexual mys-

---

against the effort of men to avert it; and in that event, it would be men, and men alone, who would have to fight, and, if need were, to die . . .' Modern armies, to say nothing of Golda Meir and Mrs Thatcher, have rendered this interesting argument obsolete.

tery and appetite, and as far removed from Patmore's respectable Honoria, or even Tennyson's Maud, as can be imagined. Moreover, he couldn't resist sending up the Victorian idea of virtue, especially sexual continence, and blasting the cant with which it was surrounded. Many of his scabrous spoofs were prudently kept from the public, being clothed in the decency of the French language. Of these, the most promising sounds to be *La Soeur de la Reine*, a play in which Queen Victoria appears as a lady of insatiable sexual appetite and her sister as a prostitute. The high point of the piece comes when the Queen is describing her first lapse from virtue, a moment of searing carnality that started her on the slippery slope of uncontrollable lust: 'Ce n'était pas un milord, ni même Sir R. Peel. C'était un misérable du peuple, en nomme *Wordsworth*, qui m'a récité des vers de son *Excursion* d'une sensualité si chalereuse qu'ils m'ont ébranlée – et je suis tombée . . .'

Swinburne tilted at the idolization of women as a way of avoiding the inner conflicts of sexuality. One feels that he would have enjoyed Nabokov's iconoclastic observation that the only reason for putting a woman on a pedestal is to get a better view of her legs. Tennyson would not have been amused by such a remark. His attitudes are complex and sometimes rather disagreeable, but they are interesting indications of the clash between warring facets of his personality. The effect on his poetry is bad where, as W.H. Auden puts it, he is trying 'to do for himself or for others by the writing of poetry what can only be done in some other way, by action, or study or prayer.'[1] Perhaps some such attempt to resolve psychological difficulties lies behind Tennyson's persistence in writing dramas, for which he had no discernible talent whatsoever. The most extraordinary of these is *The Promise of May*, which deals with the conflict between a farmer's brutish love for a country neighbour's daughter and the smooth seduction technique of a London gentleman. Philip Edgar, a heartless city sophisticate, woos Eva but backs off when he considers a lowly marriage might lose him his inheritance. Eva disappears, believed drowned. Five years later Edgar returns under an assumed name and woos Eva's sister, Dora. Eva reappears having been run down on a nearby road. Dobson, the local roughneck, is a permanent thorn in Edgar's flesh, but the

1. W.H. Auden, Introduction to *Tennyson: A Selection*, Phoenix House, 1946, p. xiii.

London man gets as far as proposing to Dora. At that very moment Eva enters, recognizes him, and in the finest traditions of Victorian melodrama shouts: 'Make her happy, then, and I forgive you.' She then falls dead.

An incidental pleasure of reading the play is to discover Tennyson's conception of stage rustic, which could, with minimal alteration, be incorporated into a future episode of *The Archers*. Before the following passage begins, Dora has just commented on the apple blossom:

Dobson:	Theer be redder blossoms nor them, Miss Dora.
Dora:	Where do they blow, Mr Dobson?
Dobson:	Under your eyes, Miss Dora.
Dora:	Do they?
Dobson:	And your eyes be as blue as –
Dora:	What Mr Dobson? A butcher's frock?
Dobson:	Noä, Miss Dora; as blue as –
Dora:	Bluebell, harebell, speedwell, bluebottle, succory, forget-me-not?
Dobson:	Noä, Miss Dora, as blue as –
Dora:	The sky? or the sea on a blue day?
Dobson:	Naay then. I mean'd they be blue as violets.
Dora:	Are they?
Dobson:	There ye goäs ageän, Miss, niver believing owt I says to ye – hallus a-fobbing ma off, tho' ye knaws I love ye. I warrants ye'll think moor o' this young Squire Edgar as ha' coomed among us – the Lord knows how – ye'll think more on 'is little finger than hall my hand at the haltar.

This scene might be played very nicely as Joe Grundy proposing to Shula. It is interesting that the verse in the play is given to the educated and higher income groups (Eva, Dora, Edgar), while the hoi polloi are relegated to prose, albeit of a rather fanciful kind.

Snobbery complicated Tennyson's attitude to women; it is most famously on display in his poem *The Lord of Burleigh*, a provincial 'Hiawatha' in which marriage turns out not to be the answer to this particular maiden's prayer. It begins as a rustic idyll with Lord B. appearing incognito.

> In her ear he whispers gaily
>> 'If my heart by signs can tell
> Maiden, I have watched thee daily,
>> And I think thou lov'st me well.'
> She replies in accents fainter,
>> 'There is none I love like thee.'
> He is but a landscape-painter,
>> And a village maiden she.

But of course he is not a landscape-painter, and she discovers after her marriage that she is now the Lady of Burleigh, an alarming prospect given the viciousness of English class prejudice:

> So she strove against her weakness,
>> Tho' at times her spirit sank:
> Shaped her heart with woman's meekness
>> To all duties of her rank.

However, it is no good. Once a village maiden, always a village maiden:

> But a trouble weigh'd upon her,
>> And perplexed her, night and morn,
> With the burthen of an honour
>> Unto which she was not born.

So she fades away and dies, which would at least have spared the wives of the local *petit nobilité* any further social embarrassment. There is, of course, an ambivalence about the poet's attitude to status in the poem, as there is in his attitude to women. The Lord of Burleigh magnanimously assumes he can bridge the class divide, but the woman's instincts are more finely attuned to the realities of English social life. Death is the easiest way of disposing of her – and of the awkward problems that lurk beneath the surface of the poem.

Stripped of their Tennysonian sophistication, snobbery and romance are the themes which underlie *The original poems of Edward Edwin Foot of Her Majesty's Customs* (1867)[1]. His poem *Jane*

1. A new edition with delightful illustrations by James Thorpe was issued by Gerald Howe, London, 1932.

Hollybrand; or, Virtue Rewarded, represents the apotheosis of Victorian gentility in verse, and is a treasure trove of obsequious platitudes. Jane is poor but virtuous. Arnold, the heir to a big estate, plucks her from her lowly cottage and installs her in his mansion, where she is groomed to be his future wife. After an absence of a year, the complacent Pygmalion returns to monitor her progress:

> He saw at once, her tutors, when they wrote,
> Had partially concealed how they were smote; –
> Not, as he naturally might have inferr'd –
> That they'd contriv'd to please him, and conferr'd
> One with another: no, this wasn't the case,
> For he beheld her now endowed with grace;
> Her comeliness and rare symmetrical form
> Surpass'd his hope, and 'flam'd his bosom warm.

Seeing that his bridal dish has been cooked to a turn, Arnold hastens to make plans to eat it:

> Lord Arnold delicately sought to name
> The nuptial-day, and urg'd the blushing Jane
> To fix the date; but she with subdued voice,
> Begg'd courteously to be excused, – 'the choice,'
> She softly said, 'dear Arnold, should be thine;
> And what your wish may be, that shall be mine.'
> He then, most fondly, kiss'd her modest cheek,
> And named it for the following Wednesday week:
> 'Shall it be so?' he said . . . 'come, dear, express
> Thy pleasure, and enhance my happiness!'
> She press'd his hand, and breathed the mono-word[1]
> To which George Hollybrand at once concurr'd:
> And silently pour'd forth this orison, –
> 'O righteous God, bless Thou this gen'rous man!'

This being agreed,

> George homeward sped;
> And Arnold Mountjoy sought his lonely bed.

---

1. 'Yes!' (Foot's footnote). (George Hollybrand is Jane's father.)

> (Twelve other nights, he[1] knew must be bygone, –
> Twelve other suns must cross the temperate zone, –
> Ere her[2] virginity – which by the law
> Is reckon'd sacred – shall be broken through.)

The poem ends with a splendid scene at the marriage feast where the local quality is as impressed with Jane as were Professor Higgins' friends with Eliza Doolittle; after which comes the moment that Arnold, Jane, and the reader have all been waiting for:

> Then gracious Somnus, with his nightly spell,
> (Beneath whose mystic beams great monarchs bend,)
> Proclaim'd – the festival was at an end:
> The good old god, who ever timely wise,
> Trod on the tender covering of their eyes;
> And bade them pay due homage unto night:
> But there was one, (the god dimm'd not his sight,)
> Whose breast was blazing with that nuptial flame,
> Which strives to ancestralize a family name;
> His sweet companion, buckling for the deed,
> Encourag'd him t'advance: her love obey'd:
> Fair Bapta[3], charitably, drew her veil,
> And bade the loving warriors doff their mail, –
> 'Twas done! – they waver'd, for the shock was great,
> The conflict ceas'd. Concordia[4] reigned in state.

The undoubted charm of *Jane Hollybrand*, with its genteel undertow of procrastinated rape, makes one wonder why Barbara Cartland has never attempted the verse form. Perhaps, had she lived in the nineteenth century, she would have done so and we should have had a version of the poem in which Jane marries a Russian boyar or an English admiral.

Tennysonian elements may also be observed in the astonishing love dramas of Alfred Austin. His poem *The Human Tragedy* (1862 – four subsequent editions) runs the whole gamut of Victorian melo-

1. Arnold (Foot's footnote).
2. Jane (Foot's footnote).
3. Bapta, the goddess of shame (Foot's footnote).
4. Concordia, the goddess of peace (Foot's footnote).

dramatic sentimentality, including unrequited love, class insults, and pharisaical self-sacrifice. In the beginning, Mary turns down Hubert, who is described as having an unusual physical composition:

> His heart in holes as from the wash when socks come,
> He must have been a most consummate coxcomb.[1]

Instead of Hubert, she marries a baronet chosen by the family (shades of Tennyson's *Maud*). Hubert wanders in Europe. Years later, he encounters Mary and her husband in Florence; the husband, Sir Gilbert, is dying of a fever. Mary and Hubert nurse him, their old passion, of course, being rekindled by propinquity. One day, Sir Gilbert wakes up, opens the door of the next room and finds Hubert and Mary in bed together (this bit is very un-Tennysonian). The scene is described in the unforgettable, if also unsayable, lines:

> . . . he, her lord, looked on with horrid ken
> Of one who, dead, had, wronged, come back again.

Hubert would like to alert Mary to this new development, but when he shakes her, he finds she has expeditiously expired. Not least entertaining are those passages of the poem where Austin adopts his 'man-of-the-world' air in discussing women:

> Who blames a pretty woman with a dimple
>   Or roguish chin for letting it be smacked?
> And yet methinks her needle, bodkin, thimble
>   Should flash to arms, to see her thus attacked.
> On all such heartless, pert, insulting flattery,
> Her eyes should scowl defiance like a battery.

There are many astonishing passages in Austin, and a great number of them occur during encounters between men and women. His stock situation is to have a lofty, intellectual (often Byronic) hero meet and court a naïve beauty of overpowering rusticity. In *A Fragment*, Sir Alured takes a walk in his woods and falls in with a maiden who behaves exactly as the author thinks women should behave: she

---

1. Reading Austin we see that Foot wasn't *so* bad a poet after all.

listens respectfully and at length to Sir Alured, a pretentious bore whose long-winded platitudes are mostly Austin's versions of remarks by considerably better authors. Then she ventures an opinion, which is suitably naïve, and shows that she has good potential as the target for a lifetime of lecturing from some superior male:

> 'God is the goal,' she said with reverent lips
> 'Then being the goal, He must be stationary,
> While we progress. Do we progress towards him?
> Do railways, or with broad or narrow gauge
> Bring us one station nearer unto Heaven?'

With Austin we descend to the realm of poetical near-misses where the entertainment is provided by the poet saying something he doesn't mean to say, or introducing associations which, if he had thought about it, he would have wished to exclude. Two examples of these not infrequently met with disasters may serve to underline the perils of poetic love-making, which was our starting-point. William Nathan Stedman (q.v.) wrote reams of unrequited love poetry for Marie Corelli, some of which is completely mad, and all of which is inappropriate considering he never met the lady. His most famous two lines are, however, a collector's item:

> . . . And when upon your dainty breast I lay
> My wearied head – more soft than eiderdown.

Equally satisfying to the connoisseur is the poem *Cupid and Euphrosyne* by Percy Goddard Stone, a Vectensian poet whose work never really made it on the mainland. The first stanza is delightful:

> Cupid and Euphrosyne
>   Played at Love – for kisses:
> At the game adept is he,
>   Not a buss he misses.

In a just world this would become a standard recitation piece.

Seven

IF NO TALENT,
JOIN A MOVEMENT

Unspontaneous overflow of powerful feelings

There weeping o'er the turf-clad ground,
  Of all existence tir'd;
He cast his streaming eyes around
  And mournfully expir'd

'Arley' (the Della Cruscan poet)

Turn and observe that lab'ring clown
  He digs an artful hole;
And puts his trap with caution down
  To catch the purblind mole.

Like him, designing men prepare
  To lure the virgin mind . . .

'Arley', *An Evening's Contemplation*

I shall go down to Bedfordshire to-morrow.

Alexander Smith (the Spasmodic),
A Life Drama

Let that thou utterest be of nature's flow,
Not art's; a fountain's not a pump's.

Philip James Bailey, *Festus*

LITERARY SCHOOLS ARE USUALLY INVENTED by the critics ('Sorry – no "Movement"; all made up by the literary editor of *The Spectator*' snaps the irascible Willoughby in Malcolm Bradbury's *Eating People Is Wrong*), and are joined with varying degrees of reluctance by the poets themselves. Croker and *The Quarterly Review* invented the 'Cockney School' to attack Keats and Leigh Hunt. The splenetic Robert Buchanan described the works of Rossetti and his circle as the 'Fleshly School of Poetry' in the *Contemporary Review* of October 1871, and was in turn labelled the only begetter of 'The Stealthy School of Criticism' by the irate poets. Southey unwisely attacked Byron and Shelley in the Preface to his tragically bad poem *The Vision of Judgement*, by branding them 'The Satanic School'. But he ought to have remembered that Satan always has the best tunes. Perhaps the eighteenth-century Graveyard Poets did think of themselves as posterity and the critics have depicted them – a sort of aesthetic gloom and doom movement. Edward Young started it with his *Night Thoughts on Life, Death and Immortality* (1742–4). *The Avenel Companion to English and American Literature* gives the following delightful summary of the movement's subsequent progress: 'Young's soliloquies on the deaths of his wife, and of his stepdaughter and her husband take place during nine nights and in each one gloom is manipulated with all the artistry of an amorist stroking a shroud.' A similar poem, *The Grave*, by Robert Blair, also achieved great success and was often printed together with Young's work. '. . . In 1817 a bumper edition of misery appeared, when *Night Thoughts* was accompanied by a paraphrase on the *Book of Job*, *The Grave*, and a homily by Bishop Porteous on the subject of *Death*.' Presumably this was the sort of thing people used to give to their mothers-in-law for Christmas.

One eighteenth-century school of versifiers self-consciously devised a title for themselves, namely, the Della Cruscans. Literary history has not been complimentary about their activities: 'at once silly and pretentious'[1], and 'the very nadir of the poetic art'[2] are two of the kinder things that have been said about them. When you actually read the Della Cruscan products, you find that such remarks are far too generous. Seldom in the whole history of sentimentality have such lamentable effusions been enshrined in print.

Their name was taken from the Florentine *Accademia della Crusca* which means the 'Academy of Chaff'. One of the ideas of the original academy, founded in 1582, was to purify the Italian language by sifting away the 'chaff'. Unfortunately, the poems of the English Della Cruscans consisted exclusively of 'chaff', notwithstanding that their leader, Robert Merry (1755–98) was a member of the Italian institution whose name he had borrowed. Between 1784 and 1787 he lived in Florence, together with Mrs Piozzi and other poetasters, and issued a stream of dreadful verse which was customarily recited at meetings of Mrs Piozzi's ridiculous salon. Some of these verses were reprinted in London by *The World*. To the readers of this journal the posturing and passion of 'Della Crusca's' poems were immediately attractive; thus, to his considerable surprise, when Merry arrived in London in 1787, he found himself hailed as a great poet. Soon he began to get used to the idea, and even contemplated a campaign for the laureateship. However, there was an even worse poet available, and the job went to the inimitable Henry James Pye.

The Della Cruscans were an odd bunch. Apart from Merry and Mrs Piozzi (a friend of Dr Johnson), there were numerous others, of whom William Parsons, Bertie Greatheed and Hannah Cowley were the most uncontrollably fertile. They affected *noms de plume* (not all of which have been penetrated) such as 'Anna Matilda', 'Reuben', 'Laura Maria', 'Cesario' and 'Bard'. Della Cruscanism was unfortunately as infectious as the German measles, and soon there were some twenty bards scribbling away. *The World* was the principal dumping ground for their productions.

Their first collection, *Miscellany* (1785), was quite favourably received. Parsons did the selection and is thus represented at nearly twice the length of his colleagues. Mrs Piozzi wrote the preface, which somewhat gives the game away: '. . . and though we have

1. *Concise Oxford Dictionary of English Literature.*
2. *Concise Cambridge Dictionary of English Literature.*

transgressed the Persian rule of sitting silent until we could find something important and instructive to say, we shall at least be allow'd to have glistened innocently in the Italian sunshine . . .' (Not, it seems, entirely 'innocently', as Merry had to leave Florence hurriedly under a cloud.) There were also some gushing references to the sweet, simple notes of the serenading Arno boatmen, who were perhaps more in evidence then than they are now.

The apotheosis of the Della Cruscans, however, which unfortunately for them brought them to the attention of a literary bludgeoner named William Gifford, occurred with the verse exchanges between Merry and 'Anna Matilda' (Hannah Cowley). On 29 June 1787 Della Crusca's *The Adieu and Recall to Love* appeared in *The World*. This at once provoked Anna Matilda (then unknown to Merry) to reach for her quill. Merry had ended his effusion, which purported to be a wail of unrequited love, with a broad hint that he was nevertheless still on the market:

> O rend my heart with ev'ry pain!
> But let me, let me love again.

Despite the excitement of her success with a West End play (*The Runaway*), life with the excellent Captain Cowley was perhaps not as thrilling as it might have been for 'Anna Matilda'. Here was her chance to escape from a rut, and she seized it with both hands:

> O! seize again thy golden quill,
> And with its point my bosom thrill

she implored Della Crusca in her unsolicited reply to his *Adieu*. 'Della Crusca' at once favoured her with some further lines of audacious absurdity, and the 'affair' between them was launched amid the sort of self-generating publicity that publishers dream about. The other poets of the group joined in, sometimes like a heavenly choir spewing crotchets of love, sometimes like an enthusiastic backing group ululating the Della Cruscan equivalent of 'Yeah! Yeah!' and 'Right on!'. 'Della Crusca' and 'Anna Matilda' did their best to outdo each other with ever more extravagant expressions and invocations:

> Ha! DELLA CRUSCA, cease to feign;
> Thy cheek with red repentance stain,
>   For having feign'd so long;
> Quick seize thy Lyre, sweep each bold string
> O'er every chord thy music fling –
>   To calm INDIFFERENCE raise thy song!

'Della Crusca' offers to do all manner of things for his love if need arise, which, happily, it will not:

> Eager I'd traverse Lybia's plain
> The tawny lion's dread domain,
> To meet thee there: nor flagging fear
> Should ever on my cheek appear;
> For e'en the forest's King obeys
> Majestic Woman's potent gaze.

For her part, 'Anna Matilda' is planning some research. 'Della Crusca', she knows, dropped a tear somewhere on the grave of Petrarch's Laura. She has to enquire of SYMPATHY which bit of mud was favoured with the tear, in order that she may drop her own on top of it:

> On Laura's grave he poured the lay
> Amidst the signs of sinking day:
> Then point where on the sod his tear
> Fell from its crystal source so clear,
> That there my mingling tear may sink,
> And the same dust its moisture drink.

As the exchange of protestations continued, Bertie Greatheed suddenly roused himself, as if a switch had been thrown in his torpid mind, and entered the lists with his own homage to Anna Matilda:

> To thee, a stranger dares address his theme
> To thee, proud mistress of Apollo's lyre
> One ray emitted from thy golden gleam
> Prompted by Love, would set the World on fire!

156

Adorn then Love, in fancy-tinctured vest
Camelion like anon of various hue;
By PENSEROSO and ALLEGRO drest –
Such Genius claimed, when she IDALIA drew.

'Anna Matilda', who liked the attention, was swift to encourage
her new admirer:

The resuscitating praise
Breathed life upon her dying lays

But Merry is at once jealous, and moves to head off this rival
'Reuben' (Greatheed):

But hark! what cruel sounds are these,
Which float upon the languid breeze,
Which fill the mind with jealous fear,
Ah! REUBEN is the name I hear . . .

This shot across the bows was enough, and Greatheed hastily retired
from the battlefield of love. Probably he had been influenced by all
the other Della Cruscans, who were chirping away to each other as
though their lives depended on it – 'Arley' to 'Eliza', 'Arno' to
'Julia', 'Benedict' to 'Melissa', 'Leonardo' to 'Laura', and 'Henry'
to 'Emma' ('Was it the SHUTTLE of the MORN/That wove upon the
cobweb'd Thorn/Thy airy lay?'). Even William Hayley[1] and Anna
Seward began a duet in *The Public Advertiser* which is every bit as
emetic as the Oscar Awards ceremony in Hollywood:

Miss Seward:	Tuneful poet! Britain's glory!
	(Mr Hayley, that is you –)
Mr Hayley:	Ma'am, you carry all before you,
	Trust me, Litchfield Swan, you do.
Miss Seward:	Ode didactic, epic sonnet,
	Mr Hayley, you're divine!
Mr Hayley:	Ma'am, I'll take my oath upon it,
	You alone are all the nine.

1. Southey said of him: 'Everything about that man is good except his poetry.'

157

Meanwhile, back at what was now *The New World*, and later *The Oracle*, the editor was planning his best publicity coup yet. Under his auspices, the two poetical canaries *were to meet*! This proved to be imprudent, and must have lost him a lot of money. In the full glare of publicity a meeting was announced and in due course took place. 'Della Crusca' was dismayed to discover that 'Anna Matilda' was all of forty-six (he was thirty-four) and not absolutely such a 'Goddess' as he had imagined. In his poem *The Interview* he attempted a smooth extraction of himself from the predicament:

> We PART! and listen, for the word is MINE
> 'ANNA MATILDA NEVER CAN BE THINE!'

'Anna Matilda' certainly wasn't about to let him slip from her grasp without a struggle, and wrote several frenzied odes in *The Oracle*, in the hope of bringing the errant lover back into line. But the game was up; 'Della Crusca' and 'Anna Matilda' faded as abruptly from public view as the name of Lord Lucan from 'Jennifer's Diary'.

If all this were not enough to kill the 'Della Cruscan' cult, the *coup de grâce* was supplied by William Gifford in his two satires *The Baviad* (1794) and *The Maeviad* (1795). The first of these two works contained some strong stuff; for Gifford was a self-made scholar, highly contemptuous of the well-padded ease of the Della Cruscans, whose private incomes were as lavish as their talents were exiguous:

> See Cowley frisk it to one ding-dong chime
> And weekly cuckold her poor spouse in rhyme;
> See Thrale's gray widow with her satchel roam,
> And bring in pomp her laboured nothings home;
> See Robinson forget her state and move
> On crutches tow'rds the grave, to LIGHT OF LOVE;
> See Parsons, while all sound advice he scorns
> Mistake two soft excrescences for horns . . .

The reference to Parsons only appeared in the second edition of *The Baviad*, because Gifford had heard that the poet was highly indignant at having been left out of the first. ' "Ha!" quoth he (wrote Gifford), "Better be damned than not mentioned at all!" He accordingly applied to me (in a circuitous manner, I confess) and as a particular favour was finally admitted, in the shape of a motto into the title page of *The Maeviad* . . .' On the other hand, those Della Cruscans who were accorded places of honour in *The Baviad*, reacted like the shady public-relations men and salivating lawyers whose Uriah Heepisms appear in the correspondence columns of *Private Eye*. Some took a high moral tone:

> Demon of darkness! Whosoe'r thou art
> That dar'st assume the brighter angel's form . . .

Others resorted to abuse. The editor of *The Oracle* wrote an angry incomprehensible sonnet in defence of his money-spinning ode-mongers. It was accompanied by even more incomprehensible foot-notes, in one of which we are informed that the Trojan horse was actually a mare. When neither high dudgeon nor low abuse worked, there was always the remedy favoured by such pillars of rectitude as Sir James Goldsmith and Mr Robert Maxwell – the writ. Della Cruscans attempted to sue all the booksellers who sold *The Baviad*; but the booksellers were making a good thing out of Gifford's *tour de force*, not least because of the footnotes, which contained some sardonic résumés of the private lives of the perfumed poetasters which hardly squared with their public posturing. The attempt to intimidate the booksellers was a miserable failure, and instead the poets stepped up production in a desperate effort to keep them-selves in the public eye. Wave after wave of brainless rhapsody hit the public prints. Gifford saw that the disease was by no means stamped out and so produced his *Maeviad*. This second battering did the trick. Harsh though it was, it contained no more than the truth:

> . . . But I sing in vain, from first to last
> Your joy is fustian, and your grief bombast:
> Rhetoric has banished reason; kings and queens,
> Vent in hyperboles their royal spleens.
> Guardsmen in metaphors express their hopes,
> And maidens 'in white linen' howl in tropes.

The success of the Della Cruscans reminds us that literary popularity often has nothing to do with quality. It is sometimes claimed that at least the purveyors of commercial trash have to believe in their own products; but it is doubtful if the Della Cruscans believed in theirs – with the possible exception of the unfortunate 'Anna Matilda'. Indeed, in the works (and life) of Merry, sincerity seems conspicuous by its absence. Nevertheless, consciously, or unconsciously, they caught the mood of the public, who were inclined to take them at face value. Until Gifford had effectively demonstrated otherwise, it seemed to them that this was real feeling expressed in real poetry.

The Victorians could also be suckers for botched art masquerading as high seriousness, and it is therefore not surprising to find that an entire school of poetry catered for their needs in this regard. The critic William Aytoun dubbed this school *The Spasmodics*[1]; like Gifford, he exposed their pretensions in a damaging satire, *Firmilian* (1854), which purported to have been written by a newly discovered spasmodic poet, T. Percy Jones.

The leading light of the Spasmodics was Philip James Bailey (1816–1902), who wrote an intolerably long poem (40,000 lines in the final edition) theoretically analogous to Goethe's *Faust*. *Festus* (1839) was a huge hit with the public, Tennyson included. It was admired, says *The Concise Cambridge History of English Literature* uncharitably, because its author 'was ambitious and appeared to be profound . . . the passages once quoted with admiration are mostly "purple" passages in the strictest sense – very purple and very patchy.' Readers of the 1889 edition were not dismayed, it seems, to read in the Preface the author's boast that he had been able to admit 'almost every variety of classifiable thought, and reasonable enlargement of purpose upon such matters as human faith, morals and human progress . . .' The result of his diligence is a poem consisting of innumerable bawled arias fabricated from extravagant metaphors and similes, interspersed with passages of recitative which make the operatic variety seem models of pith and wit. A short extract from Festus' enquiries as he is being shown round 'the Martian sphere' by a 'Guardian Angel', with 'Lucifer' in attendance, may serve to give the general flavour:

1. Because of the frequent emotional 'spasms', which recurred, like epileptic fits, in the poems.

> What mean yon souls,
> Inquisitive as they seem of every breath
> They breathe; though more ethereal than the exhaled
> Filmlet of birdling's bill, on wintry morn?
> I, on behalf of those even since arrived,
> Not less than mine own curiousness, would ask
> Of thee, kind sphere interpreter, for time
> All further search of mine forbids, what aim
> The various acts of these so various groups,
> Busied, we see, with every root of life.
> And inquest so profound as seems, of all
> They live by, and upon, regard; and thence,
> Upon what after upward shelving plane
> Such life, progressive here, wends, and its end.

Or in other words: 'I'm in rather a hurry, so could you briefly describe what it is those people are so busily doing?'

Is it possible for poetry to get any worse than this? The answer is unfortunately 'yes'. Only a few lines later we have the Archangel passing unfavourable comment on Lucifer's mode of argument, in verses that make one wonder if English was Bailey's mother tongue:

> . . . Mark the uncertain wit he words.
> Twice-shot contrariwise his thought-woof seems
> Itself to thwart reversive; not of truth
> Takes he yet hand-fast; nought of right conceives
> Indeviable . . . etc.

If General Alexander Haig writes poetry, it must be something like this. Nor do Bailey's arias let the reader off any more lightly. Pre-history, for instance, is given the full works in a passage where material culled from encyclopedias and dictionaries is jumbled up with material that can only have been culled from Bailey's eccentric mind:

> Err not, such time as fire-drakes of the seas,
> Leviathan; huge Behemoth, and the Boar,
> In vain demolished, on the morrow whole;
> Ill's choicest type, light's conqueror; deinother, [sic]

>Dreadest of brutes, limbed oak-like; and whose teeth
>As tombstones showed; aurochs, and elk enorme,
>Whose antlers, than an oarsman's oars well plyed,
>Spread widelier; mammoth huge, and mastodon;
>(These dying, deigned not fall; but bidding earth
>Close o'er them, and it would grim sepulture,
>By glacial Lena, or Nerbuddah's banks,
>Or Mississippian swamps, made they, erect,
>And their own osseous monument;) . . .

Open *Festus* at any page and you are confronted with such lines as:

>Forefated, fore-atoned for from the first . . .

or:

>But it is not more true that what is, is
>Than that what is not, is not . . .

How was it that the public did not seem to notice that, as Swinburne succinctly put it, 'Bailey had no ear and no metrical power at all?' It hardly seems sufficient to say, as does Mark Weinstein, that 'the critical field had been dominated recently by utilitarians and rationalists'[1], when the Spasmodics burst on the scene; nor to plead, as he does, that the 1839 version of *Festus* was better than the later ones into which he shoved everything he could think of from dinosaurs to dinner parties. The fact is these works were the products of a diseased sensibility that had its counterpart in intellectual fashion and popular prejudice. The heroes of Bailey's *Festus*, Alexander Smith's *A Life-Drama* (1852), John Westland Marston's *Gerald* (1842), and Sydney Dobell's *Balder* (1853) are all brooding Byronic geniuses – usually poets, or, in the case of *Balder*, a 'Poet-God'. These imagined poet-heroes distantly recall the erratic philosophical musings of Carlyle whose Hero as Man of Letters had been introduced to a susceptible public in his lectures of 1840. Carlyle's deep fascination with German literature and history was also in tune with the increasing, and often mindless, Germanism of the times. Quack-

---

1. Mark A. Weinstein, *William Edmonstoune Aytoun and the Spasmodic Controversy*, Yale University Press, 1968, p. 74.

poets, from Bailey to Alfred Austin, tried to meld in their heroes the humourless intellectual Germanic genius with the fiery sardonic Byronic personality – and the results are unimaginably awful.

The apotheosis of spasmody is reached in Sydney Dobell's *Balder*. The hero is again an ersatz Faust who has to experience 'everything' (which inevitably turns out to mean 'everything appalling') before he can complete his great poem. The ultimate experience is, of course, death; as it would limit his capacity for poem-writing and experiencing should he himself undergo it, his daughter must act as proxy, and he therefore kills her instead. But this act unsettles his nerves, and especially those of his wife. He gets over it after a while, but she goes from bad to worse, finally becoming insane. The first part ends (the second part was never completed) with Balder contemplating killing his wife as well. Although the home-life of the Balders might seem a little unsatisfactory, we are to understand that everything happens in a good cause. By means of his experiences Balder is to become a 'King of men' and 'beget a better world'. Although he is a God, he has the form of manhood, and his mission is to reform corrupt and purposeless society. In this miserable parody of an amoral Christ saviour, there is again an echo of Carlyle. His concept of the heroic strong man superseded the unsatisfactory Hero as Man of Letters – Dr Johnson, Rousseau and Robert Burns[1] were not really up to the job; Dobell's Balder is a shabby and distorted version of the Hero as King, whose glib self-justification and egotistical violence exhibit in cruder form the fascistic yearnings in Carlyle's love affair with authoritarianism.

Although Dobell is technically more proficient than Bailey – and in a different league from such windbags as Marston and John Stanyan Bigg – he has the distinction, if it is one, of having produced the quintessential spasmodic utterance with the famous lines:

> . . . Ah! ah! ah!
> Ah! ah! ah! ah! ah! ah! ah! ah! ah! ah!

(It is a little hard to read this in iambics.)

The success of the Spasmodics was partly due to the puffing they received in some of the reviews; in particular the critic George Gilfillan was a tireless and uncritical propagandist for the second

1. The three extraordinary examples cited by Carlyle.

rate, a nineteenth-century equivalent of the trend-watching journalist with an unfailing capacity to be impressed by the latest piece
of charlatanism. After Aytoun had attacked the posturing of
Gilfillan's protégés, the latter responded with a ponderous defence
that is something of a connoisseur's item: 'Surely some great poetic
orb must be nearing the verge of the horizon! What a flush of fine
poetry, both at home and from abroad, we have had lately in the
rich and eloquent writings of a Longfellow, a Lowell, a Poe, a
Croly, an Aird, a Yendys[1] (who, we are glad to hear, has a new poem
on the anvil), a Tennyson, a Marston, a Brown, the Brownings, an
Alexander Smith (who is collecting his beautiful verses into a separate form), a Scott, a Bailey, a Jameson (the author of 'Nimrod'),
and some more genuine bards of greater or less promise! We have a
strong suspicion, that somewhere or other, from among this
number, is to arise the poet of our period; and we would advise star-
gazing critics to watch *this cluster* well, to mark attentively all its
movements and mutations, to report their observations candidly,
lest in it there should appear, before their telescopes are in order,
some star brighter than his fellows forming the central sun to a great
system, and a star of hope, promise, and prophecy to the coming
age.'[2]

This is the Godfrey Talbot school of criticism with a vengeance,
and Aytoun finally decided that enough was enough. He began by
dealing with Gilfillan's factitious enthusiasm: 'We have not for a
considerable time held much communing with the rising race of
poets, and we shall at once proceed to state the reason why. Even as
thousands of astronomers are nightly sweeping the heavens with
their telescopes, in the hope of discovering some new star or wandering comet, so of late years have shoals of small critics been
watching for the advent of some grand poetical genius. These
gentlemen, who could not, if their lives depended on it, elaborate a
single stanza, have a kind of insane idea that they may win immortal
fame by being the first to perceive and hail the appearance of the
coming bard. Accordingly, scarce a week elapses without a shout
being raised at the birth of a thin octavo.'

1. Sydney Dobell wrote under the name of Sydney Yendys. Bailey, in particular,
had a great success amongst the American 'Transcendentalists', such as Emerson.
2. Quoted by Mark A. Weinstein, op. cit., as are also the following extracts from
Aytoun.

Aytoun continued his campaign by publishing in the May issue of *Blackwood's* (1854) a long review, with extensive quotation, of a supposed Spasmodic poem, *Firmilian; or The Student of Badajoz: a Tragedy*, by a poet called T. Percy Jones, whom he had invented. It is a measure of the literal-mindedness of the Spasmodic claque that this spoof succeeded all too well. As Weinstein puts it: 'To the lovers of Spasmody, the poetic extracts seemed no more suspicious than the serious productions of their favourites.'[1] Some critics complained that the review was unfair and demanded publication of T. Percy Jones' masterpiece so that the public might judge for themselves. This demand Aytoun decided to meet, and in due course the complete poem appeared. 'Firmilian' himself is an amalgam of Bailey's *Festus*, Walter, the absurd poet-hero of Alexander Smith's *A Life-Drama, Balder, Gerald*, and other hand-me-down Fausts. The poem is a lot of fun, with Firmilian rushing around the world collecting 'experiences', like his progenitors. At one point he is sitting on St Simeon Stylites column, and his best friend (also a poet of course) is climbing up to greet him:

> Together we have emulously sung
> Of Hyacinthus, Daphne and the rest,
> Whose mortal weeds Apollo changed to flowers.
> Also from him I have derived much aid
> In golden ducats, which I fain would pay
> Back with extremest usury, were but
> Mine own convenience equal to my wish.
> Moreover, of his poems he hath sold
> Two full editions of a thousand each,
> While mine remain neglected on the shelves!
> Courage Firmilian! for the hour has come
> When thou canst know atrocity indeed
> By smiting him that was thy dearest friend.
> And think not that he dies a vulgar death –
> 'Tis poetry demands the sacrifice!

Firmilian did not succeed in killing off Spasmody in the way that Gifford's *Baviad* and *Maeviad* polished off the Della Cruscans;

1. Mark A. Weinstein, op. cit. p. 123.

nevertheless, the pitch was queered, the public more cautious and even Gilfillan somewhat chastened. It should also be said in the Spasmodics' favour, that most of them apparently took Aytoun's satire in good part. Dobell and Smith remained friendly with him, and the latter seems to have taken the critic's strictures to heart, for in a few years he very sensibly gave up poetry and took to writing prose. Dobell was less of a pushover, as befits a man who had taken the trouble to work into his poems such words as 'lunation', 'susurrent', 'snood' and 'parphelion'. All the same, the public were spared anything more in the line of *Balder* – a title which irresistibly invites the addition of the suffix 'dash'.

Eight

A NOTE ON NOMENCLATURE

Names in numbers; poets lesser than their names

And while around me ocean raves,
Still warm remembrance friendship craves;
Thee, M. M. Woods, forget I'll never!

Robert Peter, *Solace of Leisure* (1875)

'There enough! Let us back. I'm a fool I know,
But I *must* see Gladys before I go.'

Alfred Austin, *The Last Night*

. . . Yet leaving here a name, I trust,
That will not perish in the dust.

Robert Southey,
My Days Among The Dead Are

(In the *Lyttelton-Hart-Davis Letters*, George Lyttelton describes these lines as 'the most pathetic thing in the Oxford Book. I except of course for a different reason, "Meet we no angels, Pansie".')

'MILTON! THOU SHOULD'ST BE LIVING AT THIS HOUR.' As every schoolboy knows, this is the opening line of Wordsworth's sonnet on *London, 1802*. It provides a comparatively rare example in English poetry of the use of an ordinary name that avoids bathos. Only four pages earlier, in the Penguin *Collected Poems of Wordsworth*, we are confronted with a sonnet that commences less promisingly with the words:

> Jones! as from Calais southward you and I
> Went pacing side by side, this public Way . . .

– which is an opening even a Welsh poet would jib at. Well into bathos is the opening stanza of the bard's remarks addressed *To the Spade of a Friend (An Agriculturist)* (composed while we were labouring together in his pleasure-ground):

> Spade! with which Wilkinson hath tilled his lands,
> And shaped these pleasant walks by Emont's side,
> Thou art a tool of honour in my hands;
> I press thee, through the yielding soil, with pride.

No doubt Wordsworth's Quaker friend was pleased with this token of his friend's esteem when it arrived through the post. One imagines his gratified smile as he read it over his porridge and ale; seldom has such a mundane instrument been so nobly serenaded:

> Who shall inherit Thee when death has laid
> Low in the darksome cell thine own dear lord?
> That man will have a trophy, humble Spade!
> A trophy nobler than a conqueror's sword.

168

Wordsworth was evidently very fond of using names in his poems, almost always with melancholy consequences. The original version of the Prologue to *Peter Bell* contained the lines:

> To the stone table in my garden
> The Squire is come, and, as I guess
> His little ruddy daughter Bess
> With Harry the Churchwarden.

Elsewhere, we are treated to a sudden display of testiness on the part of Cumberland and Westmorland's distinguished Distributor of Stamps, that would surely have gone better in prose:

> That is a work of waste and ruin;
> Consider, Charles, what you are doing.

Memorial verses are the most vulnerable to the demolition effect of a strategically placed name. Scott of Amwell has a funeral couplet which fails to get off the ground solely because the deceased was not provided with a handle the poet could use:

> Methinks of friendship's frequent fate
> I hear my Frogley's voice complain;

Even more spectacular lapses are found in the work of Miss Jane Cave. Sir John Squire tells us that her *Poems on Various Subjects, Entertaining, Elegiac and Religious* were printed at Winchester in 1783, with a remarkable frontispiece showing the author quill in hand and wearing a sort of beribboned tea cosy on top of a towering coiffure. Her volume is dedicated to the Subscribers: 'Ye gen'rous patrons of a female muse.' And with some reason. There were nearly two thousand of them, grouped by localities, 'Oxford', 'Southampton', 'Bath', etc. She, or the family which employed her in some unnamed capacity, must have systematically scoured the South of England for victims. Her character was evidently forcible, if unattractive; but her powers did not justify her evident self-complacency. She was especially fond of writing obituary poems on deceased clergymen. Here are characteristic extracts from two of these:

Hark! how the Heav'nly Choir began to sing,
A song of praise, when *Watkins* entered in.

Let ev'ry heart lift up a fervent pray'r
That old Elijah's mantle may be there,
That God from age to age may carry on
The amazing work which *Harris* hath begun.[1]

On occasion, Miss Cave adroitly turned a proper name to her advantage as in the lines: *Spoken extempore to a young Lady, whose Name was Organ, on her Return Home after a few Months' Absence.* The first six of these illustrate the poetess' rare way with a compliment:

When tuneful instruments appear,
They indicate some pleasure near,
And if an Organ we behold,
It doth a sacred theme unfold;
Its one, its chief, its grand design
Is to break forth in songs divine.

The unsolicited epitaph, which featured so prominently in Jane Cave's output, is a well-established genre which I have discussed elsewhere.[2] It is a genre which produces a good deal of intentional or unintentional humour, often revolving around the name of the deceased. Many collections of the intentional variety have been made, so a single example will suffice:

John Bun

Here lies John Bun,
He was killed by a gun,
His name was not Bun, but Wood,
But Wood would not rhyme with Gun
but Bun would.

Examples of the unsolicited variety may be found in the work of 'Poet Close' (John Close 1816–91), an amateur rhymester of Westmorland who was given a pension by Palmerston in 1860. This

1. Sir John Squire in *Women's Verse (Reflections and Memories,* Glasgow, 1927), pp. 295–6.
2. *See* Chapter 3, *Oleaginous Odes and Eccentric Elegy.*

was altered to a grant of £100 from the Royal Bounty after protests in the House. 'From this time to his death,' record Lewis and Lee, 'he added to his income by thrusting his compositions on visitors (already numbed and dazed by the Wordsworth atmosphere).'[1] They give a memorable example of his funereal manner, the lines *In Respectful Memory of Mr. Yarker*:

> And have we lost another friend?
> How sad the news to tell!
> Alas! Poor Mr. Yarker's gone –
> Hark to the tolling bell!
> Alas! how many now drop off –
> What numbers are unwell;
> Another mortal borne away –
> Hark to the tolling bell!

The author's adoption of a preferred style of nomenclature reminds us that many poetasters were granted honorific titles by their contemporaries, which were both an indication of their achievements and a mode of address commensurate with the dignity of their calling. Close's neighbouring county could also boast a home-grown poetess, Susanna Blamire (1747–94), who was known as 'The Muse of Cumberland'. There were numerous local laureates, of which the one with the most modest domain was James Waddell (*floruit* 1800–20). He was known as 'the poet laureate of Plessy and the neighbouring villages'; but there were many others, especially in the nineteenth century, such as J. Burgess, 'The Droylsden Bard', and, my own favourite, Samuel Collins 'The Bard of Hale Moss'.

Poets also attract sobriquets; apart from the 'Swans' of Mantua and Avon who need no introduction, there were other literary swans, some of whom might more correctly have been described as geese. Henry Vaughan (1622–95), 'The Swan of Usk', was a fine enough poet, but Anna Seward (1747–1809), 'The Swan of Lichfield', was not. Her father, the Reverend Thomas Seward, attempted to suppress her youthful passion for poetry – rightly, in my view. Sir Walter Scott chivalrously edited her collected poems,

1. D.B. Wyndham Lewis and Charles Lee, *The Stuffed Owl*, J.M. Dent and Sons, 1978, p. 215.

which she had bequeathed to him, but was known to have referred to most of them as 'execrable'. Her 'tinkling and tinsel'[1] verses with such titles as *Ode to Ignorance* are insufferably tedious, though we are occasionally blown off our stools by a splenetic outburst such as the line:

My inmost soul abhors the bloody French.

It is interesting that there were, in the nineteenth century, a couple of German swans paddling the streams of literature. The most successful of these was Frederike Kempner (1836–1904), known as '*der schlesische Schwan*' after the area of Germany where she was brought up and made her name. Her first poems, published in 1873, made her famous, or perhaps one should say, notorious. At any rate they were received with delight by contemporaries and have served, in the words of the *Neue Deutsche Biographie: 'bis heute als Musterbeispiele unfreiwilliger Komik.'* The appeal of her work was the way in which she tried to match platitudinous verse expression to her lofty themes, the failure of this resulting in spectacular plunges into bathos. She was an earnest activist involving herself in such matters as poverty, the problem of anti-Semitism and vivisection. In some respects she may be seen as a German version of Ella Wheeler Wilcox (q.v.), although as a Jewess holding progressive liberal views she was well to the left of the Wisconsin agony aunt. Kempner had a rival, the inimitable Julie Schrader (1882–1938), '*der welfische Schwan*'. Less well known than her *schlesische* colleague in her lifetime, Julie's verses and her eccentric *'Tagebuch'* have captured the hearts of twentieth-century readers. Her father was a railway official at Hanover; when Julie was only two, he was unfortunately run over by a coal-tender on Christmas Eve. This tragic occurrence did have one mitigating aspect – it stimulated Julie at the age of eighteen to express herself in verse:

> *Lieber Gott, ist so was richtig,*
> *Daß so Schreckliches gesschieht?*
> *Wozu sind die Züge wichtig*
> *Überall auf dem Gebiet?*

1. Oscar Wilde.

After that she wrote busily for the rest of her life, borrowing ideas and styles from other poets with gay abandon. The results are much appreciated by lovers of kitsch in the German-speaking world:

> *Mozart ist ein Wunderkönig,*
> *Fürst der Fürsten von Olymphe.*
> *Und geliebt hat er nicht wenig . . .*
> *Von der Hausfrau bis zur Nymphe.*

(Julie was herself extremely amorous, and remarkably uninhibited for the times.)

> *Beethoven, oh, Ludwig van!*
> *Hatte Gott dich auch verlassen . . .*
> *Deine Lieder pfeifet man*
> *In den Domen, auf den Strassen.*

The activities of these, and other, swans lend considerable and melancholy force to Coleridge's aphorism on the subject:

> Swans sing before they die – 'twere no bad thing
> Should certain persons die before they sing.

Those who were not honoured as swans were often given an appellation to associate them with a literary hero or household name, usually one who was long and safely dead. Admirers of McGonagall referred to him as 'The Scottish Homer', but I fear they may have had their tongues in their cheeks; Mary Robinson (1758–1800), who was for a while the mistress of a youthful Prince of Wales (he was sixteen), was referred to as the English Sappho. She was later the mistress of a great many other people as well, but relieved her spirit from any oppression attendant upon these exertions with a wonderful ode to *Chastity*:

> High on a rock, coeval with the skies,
>   A temple stands, reared by immortal powers
>   To Chastity divine!
>
>   . . . On the frozen floor
> Studded with tear-drops, petrified with scorn,

Pale vestals kneel the goddess to adore,
While Love, his arrows broke, retires forlorn.

Like many English ladies who slept their way into the highest social circles, she was eminently respectable in her conversation, and her seduction technique was as decorous as it was ruthless:

Love scorns the nymph in wanton trappings drest;
And charms the most concealed are doubly graced.

'Sapphos' were two-a-penny in the literary world, presumably because there were no other female poets of sufficient stature to emulate until the nineteenth century. America was pullulating with them – Sarah Wentworth Appleton, 'The American Sappho', Ina Coolbrith, 'The Sappho of the Western Sea', and Phillis Wheatley, 'The Black Sappho', are but a few examples. Americans are fond of associating their poets, albeit often ironically, with the literary giants of the past. Michael Wigglesworth, author of the gloomy Puritan bestseller *The Day of Doom* (1662), became 'The Doggerel Dante'. And one can see why:

The Amorites and Sodomites
Although their plagues be sore,
Yet find some ease, compared to these
Who feel a great deal more . . . etc.

Madison Cawein (1865–1914), the author of some 2,700 incredibly feeble lyrics, was 'The Omar Khayyam of the Ohio Valley'. A brief sample of his work will illustrate to what extent the title is appropriate:

Opportunity

Behold a hag whom Life denies a kiss
As he rides questward in knight-errantwise;
Only when he hath passed her is it his
To know, too late, the Fairy in disguise.

Cawein was taken surprisingly seriously by his contemporaries, so presumably his sobriquet was flatteringly intended. Others with

174

grand titles were certainly being honoured – William Cullen Bryant as 'The American Wordsworth', Edna St Vincent Millay as 'The American Female Byron' (an alarming concept!), and John Greenleaf Whittier as 'The American Burns'. Appalling poets, or those who occasioned satirical comment, had more picturesque names. Amy Lowell (1874–1925) was 'The Hippopoetess' on account of her huge bulk.[1] Eugene Field (1850–95) was known as 'The Poet of Childhood' and 'The Gay Poet'. There is a considerable irony in this. As David Loth puts it in his study of *sub rosa* erotica, Eugene Field's reputation was spotless; a writer 'with a reputation for cleaner works would be hard to find; hardly anyone except Louisa May Alcott is associated in the public mind with such blameless tales and verses . . . yet in his leisure Field set down what has been one of the pornographic bestsellers of the last few generations, *Only A Boy*, [which concerns] a boy with the prowess of the hero of *A Night in a Moorish Harem* . . . [a book that] Anthony Comstock hunted down relentlessly.'[2] This was not the only curiosity of the Field oeuvre. A poem entitled *When Willie Wet the Bed* was printed in a medical journal in the 1890s. In a sort of pastiche of his sentimental humorous style the poet describes a father reminiscing about his son when he was still a dear little chap with an uncontrollable bladder:

> Closely he cuddled up to me,
> And put his hands in mine,
> When all at once I seemed to be
> Afloat in seas of brine.
> Sabean odours clogged the air,
> And filled my soul with dread,
> Yet I could only grin and bear
> When Willie wet the bed.

'This of course,' says Loth, 'was too risqué for any family publication. And even the good doctors were afraid to publish the last stanza, for it ran:

1. Her dramatic announcement 'I, too, am an Imagiste' was not as enthusiastically received by the adherents of the movement as it might have been. Ezra Pound used to refer to her versions of Imagism as 'Amygism'.
2. David Loth, *The Erotic in Literature*, Secker and Warburg, 1962, pp. 139–40.

Had I my choice, no shapely dame
  Should share my couch with me;
No amorous jade of tarnished fame,
  No wench of high degree;
But I would choose and choose again
  The little curly head
Who cuddled up close beside me when
  He used to wet the bed.[1]

The most absurd sobriquets were sensibly reserved for the most
absurd poets. Some of these, however, could hardly have improved
on their original names – Bloodgood H. Cutter, for instance, or
Shepherd M. Dugger (though the former was also known as 'The
Poet Lariat' after the publication of his *Long Island Farmer's Poems*).
The classic example of a real poet, who nevertheless strikes one
more plausibly as an invention of Mark Twain, was J. Gordon
Coogler (1865–1901) (q.v.), founder of the Cooglerian School of
Poesy; his productions are, if anything, even more astonishing than
those from the pen of Julia A. Moore (q.v.), 'The Sweet Singer of
Michigan'. He seems to have been called many things, all of them
derogatory, the most splendid being 'The Carolina Chirper' and
'The Last Bard of Dixie'.

It has to be admitted that in the field of nomenclature, as in so
many other fields, the Americans do things more resoundingly than
the British. We cannot really match such expressive forms as 'Laureate of Darkness' (Edgar Allen Poe) or 'Poet of the Woodlouse'
(Walt Whitman). The best I have been able to unearth are Stephen
Duck (1705–56) 'The Thresher Poet' and Mrs Anne Yearsley, the
Bristol milk-woman who unfortunately signed her verses 'Lactilla'.
Stephen Duck, inevitably one feels, married a lady called Sarah Big,
and one regrets that she didn't combine her maiden name and her
married name, as is sometimes done, for Sarah Big-Duck would be
delightful. Queen Caroline gave Duck a pension and lodged him in
a house at Richmond. He was even spoken of as a possible successor
to Colley Cibber, the Laureate; but it was not to be. Instead, the
Queen made him a Yeoman of the Guard, and then Curator of her
Disneyland folly in Richmond Park known as Merlin's Cave. Unfortunately, once Duck had been taken up by the quality, there was

1. David Loth, op. cit., p. 140.

a perceptible falling off in the freshness and originality of his verse. We find him writing such stuff as:

> That moral Law, which Nature had imprest
> He blotted from the Volume of his Breast.

or:

> But, as a Child, in Thought, chews o'er
> The Sweetmeats which he eat before,
> So in his Mind Alexis keeps
> The dear Impression of her lips.

Duck took holy orders later in his life and became the Rector of Byfleet. Here he became gradually more depressed, as perhaps one would in Byfleet, and eventually drowned himself in the Thames.

The end of poor Lactilla was similarly sad. After running a circulating library near Bristol, she grew penurious and seems to have died insane in 1806. Her patroness was Hannah More who, although fundamentally well meaning, was bossy and overbearing towards her lacteous protégé. Nor was her helpful literary advice sufficiently influential to prevent 'Lactilla' from beginning an ode to the Bristol Channel with the words:

> Hail! Useful Channel . . .

The more one browses through the byways of literature the more it strikes one that persons with curious names are drawn to writing. Of course, some of them change their names, like film stars, and become Maria dell'Occidente instead of Maria Gowen Brooks, or Charles Egbert Craddock instead of Mary Noailles Murfee; but the vast majority of poetasters seem to have been endowed with names that look arresting on the page. If one picks up a vanity publication at random – say *The Autumn Anthology* of 1930[1], one is immediately struck by the reassuring array of literary-sounding names. First there is the Editorial Board, which includes such luminaries as Marie Tello Phillips (Resident, Bookfellows' Library Guild),

---

1. The London Library's copy of this volume is inscribed: 'With the author's compliments, whose poems will be found on pages 427–31.'

Margaret Ball Dickson (Valparaiso University), Carl B. Ike (President, The Ozarkians), and Edith Mirick (Editor, *Star Dust*). As for the poets, of whom there are very many indeed, some of their names *ought* to be pen names, even if they are not. They include Emma Zinke Haase, Blanche Shoemaker Wagstaff, Virginia Corin Bibb, Mary Wirt Fry (all of them, I need hardly say, of the USA); together with Stella Small of Australia, Bertram Headland of England, K. Krishnamacharya of India, Owen E. McGillicuddy, who claims to come from Canada, and E.L. Sloss. These poets do not, alas, seem to have made their names in the field of literature, but then neither did many of their interestingly-named predecessors, such as Edward Edwin Foot (q.v.), James Six and Jeremy Feeble. Perhaps, after all, you need more than a promising name to get past the guard of the critics; you may have to settle instead for being immortalized in an unsolicited and incompetent elegy by the Poet Close or Miss Jane Cave.

PART TWO

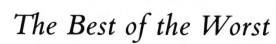

The Best of the Worst

Nine

MARGARET CAVENDISH, DUCHESS OF NEWCASTLE
1624–74
A pure lady with fantastic notions

The whole story of this lady is a romance, and all she doth is romantic. Her footmen in velvet coats, and herself in an antique dress as they say, and was the other day at her own play, *The Humorous Lovers*; the most ridiculous thing that ever was wrote but yet she and her Lord mightily pleased with it, and she at the end made her respect to the players from her box, and did give them thanks.

Samuel Pepys, *Diary*, 11 April 1667

It pleased God to command his servant Nature to indue me with a poetical and philosophical genius even from my very birth.

Margaret Cavendish, Duchess of Newcastle

A fertile pedant . . .

Horace Walpole

'HER OCCASIONAL APPEARANCE in theatrical costume, and her reputation for purity of life[1], together with her vanity and affectation, contributed to gain her a reputation for madness': so says the *Dictionary of National Biography* in its description of this most remarkable of poetesses. There does indeed seem to be a good deal of evidence of eccentricity, even allowing for the rather more flexible standards that are usually applied to persons of an artistic temperament. She paraded through the streets followed by a sort of fan club of hangers-on – as witnessed and commented on by Samuel Pepys, who tells us he went out especially to catch a glimpse of the phenomenon. And the diarist John Evelyn's wife was exceptionally rude about her, but this was partly because she was annoyed that her husband was impressed by the Duchess' conversation: 'Her discourse,' she said, 'is as airy, empty, whimsical and rambling as her books, aiming at science, difficulties, high notions, terminating commonly in nonsense, oaths and obscenity.'

The oaths and obscenity are probably a slander, but Margaret Cavendish's fascination with scientific and philosophical notions permeate her extraordinary verses, the great bulk of which she seems to have made up as the thought – any thought – struck her. A typical effusion entitled *Of Earth*, may be found in her *Poems and Fancies* (1653). She begins by explaining how 'Aire' is designed to fill all the available space:

> The reason, why Aire doth so equall spred
> Is Atomes long, at each end ballanced.
> For being long, and each end both alike,
> Are like to weights, which keep it steddy right:

1. 'Purity of life' need not necessarily be a sign of madness, one supposes; but at Charles II's court such behaviour would have been unnecessarily conspicuous.

These 'Atomes' have a hand in everything – even cholic:

> Long aiery Atomes, when they are combin'd
> Do spread themselves abroad, and so make wind:

Tiring of 'Atomes', the poetess proceeds to such matters as 'motion' and 'space' – and then to all manner of unlikely things. Verse follows verse explaining why water quenches fire ('It separates the sharp Atomes'), the reason why the sea is inclined to roar, why fire can be likened to stings, how winds are made in the air, and not in the earth, what makes echo (she is rather evasive about this) and finally: 'The Reason why Thoughts are only in the Head':

> For had the Heele such quantity of Braine,
> Which doth the Head, and Skull therein contain,
> Then would such Thoughts, which in the Braine
> dwell high,
> Descend downe low, and in the Heele would lye

> . . . As in the skull then might the Toe or Knee
> Had they an Optick Nerve, both heare and see,
> And sinewes roome, Fancy therein to breed
> Copies of Verses might from the Heele proceed.

After these novel observations, the Duchess moves on to 'Dialogues' between such entities as 'Earth and Cold', and 'An Oake and a Man Cutting him downe', in which the oak is understandably indignant but no match for the woodcutter's forensic skills. The 'Moral Discourses' are full of interesting, if not entirely fruitful, speculation:

> Who knowes, but Fishes which swim in the Sea
> Can give a Reason why so Salt it be?
> And how it Ebbs and Flows, perchance they can
> Give reasons, for which never yet could man.

The difficulty here is the same as Henry James Pye's goat with a pain in its head (*see* page 55); namely how does one interrogate the fishes on the subject?

After the philosophical speculations come the 'fancies', which are very remarkable. The Duchess was a home-loving and adoring wife (in her famous biography of the Duke, she compares him, favourably, with Julius Caesar), and had a strong interest in domestic science. Her knowledge in this field is put to good use in such poems as *Nature's Cook*:

> Death is the Cook of Nature; and we find
> Meat drest severall Waies to please her Mind.
> Some Meates shee rosts with Feavers, burning hot
> And some she boiles with Dropsies in a Pot,
> Some for Gelly consuming by degrees,
> And some with Ulcers, Gravie out to squeeze.

> . . . Some with the Pox, chops Flesh, and Bones so small
> Of which she makes a French Fricassee withall.[1]

> . . . In sweat sometimes she stues with savoury Smell,
> A Hodge-Podge of Diseases tasteth well,
> Braine drest with Apoplexy to Nature's wish
> Or swimmes with sauce of Megrimes in a Dish
> Then Death cuts Throats, for Blood-pudding to make,
> And puts them in the Guts which Collicks rack . . .[2]

Probably the poetess' most striking effort in this vein is her famous *A Posset for Nature's Breakfast*, in which human qualities and physical characteristics are enumerated in recipes for life's tastiest dishes (I have preserved the Duchess' erratic spelling and punctuation):

> Life scummes the Cream of Beauty with Time's spoon
> And drawes the Claret Wine of Blushes soon.
> There boils it in a skillet cleane of Youth,
> Then thicks it well with crumbl'd Bread of Truth.
> And sets it on the Fire of Life, which growes
> The clearer, if the Bellowes of Health blowes.
> Then takes the Eggs of Faire and Bashfull Eyes,
> And puts them in a Countenance that's wise,

---

1. Syphilis was still frequently referred to as 'The French disease' (*see* pages 97–9).
2. 'Blood' (i.e. black) pudding is a Scottish delicacy, with which the Duchess had evidently had some bad experiences. It is best eaten at breakfast.

> And cuts a Lemmon in of sharpest Wit,
> By Discretion's Knife, as he thinkes fit.
> A handfull of chast Thoughts double refined,
> Six Spoonfuls of a Noble and Gentle Mind.
> A Graine of Mirth, to give't a little Tast,
> Then takes it off, for feare the Substance wast,
> And puts it in a Bason of Rich Wealth,
> And in this Meat doth Nature please her Selfe.

The real treats (for the reader) are reserved for the 'Dissert', which is graphically described as full of tempting, but ruinous ingredients, like Viennese cakes:

> Sweet Marmalade of Kisses new gathered,
> Preserv'd Children that are not Fathered:
> Sugar of Beauty which melts away soon,
> Marchpane of Youth, and childish Macaroon.
> Sugar-Plum words most sweet on the Lips.
> And water Promises, which wast into Chips.
> Bisket of Love, which crumbles all away.
> Gelly of Feare, that quaking, quivering lay.
> Then was a fresh green-sickness cheese brought in,
> And tempting fruit, like that which Eve made sin.

'In later life,' says Colley Cibber in his *Lives of the Poets*, the Duchess 'kept a great many young ladies about her person, who occasionally wrote what she dictated. Some of them slept in a room contiguous to that in which her grace lay, and were ready at the call of her bell, to rise any hour of the night to write down her conceptions lest they should escape her memory.' To this happy provision of the Duchess we owe the preservation of much profitless speculation, and a great deal of entirely valueless scientific observation:

> All that doth flow we cannot liquid name,
> Or else would fire and water be the same,
> But that is liquid which is moist and wet,
> Fire that propriety can never get:
> Then 'tis not cold that doth the fire put out,
> But 'tis the wet that makes it die, no doubt.

185

The Duchess' enthusiasm for science was considerably greater than her understanding of it; but it was so unusual for a lady at that time to take an interest in such matters, that she was accorded a degree of respect by some of her contemporaries that does them credit. Hobbes was generous in his estimate of her, and she once made a sort of royal visit to the Academy where the assembled scientists humbly carried out some exemplary experiments for her benefit. An attempt was also made to translate her scientific verses into Latin by a scholar of Christ Church, James Bristow, but he had to give up the attempt in the face of the Duchess' intractable style and extraordinary ideas.

On the other hand, she reveals in the lengthy prefatory matter to *Poems and Fancies*, that a friend had counselled her not to add to the abundance of poetry already available:

> Besides the world hath already such a weight
> Of uselesse bookes, as it is over fraught.
> Then pity take, doe the world a good turne
> And all you write, cast in the fire and burne.

The poetess was so angry at this suggestion that she immediately rushed her verses through the press. Posterity should be grateful that she took a firm line, since otherwise we should have been deprived of such observations as that 'The Fairies in the Braine, may be the Cause of many thoughts'. The Fairies in the brain of the Duchess herself can only be described as hyperactive, stimulating a constant flow of music and opinion. The poetess described the process in her own inimitable way: the following description of her head picturesquely summarizes her creative transmutation of hot air into organ music:

> The Head unto an Organ I compare
> The Thoughts, as severall Pipes make Musick there.
> Imagination's Bag doth draw, then blow
> Windy Opinions, by which the Thoughts go.
> The small Virginall Jacks which skip about,
> Are severall Fancies that run in, and out.

'She succeeded,' wrote Virginia Woolf in *The Common Reader*, 'during her lifetime in drawing upon herself the ridicule of the great and the applause of the learned. But the last echoes of that clamour have now all died away; she lives only in the few splendid phrases that Lamb scattered upon her tomb[1]; her poems, her plays, her philosophies, her orations, her discourses – all those folios and quartos in which, she protested, her real life was shrined – moulder in the gloom of public libraries, or are decanted into tiny thimbles which hold six drops of their profusion. Even the curious student, inspired by the words of Lamb, quails before the mass of her mausoleum, peers in, looks about him, and hurries out again, shutting the door.'[2]

1. He described her Life of her husband as 'a jewel for which no casket was good enough'.
2. Virginia Woolf, *The Common Reader*, Chatto & Windus, 1932.

Ten

THE REVEREND
CORNELIUS WHUR
1782–1853

The consolations of complacency

In this imperfect, gloomy scene
    Of complicated ill,
How rarely is a day serene,
    The throbbing bosom still!
Will not a beauteous landscape bright,
    Or music's soothing sound
Console the heart, afford delight,
    And throw sweet peace around?
They may, but never comfort lend
Like an accomplish'd female friend!

from: *The Female Friend*

The sounding horn to thee conveys no charm;
Nor dost thou seek the plain where whizzing balls
Prostrate the feathered tribe . . .

from: *The Village Clergyman*

Thou pretty little jumping thing –
    Whate'er may be thine age,
Thou hast a most amusing swing
    While turning in thy cage.

from: *On A Domesticated Squirrel*

Just so the power to amplify
    Jehovah's written will;
Is never reached by heartless sigh
    Supinely sitting still.

from: *The Admirable Preacher*

THE REVEREND WHUR, ON THE EVIDENCE available to us through his writings, possessed the most pedestrian mind in English Literature; yet he makes compulsive reading. There is no barrier of art interposed between the vegetative musings of his intellect and their expression on the printed page. Every line of complacent sententiousness, every resoundingly inadequate platitude, bears the poet's unmistakable stamp of un-Samaritan piety.

Cornelius Whur was a Wesleyan minister who pursued his calling in Norfolk and Suffolk, where his sound conservative attitude to poverty and misfortune endeared him to his Anglican colleagues. It has been said that Wesleyanism was a major factor in turning the English people away from revolution when industrialists and the landed interest faced their darkest hour. Cornelius Whur seems to have played his own small part in this great drama as he perambulated the East Anglian highways observing and reporting on the spiritual health of the natives. Here, for instance, is a picture of *The Stone-Breaker*, a prey to poverty and illness, who watches with bitterness the rich gliding by in their carriages. He voices the thought that if he were Prime Minister, he would ensure that the poorer classes should have 'due and prompt relief' from their suffering. Naturally, Whur can't let such a dangerously muddle-headed remark pass without challenge:

> Unknown to Peter, I stood by,
>   And all his reasoning heeded;
> And though unasked, made this reply,
>   Conceiving it was needed.

> . . . Hast thou not learned by looking o'er
>   This vast and wide creation;
> Some must be rich, and others poor?
>   Diversity of station!

189

This is a forceful argument. Indeed only socialists and such-like persons, whom Mrs Thatcher has told us she proposes to eradicate, would have the effrontery to offer any resistance to it. It has a suitably electrifying effect on Peter the Stone-Breaker:

> I ended here, and Peter too
> Suspended every clamour;
> And while he was within my view
> He briskly used his hammer.

One of the poet's most endearing characteristics is his readiness to spray any situation involving hardship with a soothing shower of Panglossian balm.[1]

> A peasant, feeling some dismay,
> From narrow bounded view
> Was over-heard by one, to say,
> What I relate to you
> T'explain the case I must rehearse
> He had no cash! – could he be worse?

Reflecting on this, on the face of it, lamentable misfortune, the peasant is rescued by an optimistic reflection, which we may guess was also Whur's: as he possessed nothing, he need not be afraid of robbery. Moreover:

> Nor can I disoblige a friend
> By saying, I will never lend!

He will not be troubled by greedy relatives after his estate, nor pestered by beggars, nor:

> lose a single hour
> To count my yellow store.

The moral is: if you have nothing at all, you have no reason not to be happy. That is the authentic Whur note: he offers us the consola-

1.The Reverend Whur spent his earlier years as a gardener before the call came.

tions of Boethius, laced with the brusque realism of Mr Norman Tebbit, and expressed in the language of Dr Pangloss.

The Reverend Whur's first volume, *Village Musings – on Moral and Religious Subjects* (1837), which was published under the pseudonym of 'A Villager', attracted a large number of subscribers. In the Preface the author frankly confesses his 'desire and intention' of amusing and benefiting all and offending none. We do not know if he succeeded in this last endeavour, or whether any of those victims of misfortune, whom he so delighted to hymn, ever resented being trapped, like rabbits, in the glare of the Reverend's poetical headlights. It is idle – though tempting – to speculate, as to the reaction of a lady who had been immobilized for fourteen years, when presented with Whur's verses about her entitled *The Cheerful Invalid*:

> Dost thou not feel as years recede
>   Worn out distress'd and weary?
> To me it seemeth, thou hast need,
> To be from sorrow's petting freed,
>   In such a state – so dreary.
> Year after year, thou art the same,
> An invalid – remaining lame!

Surely she must envy others?

> They walking, wander anywhere,
> While thou art sitting on thy chair!

But no; the lady is blessed with many Christian visitors, the Reverend Whur amongst them:

> And therefore, though remaining lame
> I'll magnify Jehovah's name!

It is reassuring for the reader, as no doubt it was for the victims and their parents, that no matter how hopeless their condition, God had the situation in hand: 'Mere body as thou art' he writes of a little girl born without arms or legs,

> . . . not having feet
> Or hands to help thee; I, thy state divine
> As most unpromising –

He need not have worried, for the little Christian pipes up on cue:

191

Shall I, though armless, want a watchful friend?

The Reverend was as alert to the doctrinal potential of deformity and crippling disease as are armaments manufacturers to the commercial potential of wars. Readers are treated to improving discourses on a wide variety of human tragedies. There is the artist, born without arms, who nonetheless supports his family:

> 'Alas! Alas!' the father said,
>   'Oh what a dispensation!
> How can we be by mercy led
>   In such a situation?
> Be not surprised at my alarms,
> The dearest boy is without arms!'

And then there is the deaf and dumb girl who is told, in the approved Cornelian manner, that she will appreciate her sight all the more:

> Deep silence is thine only guest
>   And though earth's bliss is rare,
> Not few have pleasure in their breast[1]
>   When thou dost shed a tear
>
> 'How canst thou tell?' someone rejoined –
>   'If Heaven's ways are right,
> The maiden *deaf and dumb*, may find
>   Due pleasure in her sight!'

The author's explanatory notes, which he affixes to some of his more ambitious poems, are particularly useful to students of the sententious. Here, for example, is his description of the genesis of a poem about a lady's unexpected death, which bears a striking resemblance to some of Wordsworth's fieldwork for the *Lyrical Ballads*: 'The author, in passing through a beautiful churchyard in the county of Norfolk, was particularly struck with the appearance of a recently covered grave, which was surrounded by a profusion of roses. Afterwards, while proceeding on his journey he casually overtook the gentleman whose lady had been interred in the grave

---

1. The evident suggestion that people are enjoying the grief of the unfortunate girl appears to be a syntactical oversight on the part of the poet.

which had engaged his attention, and of whose sudden departure he
gave the following relation: he had an only daughter, who at the
period referred to was seriously indisposed, and who had been
deploring that circumstance in consequence of the inconvenience it
occasioned in the family. The lady, who at that time was in perfect
health, endeavoured to console the mind of her afflicted daughter
by exclaiming, "Thank God, I am quite well, and will alleviate your
sufferings!" But within twenty minutes the affectionate mother,
who had thus spoken, was a corpse, and in the above-named grave
her remains were reposing.' What an extraordinary occurrence!
(we cannot help exclaiming); and what an ideal subject for an effusion in verse. The first stanza says it all (although there are four
others):

> The morning arose, and its beauties were beaming
>   As they danced in her vision like snow-crested wave;
> But alas! as such splendours were brilliantly gleaming
>   She retired to repose in the rose-covered grave!

On another occasion the poet explains, apropos his poem *The
Casual Knock*, the truly remarkable event that gave rise not only to
that poem, but to the entire volume of musings. This story is so
exciting that it rather overshadows the poem itself, so I hope the
reader will forgive me if I restrict myself to quotation of the prose
footnote: 'During the winter of 1836,' writes Whur, 'the author had
occasion to visit a gentleman, who resided in another county; and
having accompanied him to a village at some distance from the place
of his abode, the gentleman in returning in the evening, passed a
respectable situation in which an intimate friend of his resided; but
who happened to be a perfect stranger to the writer. The author's
friend, without giving the least intimation of his intention, as by an
immediate impulse, gave a loud *knock* at the door. The party, compre-
hending the author, his friend, and two other individuals, were
politely invited to step in. They did so; and this *perfectly casual interview*, gave rise to the publication of this volume, and to many
important occurrences, which can never cease to be interesting to
the writer while memory is permitted to aid his retrospection.'
Note how Whur assists the reader to spot the highlights of this anecdote by cunning use of italics. As we read, we realize with a shock of
excitement that the *'casual knock'* in question is almost as momentous

193

as that of the gentleman from Porlock, and that this is the beginning
of a literary phenomenon.

Whur's first volume closes with a note threatening a sequel,
should it be well received. Apparently it was, for in 1845 he published *Gratitude's Offering – Being Original Productions On A Variety of
Subjects – By The Author of Village Musings*. This extended his range
somewhat, though there is still a residual interest in the doctrinal
possibilities of the limbless and the bereaved. Perhaps the interesting after-dinner discussions of a theological nature that he con-
ducted with his patron Dr Hall had made him aware of the other
activities of the Almighty, when not supplying comfort to the deaf
and dumb. At any rate his meditation on the sun shows a new awareness of natural phenomena, which he regards as useful visual aids
for the inculcation of true religion:

> When Jehovah spoke the word
> Thou didst hear His awful call;
> And obedient to thy Lord –
> Wert a vast and blazing ball:
> Bending thus to His decree
> Dost thou not appeal to me?
>
> Thou art likewise friend to all
> Whether pure or insincere;
> Causing rays alike to fall –
> Here and there, and everywhere;
> Being thus benignly free,
> Art thou not instructing me?
>
> . . . Thou hast rolled six thousand years
> 'Mid the changing scenes of time,
> Not annoying other spheres –
> Whatsoe'er their state or chime:
> When thy noiseless worth I see
> Ought I not to copy thee?

It will be seen that Whur has by now made the usual, and always
fatal, discovery of nineteenth-century poetasters: namely that all
the elements of nature think and act like human beings:

'Deem me not rude,' said blustering Winter –
Who swept across the flower-deserted lea . . .

is an early portent, as is, we assume, a poem entitled *The Teetotal
Bullock*. On inspection, however, it turns out not to be the bullock
that is teetotal but the farmer who bought him. Nevertheless, the
pathetic fallacy now had Whur in its grip, and we see the consequences in his poem *The Eclipse*. This is a dialogue between the
Earth and the (somewhat wimpish) Moon. The latter complains
pathetically that she is enveloped in darkness, which draws a
spirited reply from the Earth:

> . . . It is for want of better view
> That foolish blockheads, such as you,
> See with a sad repulsive frown
> A neighbour's fault, and not their own!
> Do you consider as you quake
> Like lump of clay – you're but opaque?
> If beam of light, although but one,
> Appear in you, 'tis from the *Sun*!
> Then why of lucid brightness sing,
> Since you have yours by pilfering!
> And stealing light away from me,
> Leave in its stead – obscurity!
> Nay, don't stand shudd'ring, I'm the *Earth* . . .

In reality this is not such a radical departure from the poet's
earlier manner. He had merely switched his 'buck up' and 'on your
bike' admonitions from the disadvantaged to nature herself. His
work is a seamless garment, a meandering river of piety, a glorious
garden where blow the unwithering blooms of Low Church orthodoxy. He must be accorded his niche, not only in English Literature,
but also in the annals of East Anglian horticulture. As Lewis and Lee
put it: 'In the considerable army of extinct spinsters and clergymen
who have enriched English Literature with volumes of poetry and
"pamphlets about growing roses and resisting sin", the Reverend
Cornelius Whur must henceforth occupy commanding rank . . .'[1]

1. D.B. Wyndham Lewis and Charles Lee, *The Stuffed Owl*, J.M. Dent and Sons,
1978, p. 156.

Eleven

MARTIN TUPPER
1810–89

The proverbial philosopher

[*Proverbial Philosophy* is] a singular collection of commonplace observations set forth in a form which bears the appearance of verse, but has neither rhyme nor metre, and has long since found its deserved level.

Everyman's Dictionary of Literary Biography

. . . the style, with its queer inversions, bears more resemblance to the English of an erudite German of the 19th century . . .

Dictionary of National Biography

. . . the sententiousness of Polonius, without his share of wisdom . . .

Bonamy Dobrée in *The Victorians and After,*
Introductions to English Literature, Vol IV

Death, fell cannibal, gloateth on his victim,
And carrieth it with him to the grave, that dismal
    banquet-hall,
Where in foul state the Royal Ghoul holdeth secret
    orgies.

Martin Tupper, *Proverbial Philosophy*

Shall then a man reck nothing, but hurl mad defiance at
    his Judge,
Knowing that less than an omnipotent cannot make the
    has been, not been?

Martin Tupper, *Proverbial Philosophy*

IN THE 1960S THE BEATLES MADE THE CLAIM that they were more popular than Jesus Christ; in the mid-nineteenth century, Martin Farquhar Tupper actually was more popular than Tennyson, which, in Victorian terms, was tantamount to the same thing. His perennial bestseller entitled *Proverbial Philosophy; A Book of Thoughts and Arguments, Originally Treated* was first published in 1838, and for twenty-five years never sold fewer than 5000 copies annually. By the 1860s it had clocked up 100,000 sales in England and nearly half a million in America. Victoria and Albert loved it – 'I thank you, Mr Tupper, for your beautiful poetry', said the queen when the author was presented at court in 1857 – and the middle classes seem to have given it a status in the family circle akin to that of the Bible. By 1848 there was a small industry in Tupperism, selections falling thick and fast upon the reading public with titles like *Gems from Tupper, Compiled by A Clergyman*. An 1851 compendium places Tupper amongst thinkers of similar stature – e.g. Solomon and Shakespeare – and is charmingly embellished with appropriate illustrations of Solomon's Temple, Stratford-upon-Avon, and Albury House in Surrey, where Tupper lived.

The critics, however, were not impressed. In a hostile review *Fraser's Magazine* described the work of the master as 'commonplaces in a sing-song manner' only relieved by the 'comic touches of self-satisfaction in the writer'. Later, C.E. Vulliamy was to describe Tupper's verse as 'rivulets of treacle', and George Saintsbury, in a sudden outburst, characterizes *Proverbial Philosophy* as 'incredible rubbish . . . intolerable imbecility'. When an American critic described Walt Whitman as 'the Tupper of the West' it was not intended as a compliment.

Tupper, armed for most of his life with a substantial income and a continual buzz of adulation, was able to ignore the carping minnows of the literary establishment. (Indeed, there seems increasingly to

197

be a note of desperation in the attacks of the latter: when Tupper decided to complete *Christabel*, the unfinished poem of Coleridge, *Blackwood's* could only complain helplessly: 'We are surprised by his impertinence and pained by his stupidity.') Other works flowed from his pen: works on heroes, a coronation ode, and especially works in which the author could indulge his fondness for wool-gathering. One of these was vulnerably titled *An Author's Mind* (1841), and subtitled *The Book of Title Pages.* As Patrick Scott explains, the volume 'outlined thirty-four books on everything from the souls of dumb animals to the folly of shaving – books Tupper mercifully felt that he did not have time to write out in full.'[1] 'I feel Malthusian among my nurslings,' writes the Proverbial Philosopher in a moving preface, 'I write these things only to be quit of them.' The same critic describes Tupper's *Rides and Reveries* (1858) as containing: 'all of Tupper's pet crotchets, from the value of beards and the malignancy of reviewers to the right way to solve the Irish problem and the tribulations of matrimony (the unkind story is that living with the Proverbial Philosopher had driven Mrs Tupper to drink.')[2]

Shortly before his death Tupper was able to reflect complacently on a life of distinguished service to the Muses in *My Life As An Author* (1886). The book closes with a translation from Ovid that Tupper obviously felt was appropriate to his literary standing:

> My name shall never die; but through all time
> There, in that people's tongue, shall this my page
> Be read and glorified from age to age:–
> Yes, if the bodings of my spirit give
> True note of inspiration, I shall live!

There was no reason to suppose this was a forlorn hope; if the popularity of Cliff Richard can survive two generations, clearly there is hope for us all. What Tupper relates of the esteem in which he was held by contemporaries must have encouraged a certain sanguinity regarding the future. His most striking anecdote recalls a visit to an American lunatic asylum where, on the door of every patient's

1. *The Dictionary of Literary Biography*, Volume 32, Ed. William E. Fredemann and Ira B. Nadel, Gale Research Company, 1984, pp. 288–98, *Martin Tupper* by Patrick Scott.
2. Patrick Scott, op. cit.

room, the doctor in charge had pinned up a Tupper poem entitled *Never Give Up!* The author was pleased, but of course not very surprised, to note that these lines were having a beneficial effect on the inmates; and he describes how, during his visit, he was received as a hero by 'kneeling, weeping and kissing folks'.

Perhaps there is an element of defiance in all this. Tupper was incapable of irony and he would not have perceived any in the fact that the mentally disturbed were among his very greatest admirers. In *Proverbial Philosophy* itself he explains that greatness is its own reward, and the activities of the critics a tiresome irrelevance:

> What if the prophet lacketh honour? for he can spare that
> praise:
> The honest giant careth not to be patted on the back by
> pygmies;
> Flatter greatness, he brooketh it good-humouredly: blame
> him, – thou tiltest at a pyramid.

As may be seen from this passage, Tupper relies heavily on echoes of the Bible for his best effects. *Proverbial Philosophy* is sententious, rhetorical, and pious. Biblical saws and pseudo-Augustinian meditations are stirred into an evangelical brew, to which indigestible gobbets of 'philosophy' are added. It is clear that the readers are required to swallow this brew just as recalcitrant Victorian children were required to eat up their suppers. The seriousness of the exercise and the non-negotiable nature of its premise, enables Tupper to anticipate with boldness any possible irreverence regarding its execution:

> Some have commended ridicule, counting it the test of
> truth,
> But neither wittily nor wisely; for truth must prove
> ridicule:
> Otherwise a blunt bulrush is to pierce the proof armour of
> argument,
> Because the stolidity of ignorance took it for a barbed
> shaft.
> Softer is the hide of the rhinoceros, than the heart of
> deriding unbelief,
> And truth is idler there than the Bushman's feathered reed:

In much the same manner Tupper tackles in *Proverbial Philosophy* such topics as 'Humility', 'Pride', 'Estimating Character' and 'Cruelty to Animals'. He is a valiant warrior against religious doubt, which, despite his having disposed of it once and for all in his *Probabilities* (1847), was unaccountably still around in the 1860s, and getting worse. He demolishes, to his own satisfaction, the objection sometimes raised that there is an inherent contradiction in the idea of a merciful God who allows so much gratuitous suffering in the world; victims of this, remarks Tupper briskly, are but 'the heritors of evil'. Besides, 'Pain and sin are convicts, and toil in their fetters for good.' His answer, it seems, is much the same as the one given by Willie Whitelaw to an awkward questioner at the hustings, namely: 'There it is, that's it, and there you are.'

The inquiring mind that is not very evident in *Proverbial Philosophy* was indefatigable in other fields. Tupper claimed to have invented glass screw tops for bottles, pens to 'carry their own ink' and safety horseshoes. His literary researches revealed to the world that the name 'Punch' was derived from Pontius Pilate, and that Humpty Dumpty came from a ballad satirizing William the Conqueror as '*L'homme qui dompte*'. Also that the four and twenty blackbirds in *Sing-a-Song-of-Sixpence* was a snide reference to King John's well-known greed. In *Probabilities* he took the trouble to point out that Joshua, on that famous occasion in the Old Testament, did not stop the sun and the moon, but the earth, 'the result, of course,' as a commentator in the *T.L.S.* drily observes, 'being much the same.'[1] He was also made a Fellow of the Royal Society for his archeological work on a Romano–Celtic temple on Farley Heath, acquired a Doctorate in Civil Law at Oxford and was awarded the Prussian Gold Medal for science and art. Perhaps a greater achievement than all these was to win, as an undergraduate, a theological essay prize, pushing Gladstone into second place. In fact he only took up literature (instead of law) because of his uncontrollable stammer, which he tried to cure by reading the whole of *Paradise Lost* aloud, with his chin propped on a crutch and his tongue restrained by a gag.

Tupper had energy, piety and vanity in about equal proportions. It may confidently be asserted that his works are entirely worthless

1. *Times Literary Supplement*, 26 February, 1938, p. 137, *Mr Tupper and the Poets*.

from the point of view of literature, religion and philosophy. He holds, however, considerable interest for the social historian, and perhaps no one has fixed him more evocatively in his period and context than G.M. Young. In Volume II of *Early Victorian England* he has this to say of the latter-day Polonius and his epoch: 'the circulation of some Victorian sermons is a thing to fill the modern reader with despair. If we consider the effect, beginning in childhood, of all the preachers on all the congregations, of men loud and unctuous, authoritative or persuasive, speaking out of a body of acknowledged truth to the respectful audience below them, we shall see why the homilectic cadence, more briefly, cant, is so persistent in Victorian oratory and literature. It sufficed to persuade the lower middle classes that Tupper was a poet, and the upper middle classes that Emerson was a philosopher. Mr Gladstone formed his style by reading sermons aloud and his diaries are full of self-delivered homilies. Old Sir Robert Peel trained his son to repeat every Sunday the discourse he had just heard: a practice to which he owed his astonishing recollection of his opponents' arguments and something, perhaps, of the unction of his own replies.'[1]

1. G.M. Young, *Early Victorian England 1830–1865*, Volume II, Oxford University Press, 1934, p. 425.

Twelve

WILLIAM McGONAGALL
1825?–1902

The Scottish Homer

Brutes find out where their talents lie:
A *bear* will not attempt to fly;
A founder'd *horse* will oft debate
Before he tries a five-barr'd gate;
A *dog* by instinct turns aside,
Who sees the ditch too deep and wide.
But *Man* we find the only creature
Who, led by *Folly*, fights with *Nature*;
Who, when *she* loudly cries, *Forbear*,
With obstinacy fixes there;
And, where his *genius* least inclines,
Absurdly bends his whole designs.

Jonathan Swift, *On Poetry: A Rhapsody*

Among the poets of the present day
There is no one on earth who can possibly be able for to
gainsay
But that William M'Gonagall, poet and tragedian,
Is truly the greatest poet that was ever found above or below
the meridian.

From the *Ode* in honour of William McGonagall
composed by students at Glasgow University (1891)

FEW PEOPLE HAVE ACQUIRED a niche in history by producing what nobody wanted in a manner nobody applauded. This is the achievement of William McGonagall, the son of an Irish handloom worker who had settled in Scotland, and by common consent the most consistently bad poet in the language. He is to be found in all the best reference books, and their compilers vie with each other in heaping abuse on the self-styled 'poet and tragedian': 'His naïve verses . . . have a kind of genius for the banal, stuffed with prosaic details and hilariously contrived rhymes'[1] says one; 'His poems are uniformly bad, but possess a disarming *naïveté* and a calypso-like disregard for metre which still never fail to entertain'[2] says another. George MacBeth in his prefatory remarks to *The Famous Tay Whale*, which he includes in his *Penguin Book of Victorian Verse*, writes that 'some readers may suspect that the inclusion of his work is a joke . . .' On the contrary, says MacBeth, 'By applying the simple test of whether his work is recognizable in small samples, it can easily be shown to be original. Like the Douanier Rousseau, McGonagall created a style out of a stupidity. He was the first – and perhaps so far the only widely known – naïve poet, and as such he deserves attention.'[3]

This must surely be the apotheosis of McGonagall, the recognition of a talent that he alone believed in, the sudden transformation before our wondering eyes of an indefatigable bungler into an intellectual cult. At least it ought to be, but, in fact, McGonagall's depth of ungiftedness is sufficient to defy even the intellectual's desire to create respectable justifications for enjoying him. The comparison with le Douanier Rousseau is not apt. While paintings like *The*

1. Roderick Watson, *The Literature of Scotland*, London, 1984, p. 297.
2. *Chambers Biographical Dictionary*, Edinburgh, 1975.
3. George MacBeth, *The Penguin Book of Victorian Verse*, Harmondsworth, 1969, p. 428.

Snake Charmer (1907) show a visionary power and an ability to select and transform, this can hardly be said of McGonagall. He never selects, but piles on details of utter banality in awkward rambling dirges which often end suddenly and arbitrarily with a perfunctory moral. The experience is like that of being driven unsteadily down a meandering road in a rattling old banger, which finally turns abruptly into a brick wall. Rousseau was an amateur painter, at least in the sense that he was obliged to earn his living by other means and was excluded for most of his life from the circles of professionals; but McGonagall regarded himself as dedicated to his art, the as yet unrecognized heir of Shakespeare and Burns. His visiting and/or business card, with characteristic innocence, ran as follows:

W.M. MCGONAGALL, L.I.A.R.
Lyric Inditer and Reciter
Poetry Promptly Executed

Like any dedicated professional, McGonagall never took any other work after being bitten by the Muses in 1877. As he sat lonely and pensive in his room, 'a flame, as Lord Byron has said, seemed to kindle up my entire frame, along with a strange desire to write poetry; and I felt so happy, so happy I was inclined to dance . . .' Thereafter, as Derek Wilson puts it: 'Throughout the remaining twenty-four years of McGonagall's life a torrent of verse poured from him; bad verse, excruciatingly bad verse, devoid of all metre and scansion, never dignified by any flash of poetic insight, seldom rising above the utterly banal. The poverty of his verses was in stark contrast to the magnificent subjects which inspired them. For above all things McGonagall was moved by epic events, stirring spectacles and outstanding catastrophes.'[1]

McGonagall's subject matter is monotonously repetitive and each poem handles its theme in exactly the same way. This does not rule out the unpredictable, however, for his accumulation of detail seems to have been dictated by snobbery on the one hand, and the exigencies of rhyme on the other. One of his most famous poems is the *Death of Lord and Lady Dalhousie*, which is a good example of his 'Court Circular' manner:

1. Derek Wilson, *Extraordinary People*, London, 1983.

Amongst those present at the interment were Mr
    Marjoribanks MP,
Also ex-Provost Ballingall from Bonnie Dundee;
Besides the Honourable W.G. Colville, representing the
    Duke and Duchess of Edinburgh,
While in every one's face standing at the grave was
    depicted sorrow.

While the poet's treatment of Queen Victoria is invariably respectful, his search for a satisfactory rhyme sometimes leads to a rather
brusque handling of her. Thus we are told in *The Queen's Diamond
Jubilee Celebrations*:

Her Majesty looked well considering her years,
And from the vast crowd burst forth joyous cheers;

or again in the same poem:

Oh! it was a most gorgeous sight to be seen,
Numerous foreign magnates were there for to see the Queen;
And to the vast multitude there of women and men,
Her Majesty for two hours showed herself to them.

In another Jubilee ode he seems to be even more dismissive:

And as this is her first Jubilee year,
And will be her last, I rather fear;
Therefore, sound drums and trumpets cheerfully . . . etc.

McGonagall, like many of his contemporary fellow-Scots, was
devoted to Queen Victoria. Not only had she put the Highlands on
the map by gracing them with the Royal presence at frequent intervals, but her homely appearance and evident attachment to bour-
geois mores endeared her to many of her thrifty and industrious
Northern subjects. McGonagall's indignation when a Scotsman
tried to assassinate her would have summed up the nation's feelings,
had it been better expressed. As it is, his poem on the *Attempted
Assassination of the Queen* is a remarkable exercise in sustained
bathos, complete with the poet's magnificent improvement on
some well-known lines from *Hamlet*. It begins:

> God prosper long our noble Queen,
>   And long may she reign!
> Maclean he tried to shoot her,
>   But it was all in vain.
>
> For God He turned the ball aside
>   Maclean aimed at her head;
> And he felt very angry
>   Because he didn't shoot her dead.
>
> There's a divinity that hedgeth a king,
>   And so it does seem,
> And my opinion is, it has hedged
>   Our most gracious Queen.

He goes on to express a wish that:

> Long may she be spared to roam
>   Among the bonnie Highland floral,
> And spend many a happy day
>   In the palace of Balmoral.

and ends with an adroit recapitulation of his Shakespearian allusion:

> May He be as a hedge around her,
>   As He's been all along,
> And let her live and die in peace
>   Is the end of my song.

    This poem, with its charming vision of the Queen sitting serenely inside her hedge, is one of McGonagall's most famous. It has many of the traditional elements of bestsellerdom, including royalty, crime, religion and a happy ending. Aficionados may object that it contains few of the poet's best rhymes and is, on one or two occasions, dangerously close to metrical felicity; that said, it is in every other aspect authentic McGonagall, and was no doubt amongst the verses he took with him when he tramped, in foul weather, to the gates of Balmoral, hoping to give his sovereign a private recitation. The Queen, however, having survived one horrifying experience, declined to be subjected to another.
    McGonagall's relationship with his public – he was essentially a

performer rather than a man of the printed word – was an uneven one. As the Florence Foster-Jenkins of Dundee, he drew regular and large audiences, who came to laugh and stayed to jeer. It is a mistake to think he was impervious to all this, as can be seen from his *New Year's Resolution to Leave Dundee* (1893) which strikes a note of genuine pathos:

> Every morning when I go out
> The ignorant rabble they do shout
> 'There goes Mad McGonagall'
> In derisive shouts, as loud as they can bawl,
> And lifts stones and snowballs, throws them at me;

It is heartening to see that he did not always take the attacks lying down. With splendid irony he penned the crushing *Lines in Reply to the Beautiful Poet, Who Welcomed News of My Departure from Dundee*:

> Dear Johnny, I return my thanks to you;
> But more than thanks is your due
> For publishing the scurrilous poetry about me
> Leaving the ancient City of Dundee.
>
> The rhymester says, we'll weary of your schauchlin' form;
> But if I'm not mistaken I've seen bonnier than his in a field
> of corn;
> And as I venture to say and really suppose,
> His form seen in a cornfield would frighten the crows.

The anonymous satirist had evidently concentrated his attack on the poet's appearance, which was admittedly eccentric. 'He says my nose would make a peasemeal warrior weep' complains McGonagall, 'and he criticizes the length of my hair. He forgets that Jesus himself had long hair. It is almost certain that the malicious person behind this attack must be "a vendor of strong drink".'

This seems to have been one of the rare occasions when the poet struck back directly at his critics. More often he affected not to notice either obloquy or rejection. It was typical of him to send his *Requisition to the Queen* to Balmoral, asking her to accept two of his verses. 'So heartened was he by the response, which took the form of a letter from Lord Biddulph saying that her Majesty could not possibly accept the verses, that he began styling himself "Poet to Her Majesty".[1] His early experiences as an actor may have inured him to the scabrous behaviour of the groundlings. On stage he often exhibited that serene contentment with his own prowess which also underpinned his invincible failure as a poet. He admired his own performance as Macbeth so much that it was only natural he should occasionally wish to prolong it beyond the span allotted to it by the plot. 'In an unrehearsed departure from the script [McGonagall] continued to flourish his sword for some time after being run through by Macduff; he was only finally brought to the ground by a well-placed kick from the actor playing Macduff who had lost his temper at this improvisation.'[2] The obvious delight of the audience at all this may, unfortunately, have been an encouragement to the tyro actor, who must have felt that his first struttings on the stage had gone remarkably well. Theatre managements took a different view, however, and he found it difficult to get further engagements. Nevertheless, he remained a performer, often creating sensations with his unique recitations in pubs and at banquets. Some of these were halted by the police on the grounds that they were causing a breach of the peace; at others the intoxicated locals would pelt him with rotten vegetables.

In view of this it is difficult to see why McGonagall has endured as well as he has. Without the live performance, the poems, when read at length, are liable to induce a state of catalepsy in all but the most fanatical of his admirers. That these do exist, however, is demonstrated by the fact that a publisher thought it worth issuing a complete Library Omnibus of his works as late as 1980, which was in its second impression by 1986. McGonagall saw no reason to tamper with a good title, so we find that this edition includes *Poetic Gems*, *More Poetic Gems*, *Still More Poetic Gems*, *Yet More Poetic Gems*, *Further Poetic Gems*, *Yet Further Poetic Gems*, and *Last Poetic Gems*. As for his subject matter, an analysis of his total oeuvre reveals the following: fifty-three meandering narrative poems, roughly in ballad form; forty-seven leaden elegies, odes or celebrations; thirty-nine topographical effusions; thirty-four battle poems, almost invariably in praise of stunning British heroism and incorporating abusive remarks about the opposition; twenty-nine soulful accounts of dis-

1. Catherine Caulfield, *English Eccentrics*, p. 129.
2. Catherine Caulfield, op. cit., p. 128.

asters carrying their full complements of innocent victims and amazing heroes; four expatiations on the evils of drink; two surprising poems in support of women's suffrage; a Christmas carol with temperance propaganda thrown in; a poem on the Crucifixion; the poet's leave-taking of Dundee and his riposte to the person who welcomed it; and last but not least, his account of *The Famous Tay Whale*. This is certainly not the output of what the Germans call a *Sonntags-Dichter*. McGonagall exhibits all the characteristics of the energetic Victorian writers, together with their inability to know when to stop. The peruser of his collected works is immediately engulfed in an avalanche of clichés and platitudes, the sheer weight and quantity of which have a certain magnificence. Here are the best-loved Victorian themes – the honest British tars, Tommy Atkins, injured children who stop trains before they crash down from collapsed bridges, brave Captains going down again and again with innumerable ships, infants lost and found, persons murdered or horribly drowned, amazin' spectacles that will you astound, and so on and so forth. Yet in McGonagall's verses this inherently popular material invariably disintegrates. In his incapable hands, The Light Brigade would have been pinned down by a hail of irrelevant detail instead of the Russian cannon-shot, and Sir John Moore would have been buried by the rude mechanicals. He unerringly transforms great tragedy into great comedy with a deftness of touch that has endeared him to generations of readers:

> Oh, Heaven! it was a frightful and pitiful sight to see
> Seven bodies charred of the Jarvis family;
> And Mrs Jarvis was found with her child, and both carbonized,
> And as the searchers gazed thereon they were surprised.

> And these were lying beside the fragments of the bed,
> And in a chair the tenth victim was sitting dead;
> Oh Horrible! Oh, Horrible! What a sight to behold,
> The charred and burnt bodies of young and old.

from: *Calamity in London; Family of Ten Burned to Death*

or:

> 'Tis said two lovers met there with a tragic fate.
> Alas! poor souls, and no one near to extricate.

The rail of the bridge upon which they were leaning gave
way,
And they were drowned in the boiling gulf. Oh, horror and
dismay!

The building of the Tay Bridge proved to be a godsend to the
poet. Not only was he able to hail the great construction and its
architects in three poems – *The Railway Bridge of the Silvery Tay*, *The
Newport Railway* and *Address to the New Tay Bridge* – but he could also
immortalize its dramatic collapse shortly afterwards. His service-
able Muse was equal to both occasions: in the first poem on the subject the engineers are respectfully saluted:

> Beautiful Railway Bridge of the Silvery Tay!
> And prosperity to Messrs Bouche and Grothe
> The famous engineers of the present day,
> Who have succeeded in erecting the Railway
> Bridge of the Silvery Tay . . .

While in the last poem, subsequent to the collapse, the same gentlemen are given a discreet rap over the knuckles:

> Oh! ill-fated Bridge of the Silv'ry Tay,
> I must now conclude my lay
> By telling the world fearlessly without the least dismay,
> That your central girders would not have given way,
> At least many sensible men do say,
> Had they been supported on each side with buttresses . . .

One is tempted to say that this is McGonagall at his most inimitable, but in fact he has inspired one volume of verse, *The
MocGonagall*[1] which admirably captures the spirit of the bard. It is
not all that easy to write poems as bad as the *Address to the New Tay
Bridge*, but I think the authors have come very near with their salute
to *The Kincardine Road Bridge*:

---

1. *The MocGonagall*, verses by Ross Etty and others. Illustrations by Ross Etty,
Dundee and London, 1960?

Oh splendid Forth road bridge at Kincardine
For passing over which we don't pay a farthing!
Thou also opes thy ponderous and concrete jaws
To let a boatie pass through when its whistle blaws.
Now thanks to you Kincardine housewives can travel south
And spend a cheap holiday at Bo'ness or Grangemouth:
Or, at slightly more expense, visit Edinburgh
Or Glasgow, where they can buy a copy of Ygorra.
Meantime the folk from Grangemouth any day
Can cross to Valleyfield, which will make their hearts light
    and gay.
You are a blessing to motorists too, no doubt,
Who save petrol through not having to go so far about,
But I'm sure it would have made them even more merry
If the Kincardine Road Bridge had been built at
    Queensferry.

Their apostrophization of Glencoe also has the authentic ring of
McGonagallese, particularly in the way it ends unceremoniously, as
if the front legs of Pegasus had suddenly plunged into a bog and
stuck fast:

Glencoe, Glencoe, for friend and foe
Your great grim pass is grand to show,
With a beauty so classic it could hardly be classicker,
What a pity you had such a serious disturbance.

Quite different from the MocGonagall is the spurious work entitled *The Book of Lamentations of the Poet McGonagall* (1905), with
which no true lover of the bard will have any truck. One has only to
quote a few lines to see that this is an impudent attempt to impose
upon the public; not only is the subject matter inappropriate, but it
sticks recognizably to one metre, something the Master himself
never did:

No useless trouser encircled his groin
    But in bonnet and tights we found him
And he stood like a modest tobacconist sign
    With his tartan curtain around him.

Of course McGonagall would never have used a word as indelicate as 'groin', even when he was most desperate for a rhyme. He was particularly circumspect both in his subject matter and choice of vocabulary. When he had produced his celebration of *The Newport Railway*, he was at pains to stress its absolute propriety: 'I offered this valuable contribution,' he writes, 'which contains not a single immoral line or prurient suggestion to the *British Messenger*, the *Gospel Trumpet*, and the *Christian Treasury*, by all of whom in succession it was "declined with thanks". I then offered it . . . to the Directors of the North British Railway, telling them that I had been credibly informed that, but for this descriptive masterpiece, that railway would have been one of the most disastrous investments of modern times; but there was no answer . . .'

The claim to have rescued the equity holders of the railway is an interesting one. It reminds us that the only poem of McGonagall that was commissioned and actually paid for (two guineas) was his plug for Sunlight Soap:

> You can use it with great pleasure and ease
> Without wasting any elbow grease:
> And when washing the most dirty clothes
> The sweat won't be dripping from your nose.

This must have had an impact on sales, for it was followed up by some further lines in the same vein – though not, it seems, a further two guineas.

That the author of *The Rattling Boy From Dublin* and the *Burial of the Rev. George Gilfillan* should have sunk so low as to advertise soap, is a melancholy reflection on McGonagall's situation. Throughout the whole of his life he had not enjoyed a single moment of genuine success, with the possible exception of his banquet recitations, at which, he tells us, he was kindly received. He had to pay the manager of the theatre where he performed Macbeth £1 for the privilege. When he went to Balmoral to recite his verses to the Queen, he succeeded only in selling the policeman at the gates a copy of his poems for 2d. He even went to America, but seems to have returned immediately, disillusioned and empty-handed. It never once occurred to him that he had chosen the wrong profession, or that poetry might require skill and application. He seems to have had few, if any, friends and no relationships with the opposite sex. He has achieved a posthumous fame solely for his inability to string together even the simplest verses without botching them. The best epitaph to him can be taken from his own lines *To the Rev. George Gilfillan*, another dreadful writer whom McGonagall enormously admired: they say all that can appropriately be said of the Muses' most dogged and most superfluous acolyte:

> . . . For the Bible tells us whatever your hands findeth to do,
> Do it with all your might.
> Rev. George Gilfillan of Dundee, I must conclude my muse,
> And to write in praise of thee my pen does not refuse,
> Nor does it give pain to tell the world fearlessly, that when
> You are dead they shall not look upon your like again.

Thirteen

JOSEPH GWYER OF PENGE
born 1835

England's McGonagall

I wish you Alfred now a good night;
You gives your mother great delight;
Don't you wake up and ask for baa,
Or you'll offend your dad-dad-a.

Joseph Gwyer, *To Alfred Gwyer*
[In a footnote the author explains: 'Alfred,
when asking for bread, calls it baa; and water,
waa.]

Dear Sir – I have to acknowledge the receipt of a cheque
for £1 towards the relief of the sufferers by fire at the
Alexandra Palace, and also to express to you the Lord
Mayor's thanks for your (Gwyer's) appropriate lines,
which display the talent of a most uncommon order.

R. S. Vine
Private Secretary

TWO OF JOSEPH GWYER'S GREATEST ENTHUSIASMS – royalty and potatoes – are summed up on the title page of his 1875 volume, which reads:

Sketches of the Life of Joseph Gwyer (*Potato Salesman*)
With his Poems (*commended by Royalty*).

These enthusiasms he managed to combine in the verses that streamed from him throughout a life of honest toil and compulsive versifying. His loftiest themes recall the work of the great McGonagall, a poet whom he in some ways resembles. Like McGonagall, he can seldom resist a disaster or a shipwreck; still less can he resist royalty in any shape or form. In cultivating a friendship with her Poet Laureate, Lord Tennyson, Queen Victoria little realized how many talentless, but patriotic scribblers she was encouraging. Gwyer was constantly sending his verses to Buckingham Palace, receiving in return letters of masterly evasion at which Private Secretaries excel. Unaware of the impression created by these, the poet reprints a selection at the beginning of his book. It is typical of his noble innocence that he also prints a number of reviews which he evidently takes to be favourable, and about which surely even McGonagall would have had his doubts. *Lloyds Weekly*, for instance, is quoted as saying that 'Mr Gwyer's aspirations are most praiseworthy and do him great credit, and . . . we prefer to refrain from depreciating that which is so well intentioned and so thoroughly indicative of laudable zeal and ambition.' If that was sufficiently veiled, the *Norwood News* and *Croydon Advertiser*'s references to the 'indefatigable and irrepressible' Mr J. Gwyer's work, 'a collection of the poems with which he has from time to time astonished his neighbours' is even less encouraging. The inclusion of a review from *Punch* must, one thinks, be a joke, except that else-

215

where the poet appends a note: 'Lest the public should think I only publish favourable criticisms, the following is an anonymous sample. I could easily increase them on both sides did space permit.' These, as Mark Twain once observed in another context, are not the words of a fraud, but of a 'man whose conscience is at rest, a man who believes he has done high and worthy work for his nation and his generation'.

An indication that the Penge Poet regarded himself in such a light may be found in the account of his life written by himself, and prefixed to the 1896 edition of his works. By now he was sixty years old and able to bask in the mellow glow of past triumphs: 'About this time my popularity rose to its zenith, in consequence of my writing verses on the recovery of the Prince of Wales [he wrote no less than four notably unmoving poems on the subject], which verses drew from Her Majesty the Queen, and other members of the Royal Family, many letters of appreciation; about this time also I was made somewhat popular in London and elsewhere, by the publicity resulting from my catching a swindler at London Bridge, who afterwards got five years transportation. The whole affair is described in my book, in many pages of verses.'

This is the authentic Gwyer tone – a justly deserved pride in his achievements coupled with a delicate hint or two that his labours have not gone unnoticed in the highest circles of the land, whatever the *Norwood News* might think. Occasionally, it is true, he makes an heroic attempt at modesty, but usually it does not last. Particularly charming in this respect are his introductory remarks to his *Life and Poems* (1875 edition): 'I have simply but truthfully chronicled a few of the leading incidents of my life which, it will be seen, has been one of some ups and downs; as well as put together in verse some of my thoughts on the leading topics of the day, and as they have already had many readers, received commendation from Royalty, and have been reviewed and criticized by newspapers at home and abroad, I hope the book will not be uninteresting. A noted doctor has said "that a good laugh at times does his patients more good than all his medicines"; if this book should contribute in any way to this result it will not be without merit.'

The casual reader might well find this last observation puzzling. Throughout his work Mr Gwyer appears to adopt a seriousness of tone befitting the grandeur or the gravity of his themes. One does not look for humour in a poem entitled *Alarming Collision in the Channel* – nor does one find it. Nor are the rib-tickling aspects of *In Memoriam – Lord Tennyson*, or *The Strand Explosion*, immediately apparent. In the list of contents only one title leaps out clothed, as it were, in the raiment of ribaldry, and that is: *An Apt Reply At A Temperance Hotel*. I have read this poem over and over, and the more I think about it the more I am convinced that it is in fact a very funny poem:

> Entering the house at Basingstoke,
> I thus the conversation broke;
> Please tell me now what is the charge,
> For bedroom airy, clean and large.
> Where I can lay my weary head,
> Upon a soft and downy bed,
> And rise refreshed at morning light
> Resuming work with brisk delight.
>
> The host replied, 'I cannot say,
> Refreshment comes perhaps not that way;
> But still I think you'll like my bed
> To rest tonight your busy head.
> Refreshment does depend we find,
> Upon the state of health and mind.
> But as my charge is very small,
> It suits Commercials one and all.

This has a sprightly wit that reminds one of the jest with which Wordsworth once stunned his audience. But it is hardly characteristic of the poet's work. It is his prose that reveals the strain of comedy that ran strongly beneath the surface – not quite buried by the responsibilities of the Baptist, the temperance campaigner and the potato salesman. No one stimulated this side of Gwyer more effectively than his beloved colleague and hero, the Rev. C.H. Spurgeon. Spurgeon seems to have been a very successful preacher, and perhaps something more. At any rate we learn that he was accustomed to take a summer holiday in Mentone. He and Gwyer must have had many a good laugh together, as the following remarks of the poet so delightfully describe: 'He [Spurgeon] was a master of puns, but never of those which could injure and annoy. I

217

remember once, his taking me by the arm and leading me to the bottom of his garden at Westwood, and telling me how he came into possession of that house and grounds in a most curious way, indeed most remarkable, which I am not at liberty to relate here. Suffice it to say, it was a most wonderful providence, and I know Mr Spurgeon viewed it in that light. "The privacy of the place won my affections," and now he said, "what do you think; the builders are again making inroads upon our home as you see. They have begun to build at the bottom of our garden. I have purchased these plots so that they cannot build at the back of my garden. What do you think is best to be done to make it more private that people may not be looking over?" "Well," I said, "they all like you, so they all want to look at you, but I should advise you to plant some poplar trees in front of your plots, and they would grow up almost in a night like Jonah's gourd. They would be bare of leaves whilst you are enjoying your second summer at Mentone, and the trees would be richly covered with leaves to shield you and your beloved wife from the gaze of the public when you are at home. Moreover, Mr Spurgeon, you had better have some apple trees planted so that then you can walk among the apple trees of the wood." "You are a funny fellow Mr Gwyer," said he. "As if you were not of the same type," I replied. He received this joke with a hearty laugh, which all who knew him will realize.'

This is almost as good as the apt reply at the Temperance Hotel. The alert reader will have noticed, however, that while we are promised an example of the Reverend Spurgeon's inimitable puns, what we actually get is one of Gwyer's jokes, complete with the hearty laughter it provoked.

Elsewhere in his charming sketches of his life, Gwyer once again plays Boswell to the Rev. Spurgeon – only, by some almost undetectable but inevitable process, the roles get reversed during the narration of an anecdote; the upshot is always some modestly related sally by Gwyer which is greeted with respectful applause. Sometimes it does seem as if the great orator's admiration is tinged with irony. He is reported as remarking that if Gwyer could write poems as he sells potatoes, he would make a mark in the world. He congratulates him on his poem *On the Bulwarks of England* which, he says, recalls the work of Tennyson, and adds: 'How is it you wrote that, I consider it very good, the best I have seen of yours, by all means send it to Alfred' (meaning the then Poet Laureate). 'I stood up and asked Mrs S. to rub that little praise well in between my shoulder blades, as his praise like oil was running down my back delightfully. I turned and saw that his face shook with laughter, in which his two secretaries joined heartily, then he said "you know Mr Gwyer, I only say what I think, and by all means send it to Alfred."

Charles Spurgeon was certainly a power in the land, one of the most famous preachers of his age, for whom the enormous Metropolitan Tabernacle seating 6,000 was erected in the years 1859–61. The references to his two secretaries and summers in Mentone indicate that his labours for the faith were not entirely unprofitable, and one can well believe that he was on Christian name terms with the Laureate. Gwyer seems to have met him after the 1875 edition of his *Sketches and Poems*, and by 1896, when his second volume came out, he was able to exploit the connection with the great man, who was by then safely dead. The gold stamped rubric on the cover for this volume now runs as follows: *Sketches and Poems by the Penge Poet, with Anecdotes of and Personal Interviews with the Late Revd C.H. Spurgeon. Commended by Royalty.* This technique of puffing a book by association with the great is of course as old as publishing itself – (even so undeniably successful a writer as Barbara Cartland informs us in an author's note that *Love at the Helm* was written with assistance from Earl Mountbatten of Burma). The Penge Poet is unusual in that he is attempting at one and the same time to boost the sales of his book and of his potatoes. Thus it sometimes happens that the inspiration for some of his lines appears not to be exclusively poetic, which produces an electric charge of pleasurable surprise from an unexpected emphasis or image. In his didactic *Love and Matrimony,* for instance, the importance of potato skills in prospective brides is discreetly underlined with the use of capital letters:

Many lasses know home duties well, choose your wife from such
Can cook and roast a joint, POTATOES, or anything they touch.

Perhaps the subtlety of this was too refined to stimulate sales; at any rate his New Year's Medley begins shamelessly with

A happy New Year, my readers, to you
And a happy New Year, my customers too.
My hearty best thanks for favours received
But the future; yes, future orders I need.

(That is, for potatoes, not verses.)

The significance of the potato theme in Gwyer's work was not lost on contemporary critics. *Punch* wrote perceptively of his poem on *The Alexandra Palace, Muswell Hill, destroyed by Fire* as follows: 'We consider this poem no small potatoes. It has its merits, it has its faults, but so has the *Iliad*, and so has *Proverbial Philosophy*. But, as the ancient classic poet, Horace remarks:

"Where a thousand potatoes are mealy and white
To rage that a dozen are rotten, were spite." '

Apart from potatoes, in the promotion of which even Lord Shaftesbury's remarks on the vegetable are adduced, Gwyer has three other lines of sales patter: temperance, religion, and Bentley's Relish. The last named is largely accidental and arose from the fact that he was for a while a traveller in Messrs Bentley's products. Curiously there are no verses pushing corn, coal or manure, although he was for a while engaged in the distribution of these commodities as well. The interest in temperance dates from his conversion and reform after meeting a Methodist in Peckham. In his early days in the city, after leaving his Wiltshire village, he had been a prey to sin of various kinds, not least skittle playing, to which he was addicted. His poems on drink, such as *Touch Not, Taste Not*, do not have the power of a M'Donald Clarke or an Ella Wheeler Wilcox, but his didactic and ethical effusions are charming. *Love and Matrimony* has already been mentioned; it contains some of his happiest flights of fancy, such as the following lines which effect a moving reconciliation between the requirements of Love and those of Mammon:

The Electorate of Bridesmaids, it cannot be done without,
And very often another wedding it brings about,
River Congratulation we sail pleasantly along
While Land of Presents is sometimes found a mere song.

And there is sound advice too:

> . . . You will do well to have two bears and keep them in your
>   house,
> Both are tame and harmless and each quiet as a mouse,
> Bear and forbear are their right names, please do not them forget
> And if these daily are kept at work by husband and by wife
> It most surely will help to prevent a great deal of strife.

There can be little doubt that Gwyer knew what he was talking about. Towards the end of his autobiographical notes he makes the following pregnant observation: 'I have one of the best of wives, but we cannot see alike in the matter of my writings . . . I therefore have to write my simple lays and prose under great disadvantages, writing them mostly away from home, and many poems have been written in bed in the dark.' There may be some who hold that Milton's sonnet *On his Blindness* contains a more moving statement of artistic struggle than this, but if so they are marble-hearted.

Fourteen

ALFRED AUSTIN
1835–1913

Alfred the Little

A duller dinner never was devoured
  The dishes passed, the conversation flagged;
Mary by silent stupor was o'er powered,
  Dumb were her parents, even Hubert gagged.

from: The Human Tragedy

  Through these, through all I first did see,
    With me to share my raptures none,
  That nuptialled Monica would be
    My novice and companion.

from: The Door of Humility

Go away Death!
  You have come too soon
To sunshine and song I but just awaken,
And the dew on my heart is undried and
unshaken;
  Come back at noon.

from: Go Away Death, which might be
better titled: Too Early for the Appointment

  Then I fling the fisherman's flaccid corpse
  At the feet of the fisherman's wife.

from: The Wind

Margot Asquith to George Meredith: Well, Mr Meredith
  I wonder what your friend Alfred Austin thinks of his
  appointment [i.e., to the Laureateship].
Meredith (shaking his beautiful head): It is very hard to say
  what a bantam is thinking when it is crowing.

'WHETHER THIS, MY FIRST DASH INTO THE LISTS of public opinion, bring me plaudits or discomfiture,' wrote Alfred Austin in the Preface to his anonymously published *Randolph* (1854)[1], 'it will always mortify me that I was forbidden the chivalry of heralding my name. I must not raise my visor, unknown knight though I be.' Thus, with his very first literary utterances, Austin displayed two of the most salient characteristics of his character – vanity and pomposity. This romantic picture of himself as a chivalrous knight jousting in the lists of literature is one he seems to have retained for the whole of his career. Although the plaudits were, for the most part, noticeable by their absence, he does not seem to have been much afflicted by discomfiture. Other poets, as he was later to inform the public at some length in his critical essays, were not up to much, and the critics were ignoramuses. The best attitude towards them for a man of his calibre was one of lofty indifference: 'The author has no expectation,' he wrote in the Preface to *Interludes* (1872), 'that the contents of this little volume . . . will commend themselves to that esoteric circle which just now labours, under such conspicuousness, and for the moment not without success, to direct public opinion in matters of literature and art . . .' The 'esoteric circle' were those critics who were not impressed by the mixture of pretentiousness and incompetence which were the main components of Austin's work. Nor would the contents of *Interludes* have been likely to have changed their minds. *Lady Mabel*, for instance, contains many of those embarrassing touches so often found in Austin. The first stanza has an echo of Tennyson at his most excruciatingly coy, while the second attempts an evocation of romantic languor, as in Browning's *A Toccata of Galuppi's*:

1. It sold seventeen copies.

Side by side with Lady Mabel
    Sate I, with the sunshade down.
In the distance hummed the Babel
    Of the many footed town;
There we sat with looks unstable –
    Now of tenderness, of frown.

'Must we part? or may I linger?
    Wax the shadows, wanes the day.'
Then with voice of sweetest singer
    That hath all but died away,
'Go,' she said; but tightened finger
    Said articulately, 'Stay!'

Breast to breast with Lady Mabel,
    Shrouded by the courteous night,
Baffling all the forms of fable
    To describe our dreams aright . . .

Austin himself seems to have been impervious to embarrassment, and so must his readers be if they are to peruse his works with any degree of thoroughness. Even in the only poem from his pen which could be said to have enjoyed a modest success[1], there are passages of sentimentality that surpass the efforts of the worst amateur poets. The heroine of this satire is Blanche Darley, an innocent beauty who abandons her true lover and marries a dissipated aristocrat. The marriage is a disaster, and the faithful lover dies gloriously fighting the Tartars:

He asked a sword, and hurried to the fight;
Rang out the war-cry with a Spartan wont –
'Cravens to the rear! rough riders to the front!'
Stern to the last, stemmed triumph's torrent tide;
And if unconquering, unconquered died.

Austin was at this time still attempting the Byronic pose, but he seldom gets closer to his model than a few bungled imitations of the Byronic props and trappings. As for his women, they exhibit all the

1. *The Season – A Satire*, 1861.

most revolting features of the Victorian ideal, simpering goody-
goodies endowed with a purity and sweetness that would make even
Mills and Boon readers feel slightly sick. Nevertheless, Austin is
always careful to prescribe the roles of these beatified wonders, lest
we should mistakenly believe that their great qualities entitled them
to take any initiatives on their own account. Their function is simply to remind man of his better self, to be a steady beacon of virtue
in the storm-tossed seas of the masculine existence.[1] Blanche is an
early formulation of the type; Austin describes her living in the
countryside and patronizing the farmers' wives; when not thus
engaged, she indulges in grotesque frolics with the animals:

> Far in the wolds sequestered life she led,
> Fair and unfettered as the fawn she fed:
> Caressed the calves, coquetted with the colts,
> Bestowed much tenderness on turkey poults,
> Bullied the huge ungainly bloodhound pup,
> Tiffed with the terrier, coaxed to make it up:
> The farmers quizzed about the ruined crops,
> The fall of barley, and the rise of hops:
> Gave their wives counsel, but gave flannel too,
> Present where'er was timely deed to do.

The Human Tragedy (1862 and four later revisions) was a poem
which Austin took very seriously, and is remarkable for containing
a woman who actually sins (by sexually betraying her husband with
a former lover); but she dies immediately having done so. The other
lady in the poem is more in the Blanche mould:

> And yet she was a woman, – gently framed
> For loving purposes. The murderous snare
> She never set, nor barrel deadly-aimed
> At bird or beast consented she to bear.
> E'en in the fishers' net her hands disclaimed
> All helpful service; but when none was there,
> Oft she disported 'mong the timorous tribe,
> With fearless breast ploughing the brine aside.

1. For Austin's views on female suffrage *see* Chapter 6, footnote to pp. 143–4.

It is often hard to decide which is the more objectionable – Austin's matter or his manner. His verses are stiff and lifeless, replete with archness and affectation:

> Then would a freshet runnel cross their track,
> Low-purling to itself for secret bliss,
> Now pattering onwards, now half-turning back,
> To give the smooth round pebbles one more kiss.

Norton Crowell, who quotes these lines, further observes: 'The eighteenth century rarely sank below the level of these artificial figures: "the sentient veins' abounding tide", "the bearded herds", "mortal mould . . . filled with juice divine", "the sanguine flood", "the jocund juice", "a sharp-fanged messenger of death", "the lethal hail", "messengers of doom" and (for a train whistle) "the Promethean monster's strident scream". Even these venerable clichés, however, hardly prepare the reader for such archaisms as "kith", "gyves", "leal", "fardels", "moil", "eld", "meseems", "restiff", "whilom", "sooth", "yestreen", "ruth", and "hest".[1]

All of these, together with his other defects of taste, style, and prosody, are most startlingly on display in Austin's verse dramas. One reads through them with a mounting sense of disbelief. Surely he can't have been serious? But he was, for Austin did everything with the utmost seriousness; the worse the product, the more serious was he. He had even less sense of the dramatic form than Tennyson, but relentlessly churned out his pseudo-historical abortions. A leitmotiv can be observed running through most of these; the story is usually a variation of one in which a neo-Byronic brooding hero courts a virtuous girl. She must be unsullied by the hero's religious doubts, uncorrupted by the life of power, and in many other respects unbearable beyond belief. The most satisfying absurdities are to be found in *Fortunatus the Pessimist* (1892), whose characters consist of an atheistical English Duke (Fortunatus), his friend and secretary, called Adrian, Franklin, a yeoman, Urania, his daughter, April, a forest foundling, and Abaddon, a pedlar. Incredibly, the time is designated as *Today*; and the drama opens in the Duke's castle

---

1. Norton B. Crowell, *Alfred Austin: Victorian*, The University of New Mexico Press, 1953, p. 239.

where the locals are presenting petitions. The vicar humbly craves a
new lectern:

Fortunatus:	What! Is the old worn out?
	Time makes an end sometimes of uselessness.
Adrian:	No: stolen from its place. Some virtuoso,
	Some lover of archaic furniture,
	Fancied and filched it.
Fortunatus:	Give him then a new one,
	The fellow of the old, and none will steal it.
	Our unoriginal age collects the tools,
	Spoons, corals, papboats, bellows, thuribles,
	Of man's inventive childhood. Simple vicar!
	He is the veriest curio of them all,
	He, not the lectern; and he lives and thrives
	On this strange mania for the obsolete,
	Give lectern, rood-screen, pulpit, altar-rails,
	All, anything he wills.
Adrian:	The belfry gapes.
	At the last funeral-dirge the tiles slid down
	Albeit they tolled so gingerly.

This is not a promising beginning, but there is worse to come.
The next scene discovers the Duke, as Austin might well have put it,
in a brown study on horseback. He falls in with the pedlar Abaddon,
who is evidently modelled on Autolycus. Abaddon has a terrible
line in aphorisms – 'Decoy-ducks are not put in the larder' he
remarks bewilderingly; or: 'The Ivory Gate attracts many whom
golden portals would alarm and those of brass disgust.' Abaddon
describes to Fortunatus the bucolic life of Franklin and his daughter
Urania:

> He tends the kine; Urania brims the pail
> Coaxing the udders with her lissom fingers
> Sweet as the milk they drain . . .
> . . . A wimple on her head, and kirtled short
> She pegs the snow-white linen in the wind,
> And, singing back her way into the threshold
> Compounds the custard . . .

In Scene IV Fortunatus arrives at Franklin's garden, where he finds this female paragon singing a ditty as she goes about her womanly work:

> The stiff wain creaks 'neath the nodding wheat;
>   Flit, yaffel, flit from tree to tree. [*sic*][1]
> The babe is hushed on its mother's teat,
> And the acorn drops at your dreaming feet,
>   Flit, yaffel, flit from tree to tree.
> The whimpering winds have lost their way,
>   Scream, yaffel, scream from tree to tree . . . etc.

Fortunatus is captivated by this recital ('Like to a covert nightingale she nests'), and introduces himself. Urania hospitably relieves him of his horse:

> What an equerry!
> She placed her hand upon the bridle rein
> With such a gentle empery, I could
> Not help depute my duty to her will.

However good an equerry she may be, Urania's conversation makes one's head ache:

> The early roses
> Pinched by pernicious visitings of March
> This year will blossom tardily.

'Do you not find,' she asks with excruciating politeness,

> Nature's unpunctuality retrieves
> Our too precise forebodings, filling up
> All disappointing vacancies with gifts
> Not reckoned in our calendar?

---

1. It has been remarked elsewhere (see Chapter 6) that Austin was obsessed with breasts, teats, udders, nipples, etc. A 'yaffel' (correctly 'yaffle') is a green woodpecker.

Franklin appears and shows Fortunatus round the house, while Urania and the orphan April set off for the village to do good works. In Scene V Urania dreams of Fortunatus, and in Scene VI Fortunatus dreams of Urania. He also talks in his sleep, complaining that the word 'Love' does not rhyme with 'Urania', which is one of those little culs-de-sac that poets are always running into. Act II opens with Abaddon arriving at Franklin's cottage. He has come to sell Urania some sexy underwear, but she is not that sort of a girl. Indeed, she is enraged at the very idea of a padded bra:

> And do they wear that lubricating lie,
> That fleshless falsehood! Palpitating maids
> Puff themselves out with hollow buxomness,
> To lead some breathless gaby at their heels
> A scentless paper-chase!

She buys a simple little Laura Ashley number instead. Fortunatus arrives for the haymaking. Urania gives him the picnic basket, which includes an edition of Horace that Franklin likes to read in his lunch hour. After the haymaking, Fortunatus dines with Franklin and discusses philosophical matters with him, such as the nature of 'Love':

> Lust borrows the vocabulary of Love,
> And masquerades romantically till
> Day doffs the domino [sic].

After dinner there is a romantic scene between the Duke and Urania at the garden gate in the moonlight. Here, a difficulty arises. It appears that the lady is betrothed, possibly to Nature itself. This is unwelcome news to her noble suitor, who decides to consult Abaddon about it. Abaddon in turn consults his glowworms as to who will win Urania, and they signal a favourable report on Fortunatus' chances. Meanwhile, back at the cottage, it is revealed that Franklin was really Duke Fortunatus all along, but gave up the title and opted for the simple life. Hence the edition of Horace in the picnic basket. Act III finds Urania in the garden as usual. Fortunatus gallops up to inform her that *he* is April's father – this fact having been communicated to him by Abaddon. Urania remarks that she is currently reading a book by Fortunatus, and April dies of a fever. Scene I of Act IV takes place in the Duke's castle, where the local glee clubs, composed of mowers, shepherds, etc., are singing their ditties. In Scene II Fortunatus and Urania lay flowers on April's grave, and he compliments her on her gardening. And here the play comes to an abrupt halt, as if the author had suddenly got bored of it, leaving an unresolved mess like a building project that has run out of money.

The rest of Austin's weird verse dramas contain similarly unbelievable characters, fatuous plots, and extended passages of imbecility. The reader not infrequently finds himself rubbing his eyes and going through a speech again to see if he has read it correctly; but studying Austin is a grimly fascinating task, and certainly never boring. '*Semper aliquid novi*' – in every work a new height of absurdity scaled, a new depth plumbed. *Prince Lucifer* (1887) not only has a chorus consisting of *The Matterhorn*, *The Weisshorn* and *The Visp-Thal Torrent* (something not even *The Sound of Music* attempted), but also a philosophical grave-digger, who is by no means as witty as the one in *Hamlet*:

> Men are like moles, Sir; when they go below,
> They do disturb the earth; though whether they
> Come up for air sometimes when no one looks
> What man shall say?

This gentleman has also discovered that death rules all, and repeats the fact at regular intervals, together with the observation that grave-digging is a particularly secure form of employment. *The Tower of Babel* (1874) again features the brooding unbeliever hero, this time Aran, the chief architect of the tower. The conversations between Peleg (a priest) and Eber (an astrologer) regarding the tower are beyond parody:

> . . . To Heaven its whorls ascending delicate,
> And Heaven perchance will condescend to lift
> Some feathers off your fardels.

There are also some enjoyable exchanges between the spirit Afrael, and Noema (Mrs Aran). She explains to Afrael that the idea

230

of the tower is to provide a ladder for mortals to climb up to Heaven. He sagaciously points out that it might not emerge at the top in the right place ('. . . 'twill fly wide/There's so much room to miss') – a drawback which had not occurred to the architects. The author, supplying his by now habitual comments on his own genius in the Preface, remarks that he makes no apology for anachronisms in the piece 'seeing that they are countenanced by the uniform practice of the highest dramatic authority'. Some of the anachronisms appear to be unintentional, however, as when Afrael tenderly says to Noema:

> 'Forgotten thou! not till the stars forget
> To change their watches at the appointed hour:
> Not till the sun, to suck into himself
> The froward comet's trail disorderly . . .' etc.

Leszko The Bastard, Savonarola, England's Darling (*see* Chapter 1): Austin was nothing if not industrious. It is astonishing that such diligence could have produced such uniformly poor results, but since he had no eye for quality and no sense of the ridiculous, he naturally failed to notice that anything was wrong. Even his successful prose works, *The Garden That I Love* and *Lamia's Winter Quarters*, are intolerably affected, an aspect of the Laureate that was amusingly exposed by E.V. Lucas and C.L. Graves in *Punch*:

I found Mr Austin at work in his study at Swinford Old Manor – a charming snug apartment with *Walker's Rhyming Dictionary* on the shelves. He extended a welcoming hand.

'Yes,' he said, 'I do most of my work here. *England's Darling* was written in that arm-chair: the holes in the leather were made while I was thinking of the next line. Ah, the next line – that is at once the poet's triumph and his tragedy! I would not have it re-upholstered for worlds . . . By the way, when I wrote *England's Darling* I wore woad, and the cook had orders to be continually burning cakes – it seemed to give the atmosphere.

'*The Garden That I Love* was composed in the window seat commanding a view of the geraniums. Ah! Sweet Nature – what an influence! What an inspiration! She is the best padding . . .

'And now,' said Mr Austin . . . 'if you must go' (although I had still plenty of time before me and had made no movement) 'allow me to offer you a stirrup-cup of Malmsey.'

He produced a beaker and filled it to the brim.

'Notice,' he said, in that incorrigibly poetic way of his, 'how the beaded bubbles wink.'

Thus fortified, I tore myself away, feeling that I, too, had dwelt in Arcadia.

So much abuse was heaped on Austin during his lifetime that one or two people felt obliged to put in a word for him, if only to redress the balance a little. For example, Ambrose Bierce made the entirely reasonable observation that a poet should be judged by his best work and not by his worst. The trouble is, even Austin's best work is pretty dire, and the few conventional Victorian lyrics that were included in earlier near-contemporary anthologies, largely, one suspects out of politeness, have disappeared from most modern ones. It is hard to work up much sympathy for him as a man or as a poet. Just when one is beginning to do so out of natural distaste for the spectacle of a friendless dolt being mercilessly whipped, one's eye is caught by yet another Malvoliesque performance of the Laureate, and all sympathy evaporates:

To have the esteem of the estimable, without cultivating an uneasy desire for the praise of those who are perhaps scarcely qualified to confer it, ought to content every sensible writer; and no one has had, and is daily accorded, quite enough admiration from those who are themselves admired to satiate the self-love which must be more or less the portion of all frail mortals, and to satisfy the more worthy, the more dignified, and the more discriminating ambition of which no man need be ashamed . . .

. . . an appointment . . . was made some four or five years ago by the sovereign of these realms on the recommendation of her chief minister, who doubtless acted in conformity with what he believed to be the preponderant genuine literary opinion of his fellow countrymen . . .[1]

1. i.e. the Laureateship. The extract is from *The Poet Laureate Defends Himself*, Critic XXXVII November 1900, reprinted in Norton Crowell, op. cit., p. 27.

These are the self-satisfied tones of the man who deprecated Tennyson in print (but was obsequious towards him in private), announced that Browning was not a poet at all, and placed himself at 'the head of English Literature'; a man whose bellicose jingoism and distaste for democracy could embarrass even Conservatives, who regarded Dr Jameson as a hero and who assumed that women were unfit to have the vote; and a man, finally, who attempted to inflict on the public more reams of execrable poetry than dozens of genuine poets, and who imagined he was furnishing the materials for the literary tombstone to be erected by posterity. The reality was somewhat different, and the best comment on Alfred Austin's grotesque pretensions, which might also appropriately be inscribed on his actual tombstone, was made by the *Critic* in its January 1896 issue. 'The report that Alfred Austin was to be Lord Tennyson's successor in the laureateship has been confirmed' wrote an anonymous correspondent. '. . . Mr Austin has been a prolific writer, but at sixty he has made but little reputation as a poet. One thing, however, he has in common with his predecessor: his Christian name. Tennyson has occasionally been called Alfred the Great. He will be called so oftener hereafter.'

Fifteen

JOAQUIN MILLER
1841–1913

A charlatan from the West

'Aye, now, poetry won't do. Poetry won't do, don't you know.'

> John Murray the Third, after being approached by
> Joaquin Miller, who hoped he would publish his verses.

. . . and some of the verse that earned Miller a place
in the school anthologies:

> They sailed. They sailed. Then spoke the mate:
> This mad sea shows his teeth tonight.
> He curls his lip, he lies in wait,
> He lifts his teeth as if to bite.
> Brave Adm'r'l, say but one good word:
> What shall we do when hope is gone?
> The words leapt like a leaping sword:
> 'Sail on! Sail on! Sail on! And on.'

> from: *Columbus* (1896)

JOAQUIN MILLER, ELOQUENT POSEUR and self-styled literary lion, was determined to be the hero of his own colourful imaginings, and had the satisfaction of seeing this wish largely fulfilled. He wrote a poem about the swashbuckling General William Walker, who had led an expedition to Nicaragua; and after a while he convinced himself that he had actually been 'With Walker in Nicaragua'. He also came to believe that he had taken part in the battle of Castle Crags (1855) against the Shasta Indians; but this belief had no more substance than George IV's fancy that he was a combatant at Waterloo. In later life (when he remembered) he would walk with a limp, the result (as he told a respectful audience of admirers) of a wound received at the Pit River battle against the Modocs. According to which stage of his creative autobiography Miller had reached, this was either described as a bullet wound (meaning he fought on the side of the Modocs) or an arrow wound (meaning he fought with the white men). Latterly, he settled for the arrow, but neither version cut any ice with Ambrose Bierce, who pointed out that Miller 'sometimes limps with the wrong leg'.

As a matter of fact, like many people who cannot resist embroidering their experiences, Miller did lead a remarkable, and occasionally heroic existence; but to a man of his temperament, the exact details were seldom satisfying enough: when someone told him that Byron desired to be King of Greece less than he desired to be thought the hero of his wildest poems, he thought: 'We are of accord.'[1] Byron, indeed, had a fatal attraction for the aspirant poet, who wanted to be known as 'the American Byron', and whose stock did eventually rise to the point where he was hailed the 'Byron of

1. A note in Miller's hand following *The Bride of Abydos* in the Best Edition of Byron's works confirms this. See Martin Severin Peterson – *Joaquin Miller. Literary Frontiersman*, Stanford and Oxford, 1937.

Oregon'. This homespun version of the English genius began his career, writes C.T. Kindilien, as one who 'would dramatize his own life in an exotic and picturesque world. Against the background of the Sierras, Death Valley, Nicaragua or the Amazon river, he set one strong man and one large-breasted woman and turned them loose to a variety of romantic adventurous stimulants.'[1] The process of self-dramatization began with empty bombastic poetry, and ended with autobiographical fiction.

The legend that Miller cultivated when he came to England was a vigorously hyped version of his early life in the West. There, he lived with an Indian woman whom he claimed was the daughter of a Shasta Indian Chief. For a whole year he went 'native', 'throwing away his clothes and wearing instead a soft doeskin suit and moccasins. He supplied the Indians with game, being a good shot (in his diary Joaquin claims he saw a three-year-old elk "standing across the river about 280 yards off" and then, bang, and the animal dropped dead), but most of the time he lolled about like a true brave while the women did all the work.'[2] By this lady he had a daughter named Cali-Shasta, who is supposed to have been beautiful and talented. Her mother was perhaps not so distinguished; at any rate J.H. Beadle, who visited her after she had taken up with a Mr Brock described her as coming from the Diggers, a lowly Indian tribe. 'I should say a man must needs be very crazy to live with one of them,' he wrote uncharitably. 'Their chief luxury is dried and tainted salmon and the sight and smell of most of them would turn the stomach of any other than a poet.'[3] After this romantic interlude, Miller continued to work his way across the country living off his wits; in true Wild West style he was imprisoned for horse-stealing, escaped, and was subsequently involved in a shoot out while resisting arrest. He went in for gold prospecting and newspaper editing, without any conspicuous success. He married an alleged poetess, Minnie Theresa Dyer (whom Miller called 'Minnie Myrtle'), having originally seen her verses in a newspaper. Miller arrived at her home for the first time on a Thursday and brought her to the altar the follow-

---

1. C.T. Kindilien, *American Poetry in the Eighteen Nineties*, Providence, Rhode Island, 1956, p. 43.
2. M.M. Marberry, *Splendid Poseur – The Story of a Fabulous Humbug*, London, 1954, pp. 38–9.
3. M.M. Marberry, op cit., p. 40.

ing Sunday. He became a lawyer and, then, incredibly, a judge. But all this activity was as nothing to his real ambition to be a poet, and in the 1860s he began to make serious attempts to break into literature.

His first slim volume, repulsively entitled *Specimens*, was brought out in an edition of 500 copies in 1868, priced at a dollar. Business was not brisk and the price was slashed to 50 cents after a few weeks. His second offering, *Joaquin et al* (1869), concerned the deeply unappealing Mexican outlaw Joaquin Murrieta, another of Miller's heroes[1] (the poet changed his original name of 'Cincinnatus' to 'Joaquin' as part of the identification process). Apart from a kindly notice by Bret Harte in *Overland Monthly*, this too was ignored; so a year later he decided to go to San Francisco and to become a literary lion. Arriving at the quayside he was met by Harte's associate, Charles Stoddard; Miller clambered out of the steerage 'dressed in a white linen duster, a broad sombrero and moccasins. His first words to Stoddard were: "Well, let us go and talk with the poets," ' – but unfortunately none were available.[2]

In San Francisco Ina Coolbrith (the 'Sappho of the Western Sea') took him in hand and explained the basics of poetic technique, which was in those days considered a prerequisite for the writing of verse. A year later he made his momentous decision to seek fortune and fame in England, and accordingly set off after equipping himself with a wreath to be laid on Byron's grave. New York was a little disappointing, as both Horace Greeley and Beecher refused to meet him, having no idea who he was. Only a little daunted, the poet set off for Britain in the summer of 1870.

He arrived in Scotland and immediately began a literary pilgrimage with a visit to Burns' grave. Thence he proceeded to Melrose Abbey, intending to commune with the shade of Walter Scott. Unfortunately, the drunken old lady who looked after the cemetery forgot that she had let him in, and went off with Miller's half-crown in her pocket having locked the front gates. The unfortunate poet spent a miserable night amongst the tombstones as the freezing fog

1. Of Joaquin Murrieta (c. 1832–53) the *Dictionary of American Biography* remarks: 'By Latin-American writers and by Bancroft he has been invested with a considerable degree of romantic glamour, but the probability is that he was a ruffian, brutal, avaricious and lawless.'
2. Martin Severin Peterson, op. cit.

237

crept up from the Tweed and enveloped him in the darkness. By 25 September, however, he had arrived at Byron's grave with his wreath. His interesting attire had attracted a knot of curious onlookers who were somewhat startled when he burst out with the words: 'O my poet. Worshipped where the world is glorious with the fire and blood of youth. Yet here is your home – ah well.'

The caretaker was given a sovereign, with the promise of a further one each year, to keep Miller's wreath nailed above the tablet in the church; but this arrangement apparently attracted adverse comment from the locals, who were possibly not as proud of their famous son as they should have been. The next stop was London, which he approached on foot, passing by a place where (he was told) Carlyle had once lived. 'Joaquin briskly composed an ode to be delivered at the author's grave. This unfortunately was a wasted poetic effort, for he was informed that Carlyle was very much alive.'[1] Naturally Miller at once applied to see the splenetic sage, and in due course received the now predictable rebuff.

Miller seems to have suffered from culture shock when he first arrived in London, where the natives' behaviour was scarcely less curious than that of the Digger Indians. In particular he had difficulty in adjusting to that unprepossessing institution, the English pub. In *Memorie and Rime*, he recalls his experience of it with some indignation: 'A public house here is not a tavern or an inn. I tried to get to stop at two or three of these reeking gin-mills. They stared at me, but went on jerking beer behind the counter, and did not answer. At one place I asked for water. All stopped and looked at me – women with great mugs of beer half way to their brutal big red mouths; a woman with a baby in one arm, wrapped tightly in a shawl along with herself, and a jug of beer in the other, came up and put her face in mine curiously; then the men all roared . . . I did not get the water. I now learn that one must not ask for water here. No one drinks water here. No public-house keeps it. Well, to one from Oregon, the land of pure water, where God pours it down from the snowy clouds out of the hollow of His hand – the high-born, beautiful, great white rain, this seems strange . . .'[2] It is hard not to sympathize with Miller as the protagonist of this Batemanesque scene – 'The man who asked for water in an English pub' – especi-

1. M.M. Marberry, op. cit., p. 78.
2. Joaquin Miller, *Memorie and Rime*, London, 1884, p. 20.

ally when one considers that the average pub was probably an even more disgusting establishment in 1870 than it is now. Nor can one help admiring the sheer persistence of the would-be poet, whose thick skin, allied to an eye for the main chance, ultimately brought him the rewards he longed for.

The success of 'Joaquin' Miller in England was largely due to his relentless self-promotion. Nowadays, any charlatan can shift a few books with the help of some judicious 'plugs' on radio and television; but in Miller's day the techniques were limited to exposure in the literary reviews and attendance at the parties of influential London hostesses. He excelled at the latter, appearing in a 'sombrero, red shirt open at the neck, flowing scarf and sash, trousers tucked into spurred boots, long hair down over his shoulders, and a great blond beard.'[1] He smoked three cigars at once and bit the ankles of debutantes in Mayfair drawing-rooms. This, surely, was the real McCoy, the man from the Wild West as everyone imagined him to be. Miller himself was unsentimental about his performances, remarking cynically: 'It helps to sell the poems, boys. And it tickles the duchesses.'

And indeed the poems did sell. Although his works were (rightly) spurned by the publishers at the beginning (and Miller tells us that he actually shook his fist at John Murray – once he was safely outside the publisher's office in Albemarle Street), the success of *Pacific Poems* (1871) changed all that. He published it privately, and its 'barbaric bombast thus took the critics unawares'[2]; overnight all doors were opened to him. Longmans now brought out what became his most famous volume, the *Songs of the Sierras*. He met Swinburne, and Theodore Watts-Dunton seems to have taken him under his wing. 'He would express his astonishment, wherever he went, at Watts-Dunton's profound knowledge of the art of poetry. "It's amazin'," he would exclaim. "He seems to know everything about poetry that was ever written, and much more. And here am I, a poet with a big name, and I'm darned if I could tell the difference between a hexameter and a pentameter, to save my scalp."'[3]

1. Quoted in Julian Hawthorne's memoirs of London Life.
2. C.T. Kindilien, op. cit., p. 42.
3. *The Life and Letters of Theodore Watts-Dunton* ed. Hake and Compton-Rickett, London, 1916, p. 128. Miller's idea of rhyme was sometimes as original as his approach to metre; his most engaging coup was to rhyme 'Goethe' with 'teeth'.

The influence of Swinburne on Miller's work was as detrimental as the influence of Byron on his personality. Swinburne's manner was fatally easy to imitate, and Miller at once proceeded to do so. In *Shadows of Shasta* he warbles sentimentally of:

> Sounds sweet as the voice of a singer
> Made sacred with sorrows unsaid
> And a love that implores me to linger
> For the love of dead days and their dead.

'Like Yeats,' remarks Miller's biographer tolerantly, 'he did not insist on his poems *meaning* anything'; but this heroic restraint is a good deal less impressive in the work of Miller than it is in the work of Yeats. It is a bold man who would compare the following lines of Miller's about Oregon, with even the feeblest of Yeats' lyrics:

> 'Tis a land so far that you wonder whether
> E'en a God would know it should you fall down dead;
> 'Tis a land so far through the wilds and weather,
> That the sun falls weary and flushed and red, –
> That the sea and the sky seem coming together,
> Seem closing together as a book that is read:

> Oh, the nude weird West, where an unnamed river
> Rolls restless in bed of bright silver and gold;
> Where white flashing mountains flow rivers of silver
> As a rock of the desert flowed fountains of old;
> By a dark wooded river that calls to the dawn,
> And makes mouths at the sea with his dolorous swan:

Whether the gods take more or less notice if one drops down dead in Oregon, as opposed to Palmers Green, is hardly a profitable matter for speculation. The 'nude West', the river busily making mouths and the redundant, albeit 'dolorous', swan are the characteristic trappings of Miller's verse. Too often it is begrimed with tawdry jewels, studded with spectacular vulgarities, and larded with histrionic affectation. 'Nude' is a typical Miller misfire, and he uses it on other occasions with similarly unfortunate results: the animal described in the following lines aspires to be sensual and malevolent, like the panther in Swinburne's *Laus Veneris*; but exposure to the Miller treatment produces a different effect altogether:

The nude black boar through abundant grass
Stole down to the water and buried his nose,
And crunched white teeth till the bubbles arose
As white and as bright as are globes of glass.

'Nature for Miller was essentially drama, sometimes melodrama,' explains Peterson; but in Miller's poetry it often seems
nearer to comedy; the 'nude black boar', crunching and bubbling,
evokes memories of a day at the zoo rather than an encounter in the
wilds. Sometimes the animals are merely the backcloth to the poet's
empty posturing, the whole effect being that of heavily watered-
down Swinburne:

In the place where the grizzly reposes
Under peaks where a right is a wrong,
I have memories richer than roses,
Sweet echoes more sweet than a song.

'It is not difficult to write nonsense verses in this metre,' commented J.A. Symonds when reviewing these lines from *Songs of the
Sunlands*; but his voice was one of only a few to be raised in protest.

Meanwhile the personable poseur continued to take London by
storm. Lord Houghton, a contemporary Maecenas of poets, began
to invite him to his famous breakfast parties. It was at Houghton's
house that he encountered Lillie Langtry who recalls the occasion
amusingly in her memoirs:

After dinner there was the usual reception, and presently (my
host) led up to me a very tall, lean man with a pale intellectual
face, yellow hair so long that it lay in curls about his shoulders,
a closely cropped beard, and a dreamy expression in his light
eyes. I don't remember what he wore, except that it was
unconventional. He was so new and strange, that his apparel,
whatever it was, seemed to complete the picture. After a while
he disappeared from the group surrounding me, and at the end
of the evening he returned and read me from a torn sheet of
paper the following verse:

To The Jersey Lily

If all God's world a garden were
And women were but flowers,
If men were bees that busied there
Through endless summer hours,
O, I would hum God's gardens through
For honey till I came to you.

When he had finished it, he added with a dramatic gesture:
'Let this verse stand; it's the only one I ever wrote to a living
woman.'

One can see why Miller was popular with the ladies. The poet
followed this up with an even more extravagant gesture when he
next encountered the actress: 'Two or three evenings later' (she
writes) 'I went to a concert at Lady Brassey's, who had not long
returned from a world's tour with Lord Brassey in the *Sunbeam*, and
at the foot of the broad staircase of the house stood Joaquin Miller.
He seemed to be waiting for me, and as I walked upstairs to greet
my hostess, he backed before me, scattering rose leaves, which he
had concealed in his broad sombrero, upon the white marble steps,
and saying with fervour: "Thus be your path in life." '[1]
Until quite late in his career, Miller found his American com-
patriots considerably less susceptible to his performances, literary
or social, than the gullible British. On one occasion he arrived at a
London dinner where Mark Twain and some other American
literati were also present; Miller strode in sporting round his shoulders the shaggy bearskin which was his latest party stunner. The
Americans paid no attention. Frustrated, the poet flung himself into
a chair and clapped his hand to his brow, occasionally raising his
head to stare wildly at the assembled company. The Americans continued calmly to spoon their soup. Finally, Miller suddenly stood up
and plucked out a goldfish that was swimming innocently round its
bowl in the middle of the table, and swallowed it whole. Mark
Twain glanced up, raised his eyebrows very slightly, and went on
eating.

1. Lillie Langtry, *The Days I Knew*, New York, 1925, pp. 96–7.

After a while even the Sloane Rangers of the day began to tire of their toy poet. Miller had to redouble his efforts to thrill and disconcert the company. Sometimes he would squat abruptly on the ground and chant an old Indian song that he used to sing 'when the Modocs adopted him as their chief'; on other occasions he would arrive, pause as his name was announced long enough for his outlandish garb to draw all eyes, then march to a corner and sit with his back to the company absorbed in a book. At length this whole performance was refined to a dramatic *acte de présence*, whereby he would appear at the doorway, coldly survey the assembled guests for a minute, before turning on his heel and vanishing, as if such a rabble had affronted his poetic sensibilities. Calculated rudeness does tend to diminish the supply of dinner invitations, and Miller soon discovered that he had ridden this particular gravy train as far as it would run. Moreover, even the duchesses began to suspect that there was something a bit phoney about his poetry.

For most of his career the Americans had been pretty sceptical about Miller's literary talent and even more sceptical about his exploits. Unfortunately, as gentility increases in a stabilizing society, so does the appetite for sentimentalized ruggedness and glamorized tough guys. It was this craving, to which Hollywood was later to respond with an unending stream of kitsch movies, that Miller successfully milked in the latter part of his life. In the 1890s he set up shop as a literary sage and primitive philosopher at Oakland, California. Here he 'opened his literary sideshow to all visitors, with himself as the chief exhibit; he continued to turn out novels, poems, plays, several versions of his autobiography; and he kept his jug of corn whiskey handy under his bed to sharpen the fading outlines of his incongruous life . . . when he discovered early that he had a good thing, he put off any marks of polish, and undertook a program of posturing and self-aggrandisement that would make him a replica of his own hero. The story of the lie he tried to live in his final years makes more interesting reading than the lie he passed off as romantic poetry.'[1] This analysis of Kindilien's is not the whole truth about Miller: he does seem to have taken part in many exciting events, and not always discreditably. It was characteristic of him to be so moved by his experiences when covering the Boxer rebellion in China as a

1. C.T. Kindilien, op. cit., pp. 43–4.

journalist, that he espoused the cause of the downtrodden Chinese and Japanese minorities in California. He also defended the interests of Indian tribes on more than one occasion. The real trouble was that he became, like many before and since, a victim of his own propaganda. Some of this seems to have rubbed off on the critical establishment in America, and after his death one even finds an academic writing that he was 'the greatest poet the West has yet produced'. Miller would have agreed with this. After the success of *Songs of the Soul* (1896) he gravely observed of himself: 'Yes, I think I am not only an American poet, but *the* American poet.' Following the publication of the *Complete Works* (1907) the old rogue happily declined into a celebrated and mendacious old age, a typically American monument to the higher bogusness – the Carl Sandburg of his day.

Sixteen

MRS JULIA A. MOORE
1847–1920
The Sweet Singer of Michigan

Remember never to judge people by their clothes,
For our brave noble Washington said,
'Honorable are rags if a true heart they inclose,'
And I found it was the truth when I married.

from: *Roll on Time*

When Mr Dennis does well play,
His courage is full great,
And accidents to him occur,
But not much though, of late.

from: *The Grand Rapids Cricket Club*

She knows not that it was her son,
His coffin could not be opened –
It might be someone in his place,
For she could not see his noble face.

from: *William Upson*

'Julia is worse than a Gatling gun; I have counted
twenty-one killed and nine wounded in the small
volume she has given to the public.'

Bill Nye

'I HAVE BEEN READING THE POEMS of Mrs Julia A. Moore, again,' writes Mark Twain in *Following The Equator*, 'and I find in them the same grace and melody that attracted me when they were first published, twenty years ago, and have held me in happy bonds ever since. "The Sentimental Song Book" has long been out of print, and has been forgotten by the world in general, but not by me.' And he adds that it has for him the same charm as *The Vicar of Wakefield* – 'the touch that makes an intentionally humorous episode pathetic and an intentionally pathetic one funny.'[1]

When Julia's first book – *The Sweet Singer of Michigan Salutes the Public* – was published in 1876, it was widely noticed, and achieved a *succès d'estime* overnight. The critics, without exception, agreed that Mrs Moore's was a unique talent – uniquely awful in her muddled syntax, her tin ear and her capacity for sustained bathos. Satirized as Emmeline Grangerford in *Huckleberry Finn*, her method of production is described by Huck in terms that must have been horribly near the truth: 'Buck said she could rattle off poetry like nothing. She didn't even have to stop to think. He said she would slap down a line, and if she couldn't find anything to rhyme with it she would just scratch it out and slap down another one, and go ahead. She warn't particular; she could write about anything you choose to give her to write about just so it was sadful. Every time a man died, or a woman died, or a child died, she would be on hand with her "tribute" before he was cold. She called them tributes. The neighbors said it was the doctor first, then Emmeline, then the undertaker – the undertaker never got in ahead of Emmeline but once, and then she hung fire on a rhyme for the dead person's name, which was Whistler. She wasn't ever the same after that; she never complained, but she kind of pined away and did not live long.'[2]

1. Mark Twain, *Following the Equator*, Chapter XXXVI.
2. Mark Twain, *The Adventures of Huckleberry Finn*, Thomas Nelson, pp. 138–9.

Julia's attitude to her critics was robust. On one occasion she was invited to give a reading of her work at Grand Rapids, but soon realized that something was amiss: 'Her most flowery passages were greeted with howls and hoots of uproarious laughter.' Eventually she stopped reading and said to the audience: 'You people have paid fifty cents to see a fool: I've been paid fifty dollars to look at a house full of them.'[1] When she published her follow-up volume to *The Sentimental Song Book* in 1878, the title page was adorned with a quotation from Byron:

> As soon
> Seek roses in December, – ice in June:
> Hope constancy in wind, or corn in chaff,
> Believe a woman, or an epitaph,
> Or any other thing that's false, before
> You trust in Critics.

(Evidently she believed it was worth stomaching the casual insult to her sex for the sake of the greater insult to the critics.) Included in this volume – indeed, they constitute the bulk of it – are what she describes as 'Reviews and Commendatory Notices' of its predecessor. Amongst these there is complete unanimity, and Julia seems to have taken every word literally; her capacity for overlooking ridicule is therefore as much to be wondered at as her incapacity to stumble, even by chance, on a form of words that would make an acceptable line of verse. *The Rochester Democrat* concludes a long review of coruscating irony with the following words, which the 'Sweet Singer' complacently reprints: 'We never felt the inadequacy of an ordinary newspaper as we do to-day. We should like to coerce the entire pamphlet, but space forbids. We are obliged to drop Julia A. Moore right here, crushing a flood of the best emotions of the human heart back into our true inwardness and hiding the light of our countenance for many consecutive moments in the soothing but most unsatisfactory bandana handkerchief. Nothing like this book has ever before been printed. William Shakespeare, could he read it, would be glad that he was dead; and as for Bryant, Whittier, Longfellow, and a number of other venerable poets, their

1. Quoted in Jack Loudan, O *Rare Amanda! – The Life of Amanda McKittrick Ros*, Chatto & Windus, 1954.

gray hair must inevitably go down with sorrow to the grave. If Julia
A. Moore would kindly deign to shed some of her poetry on our
humble grave, we should be but too glad to go out and shoot ourselves tomorrow.'

The 'Reviews and Commendatory Notices' are quite something
– and often rather more fun than the 'Sweet Singer's' poetry itself.
The Connecticut Courant, which headed its review with the words: 'A
Gifted Poet', and possibly thus misled the authoress or her publisher into thinking the piece would pass muster as an endorsement,
began by reprinting in full the letter her publisher had sent with the
review copies:

Cleveland, O. October 1877.

Dear Sir

Having been honored by the gifted lady of Michigan, in
being entrusted with the publication of her poems, I give
myself the pleasure of handing you a copy of the same,
with my respectful compliments.

It will prove a health lift to the overtaxed brain; it *may*
divert the despondent from suicide. It should enable the
reader to forget the 'stringency', and guide the thoughts
into pleasanter channels.

It opens a new lead in literature, and is sure to carry the
conviction.

It *must* be productive of good to humanity.

If you have the good of your fellow creatures at heart,
and would contribute your mite towards putting them in
the way to finding this little volume, the thanks of a
grateful people (including authoress and publisher) would
be yours.

If a sufficient success should attend the sale of this work,
it is our purpose to complete the Washington monument.

Very truly yours,

J.F. RYDER.

The literary editor of *The Connecticut Courant* must have found it
hard to resist such an eloquent appeal to his better nature. Perhaps
the selfless patriotism of the authoress' gesture regarding the Washington monument tipped the balance. At any rate, he gave the book

plenty of space, beginning with a few observations of a personal nature: 'It seems to us – though we are not judges of beauty – that the "Sweet Singer", the gifted One, has made a mistake in printing her portrait in this volume. It gives us a notion that she might build the Washington monument with her own hands, but it knocks our ideas – if we may use such an expression – of a poetess. We should say that the picture represented the effects of the Magnolia Balm upon the head of a discontented parricide. To be sure the hair is arranged on top in the form of a crown, and thence flows in Magnolia masses about the shoulders, but the broad face with its wide mouth wears a look of painful surprise at its situation. We are sure that this wretched wood-cut does Julia A. Moore great injustice; for no one could write these poems who was not as beautiful as the poetry. And the volume is evidence not only of the loveliness but the heroism of the poet. She is the first poetess so far as we know who has been willing to tell her age; usually you cannot discover the age of a poetess in the biographical dictionary. They live to us in the bloom of perpetual youth. But Julia A. tells us, in what minstrels would call her "opening lode" that

> My parents moved to Algoma
> Near twenty-five years ago,
> And bought one hundred acres of land,
> That's a good-sized farm you know.

If we add this information to that contained in the preface, which says that she lived ten years in Plainfield before going to Algoma, we find our author's age to be thirty-three, and that she is consequently in the full maturity of her genius. These poems are not the crude early crop of genius, but the matured fruit. We may expect nothing better; and nothing worse.

> His parents parted when he was small
> And both are married again.
> 'Tis said his father's second wife
> That she did not use him well.

> He was a small boy of his age,
> When he was five years or so,
> Was shocked by lightning while to play
> And it caused him not to grow.

Struck by lightning himself and his parents divorced, it is no wonder that he withdrew at fifteen, as he did to the tune of 'Three Grains of Corn' . . .

The most effusive tribute to Julia's talents is printed at the head of the reviews and comes from a Mr Peirce, Chairman of the Committee of the Board of Education in Grand Rapids. The poetess and her publisher might be pardoned for not suspecting any irony from such a source, and the first paragraph of his letter is entirely innocent of any undertow of irreverence:

'Honoured Madame – I had the pleasure of presenting to the Board of Education of our city, for the use of the library, a copy of your Centennial poems, which was unanimously accepted, and I am directed to make a proper acknowledgement of the donation. In performing so important a duty I beg, on behalf of the Board, to offer at the shrine of your muse the following.' At this point Mr Peirce begins to demonstrate that he is no ordinary dry-as-dust bureaucrat, but a man gifted with a rare turn of phrase. Obviously the congenial task of thanking the Michigan poetess presented him with an opportunity to exercise a repressed vein of satire which his other more mundane duties had tended to stifle. This opportunity he seems to have seized with both hands:

'Ever since the morning stars sang together, for joy, at the creation, or the sweet singer of Israel in a lachrymose mood, sat down on the greensward by the waters of Babylon and suspended his harp upon a willow, poesy has filled no inconsiderable space in the education of a refined and intellectual people. Dante and Shakespeare, Milton and Schiller are doubtless familiar to you, as lofty examples of an age preceding the close of our Centennial, while Hosea Biglow, and Prof. Everett, Mark Twain and Orpheus C. Kerr[1] are living examples of the present moment.

1. This is a deliberately upstaging list of American patriots and publicists. Hosea Biglow was the critic and poet James Russell Lowell. Edward Everett was the first American to be granted a Ph.D. – at Göttingen in 1817. At the dedication of the National Cemetery in Pennsylvania he spoke for two hours without notes. Abraham Lincoln was also present, and spoke for two minutes only, to the chagrin of reporters. Everyone agreed that his Gettysburg address had been a pale shadow of Everett's, and inappropriate to boot. Orpheus C. Kerr was the pseudonym for Robert Henry Newell, a New York journalist and soi-disant humorist. For a short while he was married to the formidable Ada Isaacs Mencken, who was sent along by Rossetti to provide Swinburne with sexual therapy, but gave the job up because of unspecified difficulties with the patient.

'Still a void, a vacuum, so to speak, existed in the potential firmament, until comet-like, your very meritorious production was projected into the ethereal firmament of public opinion through the typographical persistency of C.M. Loomis, of this city, causing an astonishment greater than the introduction of blue glass or the meazles amongst us. There is much in your work that touches the heart, and raises sad but tender emotions, reminding the reader of Sappho, who, with her golden lyre, sent forth her mellifluous rhapsodies to sooth the troubled breast of her iconoclastic country-men, and caused the heart bowed down with sorrow to expand with hope and elecampaine.'[1]

After quoting from some of the verses, Peirce singles out one poem in particular as having impressed the Board of Education: 'But what seemed to strike the Board with the force of a ten-ton boomerang, and one that imparted joy to their solemn counte-nances, was the brochure on Grand Rapids. Eben Smith, one of our more adolescent members, required its reading several times in order to catch the prophylactic of its hexameter, and comprehend attitudinarily its doric structure:

> When Campan settled in Grand Rapids
>   No bridge was across the river;
> The Indians in their light canoes,
>   Would row them across the water.
> The railroads now from every way,
>   Run through the city of Grand Rapids,
> The largest city in Western Michigan,
>   Is the city of Grand Rapids.

Peirce concludes his remarks with two graceful images of the poetess, as a meteor, and as a soaring song-bird in the realms of poesy: 'But I must not longer draw from the rich fountains of your meritorious work – so cheap at twenty-five cents – but have to con-gratulate you on the success which has attended your meteoric appearance in the realms of one of the most divinest of arts, that of a poet; soaring aloft on the wings of fancy with "your garlands and singing robes about you," as Dryden says.'

1. Correctly 'Elecampane' – i.e. a healing balm. According to Pliny the Elecampane plant, much used in ancient herbal remedies, sprang from Helen's tears.

In view of what she evidently took to be generally rapturous notices, it is almost surprising that Julia deemed a defence of her work to be necessary. Perhaps some of the public readings, like those in Grand Rapids, had not gone too well; and then again, like many well-known writers, she may frequently have been pestered with letters containing ignorant and hostile comments on her work. Whatever the reason, in 1878 she issued her volume entitled *A Few Choice Words to the Public, With New and Original Poems*. The 'choice words' are, in fact, Julia's equivalent of Wordsworth's Preface to the *Lyrical Ballads*. She begins by making it sadly clear that, notwithstanding the glowing critical encomia in the popular press, the public have failed to grasp the seriousness of her work and have even written in to tell her so. 'I was very foolish, I admit,' she writes, 'in signing my original name to that little book, when a ficticious [*sic*] name would have done just as well. And another foolish act was when I told where I resided.' She does admit that her verses might have needed just a little more work to get them absolutely right before giving them to the world: 'I wished for something different from all literary work, something to catch the public eye, and I think I have it in that little book. Its rare combination caused a great many literary people to laugh at my ignorance, yet at the *same* time, some of them could not help thinking that the sentiments were good, although so rarely constructed in poetry. That little book reminds me of what I have heard said about my uncle when a boy while learning music. He had been learning a very difficult piece of music. He had learned it so he could play it quite well. He said to the professor, "What do you *think* of it." The gentleman smiled and said, "My boy, the work is well laid, but it needs a little more filling." Now, dear readers, that is just what is the trouble with my little book. It needs a little more filling. Poetry, in its high perfection, is thought, feeling, imagination and music expressed in versification. The individual that can, with science, combine these four properties together in good moral sense, and make it beneficial to mankind, is indeed a true poet. Literary is a work very difficult to do. It needs to be thoroughly studied to make it as it should be.'

Despite her determination to put 'a little more filling' in her poems, Julia's later work is largely indistinguishable from her earlier pieces. As the *New York World* put it, her pegasus was 'never happy except between the shafts of a hearse', though in Lord Byron she had a more interesting hero (or anti-hero) and a more exalted death than was usually the case. The first stanza runs:

'Lord Byron' was an Englishman
A poet I believe.
His first works in old England
Was poorly received.
Perhaps it was 'Lord Byron's' fault
And perhaps it was not.
His life was full of misfortunes,
Ah, strange was his lot.

After some animadversions on Byron's character, leavened, how-ever, with a poet's fellow-feeling for his treatment at the hands of the press, we reach the celebrated moment of his demise, which Julia handles with characteristic aplomb:

He had joined the Grecian Army;
This man of delicate frame;
And there he died in a distant land,
And left on earth his fame.
'Lord Byron's' age was 36 years,
Then closed the sad career,
Of the most celebrated 'Englishman'
Of the nineteenth century.

Julia's late period does contain one surprise in the form of a song that has succeeded in surviving despite having been written by her. *Leaving off the Agony in Style* was resurrected in the 1950s and became, with altered words, a popular hit for Lonnie Donegan, the Julia A. Moore of skiffle:

People in this country they think it is the best;
They work hard for money and lay it out in dress;
They think of the future with a pleasant smile
And lay by no money while putting on the style.

Leave off the agony, leave off the style,
Unless you've got money by you all the while,
If you look about you you'll often have to smile,
To see so many people putting on the style.

253

This reincarnation of the poetess as the age of austerity's librettist is not quite as unlikely as it might seem. Most pop songs of the fifties shared with Julia's work a number of characteristics, such as linguistic poverty, rhymes that would worry even an advertising executive and a relentless mind-numbing banality. This didn't prevent them getting into the brain unawares and being quite hard to get out again. Julia's verses are not memorable in that way, because her rhythms are so chaotic; but occasional infelicities stick to the reader like burrs:

> And now kind friends what I have wrote
> I hope you will pass o'er,
> And not criticize as some have done,
> Hitherto herebefore.

Usually it is the last line of a stanza, like the one above, that lingers in the brain, fading only gradually from one's consciousness like the irritation from a nettle sting. One of her most famous and least moving verse sagas concerns *John Robinson* (which she tells us should be sung to the air of 'The Drunkard'), an orphan who was sent to California to stay with his Uncle Zera French. The visit was not a success, and he was soon writing home asking for money for the return trip:

> The doctor says I must soon return,
> If I wish my home to see,
> For if I stay my life is short
> For the air disagrees with me.

Too late, his brother sets off to fetch him home:

> For he was sick, and very bad –
> Poor boy, he thought no doubt,
> If he came home in a smoking car
> His money would hold out.
> He started to come back alone –
> He came one-third the way –
> One evening in the car alone
> His spirit fled away.

No friend was near to speak to him,
　Or hear his dying moan;
How sad, how sad it must have been
　To die there all alone . . .

John Robinson is deservedly a favourite amongst Julia's fans. It exhibits many of her most striking qualities – a Wordsworthian adherence to the language of common men, a naturalistic representation of the rhythms of ordinary speech, and a theme of almost unbearable pathos. These qualities are even more evident in her famous threnody concerning the *Ashtabula Disaster*, which soars to heights that were beyond the reach even of the Great McGonagall:

Have you heard of the dreadful fate
　Of Mr P.P. Bliss and wife?
Of their death I will relate,
　And also others lost their life;
Ashtabula Bridge disaster,
　Where so many people died
Without a thought that destruction
　Would plunge them 'neath the wheel of tide.

Swiftly passed the engine's call,
　Hastening souls on to death,
Warning not one of them all;
　It brought despair right and left.

It is this plainness of thought and bluntness of expression that has endeared Julia A. Moore to generations of readers, and even earned her a place in *The Oxford Book of American Light Verse*, whose editor describes her in his Introduction as 'a writer so transcendently, surpassingly, superlatively bad that . . . she belongs in a special genre in which normal rules and habits of judgement are magically suspended.'[1] But perhaps the best summing up of her peculiar contribution to literature was that provided by the *Worcester Daily Press* which Julia reprints among the other 'Commendatory Notices' of her first volume: 'This saccharine songstress', writes the anonymous critic, 'has issued her poems in book form, introduced by a preface

1. *The Oxford Book of American Light Verse* Ed. William Harmon, OUP, 1979, p. xx.

which at once lays hold of the reader with the familiar grip of a liver pill and makes resistance useless. The aim of the author seems to have been the amalgamation of those two antagonistic elements, truth and poetry, into a substance that would preserve the utility of the one and the beauty of the other, but never to permit poetry to in any respect or degree get the better of truth.'

Seventeen

ELLA WHEELER WILCOX
1850–1919

The wisdom of Wisconsin

A harsh and homely monosyllable,
Abrupt and musicless, and at its best
An inartistic object to the eye;
Yet in this brief and troubled life of man
How full of majesty the part it plays!

from: *The Bed*

Laugh, and the world laughs with you:
Weep, and you weep alone;
For the sad old earth
Must borrow its mirth,
It has trouble enough of its own.

from: *Solitude*

'I may lie in the mud of the trenches,
I may reek with blood and mire,
But I will control, by the God in my soul,
The might of my man's desire.
I will fight my foe in the open,
But my sword shall be sharp and keen
For the foe within who would lure me to sin,
And I will come back clean.'

from: *Come Back Clean*

(Just before her death Ella Wheeler Wilcox travelled to
the Western Front to read her poems to the troops and
deliver talks on the two great enemies – the Germans
and sexual incontinence.)

'THERE WAS SO MUCH I WANTED! I wanted to bestow comfort, ease and pleasure on everybody at home. I wanted lovely gowns – ah, how I wanted them – and travel and accomplishments. I wanted summers by the sea – the sea which I had read of but had never seen – and on moonlight nights these longings grew so aggressive I often pinned the curtain down and shut out the rays that seemed to intensify my loneliness, and I would creep into my little couch under the sloping eaves, musing, "Another beautiful night of youth wasted and lost." And I would awaken happy in spite of myself and put all my previous melancholy into verses – and dollars.' So wrote Ella Wheeler Wilcox looking back on her youth in *The Story of A Literary Career*[1] – that is, the story of a writer who appears in no critical works and in no anthologies of a literary nature, and whose appearance in reference works usually consists of a few abusive remarks. The passage illuminates many of the contradictory elements in Ella's character – her *naïveté* mixed with shrewdness, her cloudy romanticism half subdued by severe practicality, her love of pleasure tempered with self-discipline. And the bottom line is dollars, as befits a writer who discovered at the age of sixteen, when her first book was published, that she could support a family of failures with her pen.

This first volume (*Drops of Water*, 1872) consisted of verse that was exactly what the doctor – or the editor – ordered. The magazines could print temperance tracts, so Ella Wheeler supplied them. The sentiments were those required, as was the length of the poem; and the poetess was prolific and punctual. Once it was established that the public liked her, she was an editor's dream. Nor was she merely a pale and prolix imitation of others – a 'periphrastic study

1. Originally published in Massachusetts, 1905, in response to the many requests for information about the poetess from her fans. The British Museum copy comes from 'The Higher Thought Centre', 10 Cheniston Gardens W8.

in a worn-out poetical fashion'. Ella's originality and personality
are powerfully present in all her writing:

> When the west grew red, and the sun's bald head
>   Dipped into a sea of gold,
> My love came down from the busy town,
>   Came down like a knight of old,
> On a steed sloe-black, whose fiery track
>   I saw through the gloom afar
> As on he came, with his hoofs aflame,
>   Like the trail of a falling star.
>
> And my love drew rein at the lattice pane,
>   And he sprang to my side in glee;
> And he cried, 'Complete is the world, my sweet,
>   In this twilight hour with thee.'
> And he held me fast, and he said, 'At last
>   I claim thee as mine – all mine.'
> But I turned my face from love's embrace,
>   For the dew on his lips was *wine*.

This is certainly as effective as TV advertisements that feature
smoker's breath, or the horrors of people who do not use Amplex.

The early fathers of the Orthodox Church laid down rules for the
painting of frescoes, rightly fearing that irrelevant pleasure in the
depiction of the story line might hinder the transmission of stern
theology; part of the pleasure to be derived from Ella Wheeler's
didactic verse is that the story and its recitation is good fun anyway;
the message is not allowed to get in the way: 'It was part of her
skill', writes Naomi Lewis, 'to invest any form of abstinence, if the
context required, with a positive and even exhilarating quality. We
see this in her first published work, those temperance verses which
were so remarkably like drinking songs . . .'[1] Well, not *exactly* like
drinking songs. The poem just quoted ends on an appropriate note
of squalor which topers would have to be pretty far gone to sing
with any degree of relish:

---

1. *A Visit to Mrs Wilcox*, Naomi Lewis, The Cresset Press, 1957, p. 20.

Then he mounted his steed, and he rode indeed
   Like a knight of the old crusade;
And he wedded soon, e'er the fall of the moon,
   A queenly and haughty maid;
And he drank up his health, and drank up his wealth,
   And his youth, and strength and grace
And now bereft, he has nothing left
   But a bloated, hideous face.

On the other hand, Miss Lewis's point is well taken. Ella Wheeler's poems invariably go with a swing, the result partly of her choice of metre, and partly of her unquenchable enthusiasm for life.

It is this latter quality which lay at the heart of her success. Her general message is no different from that addressed to the purchasers of what the record shops designate 'Easy Listening' albums, with titles like 'Get Happy' or 'Smilin' Through'. 'The particular virtues extolled', writes Miss Lewis, 'the consolations offered are acceptable chiefly to a settled, middle-class community, not quite illiterate, of few and small ambitions, many and small anxieties, and a modest standard of behaviour to maintain.'[1]

Smile a little, smile a little,
   All along the road;
Every life must have its burden,
   Every heart its load.
Why sit down in gloom and darkness
   With your grief to sup?
As you drink Fate's bitter tonic
   Smile across the cup.

This is a very special type of smile – not the one that can freeze you at ten paces, like Angela Rippon's; nor the one that makes you instinctively check your wallet, like Roy Hattersley's. It is the courageous little smile of the domestic martyr – a peculiarly Anglo-Saxon phenomenon. Obviously it was seldom absent from Ella Wheeler's own face as she penned the thoughts which, in the words of one hagiographer, 'were helping the world to be more loving and

1. Naomi Lewis, op. cit., p. 17.

cheerful, more humane, more philosophic and more progressive.'[1]

Nowhere are these aims of the poetess more in evidence than in her collection of fictional letters of advice to persons in different stations of life entitled *A Woman of the World*.[2] In these, good advice is poured over the recipients like buckets of cold water. A young man greatly smitten with the middle-aged and happily married Ella Wheeler Wilcox is dealt with in terms that would certainly have cured him of his affliction. Another lady, apparently writing while still on her honeymoon, wants to know how to preserve romance in her marriage. This was an area where Ella was something of an expert, and accordingly her correspondent gets the full treatment:

'Husbands are like invalids, each needs a special prescription, according to his ailment.

'But as all invalids can be benefited by certain sensible suggestions, like taking simple food, and breathing and exercising properly, and sleeping with open windows or out-of-doors, so all husbands can be aided toward perpetual affection by the observance of some general laws, on the part of the wife.' This realistic assessment of the male is followed up by a realistic prescription for treating his weaknesses: 'A woman who knows how to praise more readily than she knows how to criticize, and who has the tact and skill to adapt herself to a man's moods and to find amusement and entertainment in his whims, can lead him away from their indulgence without his knowledge.

'Such women are the real reformers of men, though they scorn the word, and disclaim the effort.'

If this is all rather crushing for the male ego, there is no room for complacency on the part of the female either: 'If you wish to be thought spotless marble,' writes Ella Wheeler scathingly, 'instead of warm flesh and blood, you should have gone into a museum, and refused marriage. Remember God knew what He was about, when He fashioned woman to be man's companion, mate, and mother of his children.' Above all: 'Do not thrust upon the man's mind continually the idea that you are a vastly higher order of being than he is. He will reach your standard much sooner if you come half-way and meet him on the plane of common sense and human understanding.' As with Lord Chesterfield's Letters – as, indeed, with a

1. The words are those of Ella Giles Ruddy.
2. I assume they are fictional. If not, one feels rather sorry for the recipients.

great deal of solicited advice – one rather feels that there are parts of it the recipients may not have welcomed. To a 'new woman' contemplating matrimony, she writes: 'Your heart is awakened from its stupor, caused by an overdose of intellect'; and a recently divorced attractive young female is told sharply: 'A grass widow whets the appetites of bovines.' Ella Wheeler was not only a successful poetess; she was also an excellent Marjorie Proops, ladling out good advice with relentless good humour and, where necessary, administering a well-aimed smack: 'Do not mistake frigidity for serenity', she tells a correspondent with a tendency to self-righteousness, 'nor austerity for self-control. Be affable, amiable and sweet, no matter how much you know. And listen more than you talk.'

In her autobiography, the poetess also has advice for aspirant writers. She remarks sternly that she found her way into print 'by sheer persistence', and so should they, relying on the 'Divine Power and the divinity within us'. One of her own stories 'was declined by nine editors (and ridiculed by the ninth on the margin)' but 'brought seventy-five dollars from the tenth . . .' Then, of course, fecundity is required as well as persistence: 'A day which passed without a poem from my pen I considered lost and misused . . . two each day was my idea of industry, and I once achieved eight.' And indeed, her three volumes of *Collected Poems*, issued in England in 1917, is eloquent testimony of her indefatigableness. They contain about a thousand poems, but are by no means her complete oeuvre. Reading through them, the nature of Ella Wheeler's achievement becomes clear: she succeeded in turning the whole notion of poetry into a species of kitsch:

> Only a simple rhyme of love and sorrow
>   Where 'blisses' rhymed with 'kisses', 'heart' with 'dart',
> Yet reading it, new strength I seemed to borrow,
>   To live on bravely, and to do my part . . .

She was a particularly successful scion of a flourishing line of 'domestic bards', as Naomi Lewis aptly calls them. Her poems are often Protestant homilies which, stripped of overt theology, leave the reader with a mixture of platitudinous advice and moral uplift. Much of what 'counselling' and 'analysis' seek to do for their clients today, Ella Wheeler was able to provide for her readers:

As the ambitious sculptor tireless, lifts,
   Chisel and hammer to the block at hand,
Before my half-formed character I stand
And ply the shining tools of mental gifts.
I'll cut away a huge unsightly side
   Of selfishness, and smooth to curves of grace
   The angles of ill-temper.

                      And no trace
Shall my sure hammer leave of silly pride,
Chip after chip must fall from vain desires,
   And the sharp corners of my discontent
   Be rounded into symmetry, and lent
Great harmony by faith that never tires.
   Unfinished still, I must toil on and on,
   Till the pale critic, Death, shall say, ''Tis done.'

This is the note that made her, in the happy phrase of *The Times* obituary writer, 'the most popular poet of either sex or age, read by
thousands who never opened Shakespeare . . . the chief moral and
aesthetic support of innumerable readers from the palace to the
cottage.' Her successors, such as the prose-poem manufacturers
Wilhelmina Stitch (q.v.), and Patience Strong, or the whimsical
purveyors of narcissism, like Rod McKuen, similarly appeal to a
public for whom poetry is gift-wrapped platitude and religion a
dose of valium. What makes Ella Wheeler, even today, more readable than the hideous affectation of McKuen or the wearisome
sanctimoniousness of Stitch and Strong, is her capacity to surprise
us:

     If the sad old world should jump a cog
       Sometime, in its dizzy spinning,
   And go off the track with a sudden jog,
       What an end would come to the sinning . . .

     With not a sigh or a sad good-bye
       For loved ones left behind us,
     We would go with a plunge and a mighty plunge
       Where never a grave should find us.

What a wild mad thrill our veins would fill
  As the great earth, like a feather
Should float through the air to God knows where
  And carry us all together.

No dark damp tomb and no mourner's gloom,
  No tolling bell in the steeple,
But in one swift breath a painless death
  For a million billion people . . .

This almost breaks a taboo of kitsch uplift, where 'Death' usually
has to be presented as an austere headmaster holding the tape at the
end of the sports day marathon. Its spirit seems closer to sentiments
such as:

Beyond all this desire of oblivion runs . . .

or even Tom Lehrer's:

We will all go together when we go,
Every Hottentot and every eskimo;
. . . When the air becomes uraneous
We will all go simultaneous . . .

'As I read over my own works, and painfully realize their great
defects', wrote Ella Wheeler, 'I am moved to wonder why I have
been accorded such unusual success, when many writers who far
excel me as poets and artists have failed to win recognition or remu-
neration'; and she goes on to lament her inability to perceive that
'the manner of expression is as worthy of consideration as the
thought to be expressed.'[1] Although she later put aside this engaging
modesty, Ella Wheeler never behaved with the arrogance of the
eccentric or the fraud – of an Amanda Ros or a Joaquin Miller. Her
sense of humour was an effective bulwark against overweening
pride. When Charles A. Dana attacked her poems in the New York
Sun as over-erotic, unwisely quoting half a column of lines all containing the word 'kiss', she notes that scores of readers wrote in asking where they could purchase the book. A grateful Ella Wheeler
accordingly wrote a note to Charles Dana thanking him for the

1. *Lippincott's Magazine*, 1886, quoted in Naomi Lewis, op. cit., p. 16.

reviews; whereat, she adds drily, 'Mr Dana was exceedingly wroth.'
At other times one wonders if she was intending to be humorous or
not – as in the delightful way in which she describes the inspiration,
based on an actual incident, of her famous poem *The Waltz-
Quadrille*: '[This poem], one of my most popular early verses, was
similarly conceived [as *The Dirge*]. I had promised the quadrille at a
commencement ball at Madison University to a man on the eve of a
journey who was unable to find me when the number was called.
Although I did not have the pleasure of a dance with him, I wrote
the poem and sent him a copy of it, saying, "This is the way I should
have felt had I been in love with you and had I danced the waltz-
quadrille with you just before your departure from Madison . . ."
Unfortunately we do not have the young man's reaction to this
amusing and practical *billet* of Ella's; but no doubt he was proud
enough to have been instrumental in supplying the necessary props
for her poem.

> A clamour, a crash, and the band was still
>   'Twas the end of the dream and the end of the measure:
> The last low notes of the waltz quadrille
>   Seemed like a dirge o'er the death of Pleasure.
> You said good-night, and the spell was over –
> Too warm for a friend, and too cold for a lover –

That is the romantic side of Ella Wheeler, the part of her with
potential experiences all bottled up and just waiting the opportunity to happen – on paper of course. After her marriage in 1884 to
'one of God's truest noblemen' the passionate element in her verses
is increasingly tinged with metaphysics and half-digested spiritual-
ism. While this lent her poems a spurious air of profundity, the
down-to-earth and pleasure-loving side of her was never far below
the surface. Visitors to her Connecticut coast bungalow admired
her energetic swimming – a life-long passion – and her even more
energetic dancing (she invented a dance called the Ella Wheeler
Wilcox Glide). Meanwhile, she continued to write her sensible
Proopsisms for the Hearst press. If there was any evidence of
crankiness, it was only perceptible in an excessive faith in the
idea that all unpleasantnesses in life are susceptible to common-
sense solutions – a recurrent weakness of the Anglo-Saxon

Weltanschauung – and a belief that 'science', properly employed, could 'cure' crime and build a race of 'demi-gods' from genetic selection:

> I look to Science for the Coming Race
> Growing from seed selected; and from soil
> Love fertilized – and pruned by wisdom's hand
> Till out of mortal man spring demi-gods,
> Strong primal creatures with awakened souls
> And normal passions, governed by the will,
> Leaving a trail of glory where they tread.

A hymn to 'normal passions' is really quite an achievement, especially as our enthusiasm is so often solicited for abnormal ones. It would have appealed to her decidedly normal audience. She was the voice of their hearts, the shaper of their not very outrageous dreams. 'I think,' she once said, 'the word "poetess" to the average American, until recent years, suggested a sentimental person with ringlets and an absence of practical good sense.' Well, she changed all that.

Eighteen

AMANDA McKITTRICK ROS
1860–1939

A euphuistic lady from Ulster

This inventive production was hatched within a mind fringed with Fumes of Formation, the Ingenious Innings of Inspiration and Thorny Tincture of Thought.

> Amanda Ros, introducing her volume of poems
> entitled *Fumes of Formation* (1933)

Love is the rolling stone of all,
And often makes large matters small:

> from: *Eastertide*

Reading could destroy my instinct for what is popular.

> Mr Paul Raymond (of the Revuebar)

'MY CHIEF OBJECT OF WRITING *is* and always *has* been, to write if possible in a strain all my own. *This* I find is why my writings are so much sought after.' The writer of these words triumphantly succeeded in her object, and she is perfectly correct in supposing that her unique approach to literary composition is the magnet that attracted connoisseurs of taste to her work. Indeed, like Elvis Presley, she had her own appreciation society, which was established at Oxford in 1907. Its members met irregularly to read aloud specimens of her work, which certainly do make good reading. Here, for instance, is a memorable passage from her novel *Delina Delaney* (Lady Gifford returns home to discover that her son, Lord Gifford, has been kissing Delina, a mere fisherman's daughter, in the conservatory of Columba Castle. She is outraged):

> 'Home again, mother?' he boldly uttered as he gazed reverently in her face.
> 'Home to Hades!' returned the raging high-bred daughter of distinguished effeminacy.
> 'Ah me! what is the matter?' meekly inquired his lordship.
> 'Everything is the matter with a broken-hearted mother of low-minded offspring,' she answered hotly . . . 'Henry Edward Ludlow Gifford, son of my strength, idolized remnant of my inert husband, who at this moment invisibly offers the scourging whip of fatherly authority to your backbone of resentment (though for years you think him dead to your movements) and pillar of maternal trust . . .'

The shock proves to be too much for Lady Gifford, and she presently joins her inert husband. Her death provokes a wail of remorse from the wayward 'idolized remnant':

'Is it true, O Death,' I cried in my agony, 'that you have wrested from me my mother, Lady Gifford of Columba Castle, and left me here, a unit figuring on the great blackboard of the past, the shaky surface of the present and fickle field of the future to track my life-steps, with gross indifference to her wished-for wish? . . . Blind she lay to the presence of her son, who charged her death-gun with the powder of accelerated wrath.'[1]

Amanda Malvina Fitzalan Anna Margaret McKittrick Ros resided at 'Iddesleigh', Larne, Co. Antrim. The house is named after her most famous novel *Irene Iddesleigh* (1897), the profits from which, she claimed, had partly financed its construction. Her visiting card ran as follows:

AT HOME ALWAYS TO THE HONOURABLE
MRS AMANDA M. ROS
AUTHORESS

Iddesleigh	Telegrams
Ireland	'Iddesleigh, Ireland'

From this bastion of literary isolation she issued a stream of colourful abuse against such critics as Barry Pain and Wyndham Lewis, who seldom neglected to notice her work, always unfavourably. These outbursts exhibit some of the euphuistic tendencies which Aldous Huxley draws attention to in her novels; 'auctioneering agents of Satan' has a fine Elizabethan ring about it, as do the more picturesque and obscure insults like: 'crowdrops', 'talent wipers of a wormy order', 'poking hounds' and, my own favourite, 'tree of rebuff'. All this and more is to be found in the privately printed *Bayonets of Bastard Sheen* (1949), a selection of her letters written between 1927 and 1939. There is an interesting sidelight on her self-confidence in a letter dated 9 April 1930, in which she writes: 'I enclose in conjunction with this critique a cutting from a recent paper and I hold according to this critique that I should make a dart for this Prize!' It seems that the Nobel Prize for Literature had just come to her notice; in an enclosed newspaper cutting she had

1. These two passages are quoted by Aldous Huxley in his essay on Amanda Ros entitled 'Euphues Redivivus' in *On the Margin*, London,1923, pp. 134–40.

underlined a reference to the award of £9,608 for outstanding literature of an idealistic tendency.

It cannot be denied that her poems do exhibit such a tendency,
amongst others that make them less suitable for consideration for
the Nobel Prize. In particular, she waged unceasing war against the
abandonment of Victorian sartorial standards in her volume *Fumes
of Formation* (Belfast, 1933):

> The petticoat faded away as we do
> In circumference it covered not one leg but two,
> Its successor exposes the arms, breasts and necks,
> Legs, knees and thighs and too often – the — .

That eloquent final dash is masterly, forcing the reader to supply
what the poetess is too delicate to mention by name. Elsewhere, she
returns to the attack:

> Seasons altered – fashions too
>   Don't hide from view
> That brazen faced immodest form
>   Exposed to storm,
> Open to ills of any kind
>   Before – Behind.

Another target – and here she was well in advance of her time –
was nicotine abuse. She praises a girl's lips that:

> . . . form the sweetest mouth e'er made
>   Void of that horrid smell
> Of cigs, so many female grades
>   Prefer to Heaven or — !

Her own preferred drug was a tankard of the blushful Hippocrene,
whose workings she described on the volume's title-page: 'This
inventive production was hatched within a mind fringed with
Fumes of Formation, the Ingenious Innings of Inspiration and
Thorny Tincture of Thought.' Part of her 'Thorny Tincture' may be
seen, I think, in her patriotic verses; to adapt the Duke of Wellington's remark, they may not have frightened the enemy, but they
certainly frighten the reader. Of the Kaiser she writes:

> Not long ago you tried full hard
>> To grease your bones with English lard!
> But take from me 'in lodge' a tip
>> That in its fat you'll never dip.

Her wartime broadside *A Little Belgian Orphan* has a blood-thirsty fervour which was not untypical of those who were themselves in no danger of being sent to the front:

> Go! Meet the foe undaunted, they're rotten cowards all,
> Present to them the bayonet, they totter and they fall,
> We know you'll do your duty and come to little harm
> And if you meet the Kaiser, cut off his other arm.

When not dishing it out to immodest maidens and the frightful German emperor, Amanda turned her attention to the legal profession, which is undoubtedly her King Charles' head. In a letter to an admirer she writes: 'My next work (*Poems of Puncture*, 1932), which could not appear too soon, is written chiefly to cut up the lawyers, a gang I absolutely detest. When it appears they will get a chance then of snarling and biting and guzzling each other in their dog beds of injustice. They'll get a tiny "drop" when they swallow its intestines.' For good measure she adds: 'I've thrashed the clerics too and Royalty won't laugh over its pages.'

Like many people with an obsessive hatred of lawyers, she never stopped litigating, almost invariably without success. Her failure to realize that lawyers were delighted to encourage her in this, and quite indifferent as to the outcome of a case as long as they received their fees, meant that she continually put herself in the hands of her enemies. To her, all lawyers were Uriah Heep incarnate, a point of view that would engender enthusiastic support if it were better expressed:

> Readers, did you ever hear
> Of Mickey Monkey face McBlear?
> His snout is long with a flattish top,
> Lined inside with a slimy crop:
> His mouth like a slit in a money box,
> Portrays his kindred to a fox.

271

> . . . His head, shaped like a rotten pear, has bumps stuck
> round it here and there,
> Stuffed with muddy brains and batter, with a slit in front
> whence oozes clatter.

There is certainly one line here that strikes a glancing blow on the target – 'His mouth like a slit in a money box' admirably sums up a grasping representative of the world's most restrictive profession; but the next line ruins it, and the accidental flash of Byronic impudence is immediately buried in a welter of energetically thrown mud.

Occasionally, very occasionally, Amanda abandoned hostilities against lawyers or what she called the 'random hacks of illiteration' (or 'corner boy shadows of criticism', or 'maggoty numbskulls') and indulged her elegiac strain. It does not come easily to her. Her *Ode to Easter* begins unpromisingly with:

> Dear Lord, the day of eggs is here . . .

and elsewhere she attempts a philosophical mode that looks forward to the Christmas cracker aphorisms of Ella Wheeler Wilcox (q.v.):

> Love is the rolling stone of all,
> And often makes large matters small:

If one substitutes the word 'verse' for the word 'love' here, these lines reveal a poignant truth about poetasters in general and Amanda Ros in particular. Her poem *On Visiting Westminster Abbey* succeeds beyond all expectation in making 'large matters small'. It is as if Pam Ayres had been asked to rewrite Gray's Elegy in her own inimitable manner:

> Holy Moses! Take a look!
> Flesh decayed in every nook,
> Some rare bits of brain lie here,
> Mortal loads of beef and beer.

The alliterative bang and crash of her style, while ensuring that the reader is continually amazed and startled, fails to convey the full pathos of her subject matter. The same is true of her prose, as may be seen from the description of Lord Gifford's enforced departure from his beloved Delina in *Delina Delaney*. He tries hard to rise to the dignity of the occasion, but something has gone seriously wrong with the author's metaphor mixer:

'I am just in time to hear the toll of a parting bell strike its heavy weight of appalling softness against the weakest fibres of a heart of love, arousing and tickling its dormant action, thrusting the dart of evident separation deeper into its tubes of tenderness, and fanning the flame, already unextinguishable, into volumes of burning blaze.'

When Delina takes herself off to a convent, the machine breaks down again, this time even more spectacularly:

'Two days after, she quit Columba Castle and resolved to enter the holy cloisters of a convent where, she believed she'd be dead to the built hopes of wealthy worth, the crooked steps to worldly distinction, and the designing creaks in the muddy stream of love.'

It will be seen from this that Amanda Ros considered herself to be an artist. There was, indeed, nothing natural which she could not make grotesquely artificial, and nothing affecting which she could not make laughable. She believed herself to be in the front rank of writers and took a lordly view not only of the competition, but even of her professed admirers. The insolence with which she favoured one of them, who humbly asked for an inscription in the front of his copy of *Irene Iddesleigh*, is breathtaking:

Extempore

On being asked by a digit of dollardom, USA, to write a few lines on the front page of 'Irene Iddesleigh', I gave him the following:

> What a fool art thou my dear man
>   To ask for a daub of my pen
> With which to enrich your ambition
>   And place you above other men.
> Assuming you're wise I now send you
>   A stroke of my purest and best:
> So here's to your health when I'm dreaming
>   Of you and your foolish request.

The mixture of pretended modesty and serene egotism is worthy of Alfred Austin. Of course, unlike the latter, she never actually said she was 'at the head of English literature', but her decision to apply for the Nobel Prize implied that she knew her rightful place. She had no need to compare herself with the competition, of which she seems to have been largely unaware. Her biographer says of her: 'Her opinion about the nobility of the author's calling was sincerely held, but she applied it mainly to herself. She had few books in her house except her own. She neither bought the works of contemporaries nor borrowed them at the library. She was not, in fact, a reader.'[1]

So lived Amanda Ros, a literary recluse who nevertheless adopted an extraordinarily high profile, and gave much pleasure to thousands of readers.

1. Jack Loudan, *O Rare Amanda! The Life of Amanda McKittrick Ros*, London, 1954, p. 160.

Nineteen

J. GORDON COOGLER
1865–1901

A manufacturer of verse to order

Alas for the South, her books have grown fewer –
She never was much given to literature.

from: *Purely Original Verse* (1891 and seq.)

From early youth to the frost of age
    Man's days have been a mixture
Of all that constitutes in life
    A dark and gloomy picture.

from: *A Gloomy Picture*, op. cit.

Alas! Carolina! Carolina! Fair land of my birth,
    Thy fame will be wafted from the mountain to the sea
As being the greatest educational centre on earth,
    At the cost of men's blood thro' thy 'one X' whiskey.

Two very large elephants[1] thou hast lately installed,
    Where thy sons and thy daughters are invited to
        come,
And learn to be physically and mentally strong,
    By the solemn proceeds of thy 'innocent' rum.

from: *Alas! Carolina!*

For what tho' I obtain the praise
    Of human lips both far and wide,
A worm of dust I still must be,
    Drifting on life's gloomy tide.

from: *I Dislike A Vain
And Haughty Man*, op. cit.

1. i.e. Winthrop and Clemson colleges.

'IN PRESENTING THIS VOLUME I SHALL repeat the words contained in the introduction of my former ones: "My style and my sentiments are MY OWN, purely original." ' These defiant words are to be found in the prefatory remarks to J. Gordon Coogler's *Purely Original Verse. Complete Works And A Number of New Productions In One Volume, Revised, Illustrated And Printed By The Author*, Columbia S.C., 1897. Although he was only thirty-two, this edition may be taken as the definitive collection of the poet's oeuvre. It contains all those poems which he wished to preserve (i.e., all of the ones he had written), together with some new offerings, and thirty-three pages of extracts from reviews. His distressing facility, and especially his willingness to oblige customers (the window of his printshop in Columbia boasted a sign: 'Poems written While You Wait'), would have ensured a much greater output had he lived; but within four years the poet was dead, having reached only his thirty-sixth year. His last poem was brimming with intimations of mortality and carried the prophetic title *Let Me Hang Up My Harp*.

Like Julia A. Moore, Coogler attracted ambiguous tributes from far and wide. He was unselfconsciously proud of these and needed little persuasion to bring out his file of cuttings to show the visitors to his printshop. In Atlanta a Coogler fan club was formed, which was to be the first of many. The poet sent them a copy of his complete works and a large portrait of himself. Mr Henry W. Grady wrote a graceful letter of thanks, which is reprinted in the *Complete Works* of 1897: 'To say that the members of the club are delighted with the picture and grateful for your interest in the organization but mildly expresses their feelings. Each and every member wanted to take the picture from the packing with his own hands . . .' 'We have,' wrote Grady, 'every day requests from people to become members of the club, but we are careful about admitting new brothers, as we have now an organization to be proud of and desire to have in it only the most appreciative literary spirits.'

The selection of critical comments that Coogler included in the *Complete Works* exhibits a disarming frankness – or perhaps one should say, a blind self-confidence. The *Atlanta Constitution*, it is true, is quoted as saying: 'There must be something in the writings of a man who can attract attention and win applause when corn is thirty cents a bushel and potato bugs have become a burden'; but other contributions seem less flattering. Some are downright hostile; for instance, *Puck's* 1894 review of his third purely original volume: 'Wretched taste', complains the critic, '. . . is shown in some *Lines to Byron*:

> Oh thou immortal Byron
> Thy grand inspired genius
>   Let no man dare to smother;
> May all that was good within thee
> Be attributed to heaven;
>   All that was evil – to thy mother.

'Byron's mother may not have been an admirable woman; she may have had the gravest of faults; but she died many years ago, and we protest that J. Gordon Coogler has no right to rake up any old scandal about her, especially in an ode to her talented son . . . Let us not Mr Coogler, be cruel and vindictive toward one who, whatever her failings, was once a woman. Remember your own "Lines to Woman":

> Oh that inexhaustible subject
>   Filled with celestial fire
> On which no seraph's song can cease,
>   No poet's pen expire.'

The subject of womanhood does indeed loom large in Coogler's work. He was nothing if not a romantic, and wrote his first love poem to a certain 'Minnie' when he was still a schoolboy (unfortunately she went to Galveston and was drowned in a hurricane). Coogler followed this up with numerous poems that are always chivalrous, but also show a strong awareness of the weaker sex's temptations:

Woman's Folly

Alas! poor woman, with eyes of sparkling fire,
Thy heart is often won by mankind's gay attire;
So weak thou art, so very weak at best,
Thou canst not look beyond a satin-lined vest.

I've seen thee ofttimes cast a winning glance
And be carried away – as it were within a trance –
By the gay apparel of some dishonest youth,
Whose bosom heaved with not a single truth.

Alas! for thee – I would that thou couldst learn
That love does not in such quicksilver burn;
That he who lurks beside thy virtuous path
When thy good name is gone, will gaze on thee and laugh . . .

It comes as no surprise to learn that Coogler taught Sunday School at the local Methodist church when one considers the gentle didacticism of poems like *She Fell Like A Flake of Snow*:

She was beautiful once; but she fell,
And some said 'let her go,'
For she can never shine again
Like a beautiful flake of snow.

Or the noble indignation he displays towards sexual gossip in the lines entitled *Destroy It Not*:

Go shatter the walls of some beautiful city
That is noted for grandeur and fame,
Rather than cast a suggestive remark
To destroy a woman's fair name.

The walls of a city can be erected again,
Their beauty be grander than ever;
But a woman's good name once destroyed
Can ne'er be reclaim'd, no never.

All Heaven has no water soft enough,
Nor earth no cleansing soap,
That can wash the crimson from the heart
That destroys a woman's hope.

Although there is no doubting the intensity of Coogler's feelings, it has to be admitted that his approach is rather impersonal. It is the general idea of female company that attracts him, not the specific endowments of one matchless beauty:

> How sweet when our lonely soul grows weary
> And our tired feet need rest,
> To recline 'neath the shade of the willow tree,
> Pillow'd on a maiden's breast.
>
> To feel a passion pure within us,
> And not the one that seeks to rob
> That beautiful virtue underlying
> Her peaceful bosom's throb.

Only once does passion break through in a moving couplet which the parsimonious printer used, as was his wont, to fill up a white blank at the bottom of page 62:

> I have promised her ne'er to mention her sweet name again;
> But, oh, how the fulfillment of that promise gives me pain.

These pregnant lines are all we have to go on, but they bespeak volumes of the poet's silent suffering – rather more, in fact, than all the rest of his Purely Original Verses. Reading between these two lines, we may surmise that women were something of a disappointment to Coogler. This impression is reinforced by his great denunciatory masterpiece in the manner of *Ecclesiastes*, with its unforgettable title *More Care For The Neck Than For The Intellect*:

> Fair lady, on that snowy neck and half clad bosom
> Which you so publicly reveal to man,
>   There's not a single outward stain or speck;
> Would that you had given but half the care
> To the training of your intellect and heart
>   As you have given to that spotless neck.
>
> For Time, alas! must touch with cold unerring hand,
> That fair bosom's soft, untarnished hue,
>   Staining that lily-leaf of your sweet sex;

Then in ignorance you will journey here below,
Hiding that once fair bosom 'neath a veil,
    With a standing collar 'round your wrinkled neck.

It was not likely that poetry of this quality would long be over-looked by the public, and it is pleasing to learn that Coogler had appropriate recognition and commensurate financial success in his all too brief career. Some 5,000 copies of the two Purely Original Verses were sold, latterly at a dollar each, or $1.10 by mail. Professor Claude Henry Neuffer estimates the bard's earnings at about $3,600 – and this at a time when corn was thirty cents a bushel and potato bugs were rampant![1] By the time of his death his fame had spread well beyond South Carolina and there were many fan clubs in far-flung corners of America that eagerly awaited his next effusion. Moreover, his critics must surely have been put on the defensive after his ringing declaration headed *Impossible*:

> You may as well try to change the course
>   Of yonder sun
>   To north and south,
> As to try to subdue by criticism
>   This heart of verse
>   Or close this mouth.

Alas! Death achieved what was beyond the powers of the critics, and the obituary writers seemed incapable of understanding the extent of the nation's loss. 'An Excellent Young Man', ran the headline in the *Charleston News and Courier*, 'who unfortunately thought he was a poet.' Coogler would have been equal to that, however. His answer is prophetically contained in the lines he wrote 'On being asked by a young lady, just after a renowned Northern journal had given my works a page of complimentary review, if my hat was not "too small for my head".'

You'll never see this head too large for my hat,
    You may watch it and feel it as oft as you choose,

1. *See* the Introduction to the 1974 photographic reprint of *Purely Original Verse* by J. Gordon Coogler (1897) by Claude Henry Neuffer, Professor of English, University of South Carolina, Columbia S.C.

But you'll learn, as millions of people have learned,
   Of my character and name thro' my innocent muse.

You'll never see this form clad in gaudy apparel,
   Nor these feet playing the 'dude' in patent-leather shoes;
But your children's children will some day read
   Some pleasant quotations from my innocent muse.

Twenty

JOHN GAMBRIL NICHOLSON
floruit 1890–1930

A dangler after boys

Fit setting such for unripe Boyhood's pose!
  In this fair picture of Love's fortunate hour,
  Youth calls on Passion with a wondrous power;
But ere you come where laughing lips unclose,
Mark the symbolic rod and shun its blows –
  Poor fox, methinks again the grapes are sour!

from: Sour Grapes (For A Photograph)

He writes the dearest letters, his love to me he sends,
He is not shy when he and I are spoken of as friends.
He welcomes me as visitor, he deigns to be my guest,
Accepts my plan whene'er he can, and does as I think best;
My gifts he shows where'er he goes, nor cares what people say:
But when I offer him my love – he waves that gift away!

from: Thus Far –

IN HIS BOOK *THE PUBLIC SCHOOL PHENOMENON* Jonathan Gathorne-Hardy vividly describes the hot-house culture of such schools, with their mixture of naïve chivalry and institutionalized sadism, of Platonic passions and furtive erotic manoeuvres. This culture had its own painter in Henry Scott Tuke (1858–1929) 'who could do for boys' flesh what Renoir could do for women's. Year after year, in those unknowing days, he could exhibit at the Royal Academy or have hung in the Tate vast glowing paintings of naked boys or youths, posed on boats so that their buttocks caught the reflections of water, and no-one so much as blinked.'[1] According to one of Tuke's ex-models, he used to assemble his 'perfect' boys from different bits of his sitters – 'here a calf, there a buttock, somewhere else a head . . . His own lover was then aged forty, but he'd kept his figure and quite a lot of him could still be used in the paintings.'[2]

If Tuke was the leading paedophilic painter, John Gambril Nicholson and the Reverend E.E. Bradford (q.v.) were his counterparts in poetry and prose. Some of the titles of Nicholson's books indicate his preoccupations – e.g. *A Garland of Ladslove* and *The Romance of a Choirboy*. These, however, were privately printed, and those readers who manage to run them to earth in the British Museum will not find it hard to see why. At the same time as he was writing of a clergyman's passion for a chorister, however, he was also contributing stories full of fresh air and fun to such blameless periodicals as *Chums* and *Boys*.

Nicholson himself was a schoolmaster and a friend of Frederick Rolfe, 'Baron Corvo', who had taught him at a school in Saffron Walden. This is not a very promising beginning for one destined to be *in loco parentis* for most of his career, and not the least surprising

1. Jonathan Gathorne-Hardy, *The Public School Phenomenon*, London, 1977, p. 214.
2. Op. cit., p. 214.

aspect of Nicholson's life is that he appears to have kept out of trouble and never suffered the fate of William Johnson Cory.[1] But Cory's platonic yearnings pale into insignificence beside the effusions of Nicholson in *Love in Earnest* (1892), the above-mentioned *Garland of Ladslove* (1911) and *A Chaplet of Southernwood* (1896). Nor is it likely that he entirely confined himself to celebrating the fleshly attractions of small boys in verse: according to Gathorne-Hardy, his 'old boys' used to return regularly 'to have photographic records kept of their growth'.[2]

Love in Earnest represents the respectable face of the poet. Although the topic is love, the actual gender of the loved one is left discreetly vague, and the nature of the relationship only a little less obscure than that in Shakespeare's sonnets; at least it would have been for readers of *The Athenaeum* and *Cassell's Saturday Journal*, where many of the poems had previously appeared.[3] The dedication is to his mother, who 'incited me to (the book's) publication, but fell asleep ere she saw its fulfilment'. Probably it was just as well that his mother had fallen asleep before seeing the contents of his follow-up volume in 1911, *A Garland of Ladslove*. The flavour of this work is immediately clear from the Frontispiece. It is a photograph of a naked boy standing beside a boat on a mudbank; in front of him is a large golden retriever, apparently staring at his genitals. The First Part of the volume is dedicated to *Verses for Victor* (1902–10), some of which are rather odd:

1. The unfortunate author of *Heraclitus* left Eton abruptly, where he was a master, after an indiscreet letter he had written to one of the boys was intercepted.
2. Jonathan Gathorne-Hardy, op. cit.
3. Nicholson was writing at a time when the Victorians were 'tying themselves into knots about the sonnets' (Philip Henderson, *Tennyson, Poet and Prophet*, London, 1978). Palgrave simply left out Sonnet 20 in his 1861 edition, because he erroneously thought it demonstrated a physical relationship between Shakespeare and Mr W.H. 'We cannot understand', he wrote, 'how our great and gentle Shakespeare could have submitted himself to such passions.' Samuel Butler was less inclined to *suppressio veri* than the virtuous Palgrave, but his gloss on the topic is a masterpiece of wishful thinking laced with cant: he asserts that the offence 'never went beyond intention and was never repeated . . . The marvel, however, is this: that whereas the love of Achilles for Patroclus depicted by the Greek poet is purely English, absolutely without taint or alloy, the love of the English poet for Mr W.H. was, though only for a short time, more Greek than English.' A brief lapse then, not a congenital disposition.

. . . But ere you come where laughing lips unclose,
Mark the symbolic rod and shun its blows, –
Poor fox, methinks again the grapes are sour!

There are rondeaux to Victor's eyes, an account of hand-holding at
dusk, and a version of 'the second time around' theme – only on this
occasion it's the third time around:

> You've had your predecessors,
>   Of whom you've scarcely heard,
> There was Ernest, and there was Alec,
>   And you, my Victor, are the third.

This sounds alarmingly like Bluebeard warming up, an impression
not dispelled by lines from *Triolets of Conquest*:

> Victor's coming on our yacht, –
>   Fate, be kind to little Victor!
> What may happen? What may not?

One gets the distinct impression afterwards that the yacht may have
had the desired effect:

> When I lie in the darkness, pondering
>   The problems of Wrong and Right,
> A soft little hand comes wandering
>   Out of the wakeful night.

On the other hand Victor was obviously not a pushover, as is
revealed in another 'Triolet' which owes much to Leigh Hunt's
poem in similar vein:

> Just for once my Victor kissed me –
>   Ah, his cheek was soft as satin!
> Cynics say that Fortune's missed me, –
> Just for once my Victor kissed me,
> And when with the lost they list me,
>   Let them, anyhow put that in!

> Just for once my Victor kissed me –
> Ah his cheek was soft as satin![1]

The declining course of the poet's affair with Victor is charted in a series of poems, some of which are not without pathos. A note of self-reproach enters in when Nicholson refers to his age, 'six and thirty chequered years', and is evident again in a poem called *Vigil*. At night, a still small voice reminds him of the error of his ways, but in a fine Lawrentian outburst he rejects the stale saws of conventional morality:

> Satan, thy words do *not* from God proceed,
> Nor shall the letter of an ancient creed
> Against Love's new and living law prevail.

The affair with Victor is beginning to burn itself out, however. One of the last poems to feature him describes in Betjemanesque terms an encounter on the tennis court; the description of his beloved's 'alert and nervous limbs' anticipates the rosy thighs of the late Laureate's nubile Surrey maidens:

> Flinging off his hat and jacket
>   Standing out of court
> Shouting as I raise my racket,
>   'Ready! any sort!'
>
> That's how Victor waits my service,
>   When I open play;
> All his limbs alert and nervous
>   Eager for the fray.

1. I append the justly acclaimed original (1838) of these verses for those interested in Nicholson's literary influences:

> Jenny kissed me when we met,
>   Jumping from the chair she sat in;
> Time, you thief, who love to get
>   Sweets into your list, put that in:
> Say I'm weary, say I'm sad,
>   Say that health and wealth have missed me,
> Say I'm growing old, but add,
>   Jenny kissed me.

Perhaps this tribute of Hunt to Jane Welsh Carlyle has a slight edge over Nicholson's tribute to Victor, but the rondeau is a form notoriously difficult to handle in English.

And at the end the poet is left with his memories and, it seems, disappointments:

> All that to ardent boyhood beckoneth
> Has never lured you yet from Honour's line . . .

Not, one feels, for want of effort on Nicholson's part.

Although the figure of Victor broods over the *Garland of Ladslove* as that of Beatrice looms over *La Vita Nuova*, the poet nonetheless allows himself occasional excursions into more abstract zones. In *A Tragedy*, which (it is claimed) is 'translated from the French of E.Q.', he taps a Wordsworthian vein of rusticity. The language is as simple and moving as that of *The Thorn*, and the imagery even more richly suggestive:

> As I wandered forth (said the Poet to me)
>   On one of my country rambles,
> A ripening berry I chanced to see
>   Peeping forth from a bush of brambles.
>
> On the end of its slender stalk it swung
>   Half-hid in the thorny thicket,
> And I put my hand the briars among
>   And was just on the point to pick it.
>
> But when I felt it was immature
>   I pitied the poor little fellow,
> As I turned it over I saw it was sure
>   To grow more luscious and mellow.
>
> But would it be there another day?
>   I felt it was vain to ask it, –
> Some village girl would have come this way
>   And have tumbled it into her basket.
>
> So I thought of the bird in the hand, you know,
>   And I deemed it folly to linger,
> While bigger and bigger it seemed to grow
>   Between my thumb and finger.

A moment my lips above it hung,
   And I felt its destiny waver;
The next, I was rolling it over my tongue
   To catch its delicate flavour.

And I swear my soul will ne'er forget
   That moment of perfect rapture, –
Tinged with enjoyment, the touch of regret,
   And the pride of early capture!

It would be interesting to see the French original of this.

Nicholson gives no other evidence of Francophilia, despite the interest of many contemporary poets in Baudelaire, Verlaine, and Rimbaud. His character is unrepentantly Anglo-Saxon, an incandescent mixture of burning conscience and inflamed lust. A surprising bonus at the end of the book is a selection of his verses done into German by Bernard Esmarch. What hopes can Nicholson have entertained of the export market, one wonders?

Nicholson's next book was, if anything, even more privately published than *Ladslove*. *A Chaplet of Southernwood* was available in a limited edition issued by Harpur and Murray of the Moray Press Derby 'from Plants grown by John Gambril Nicholson and offered to Collectors by Frank Murray at his Country House "Leidernot", Ashover, Derbyshire on May Day 1896; Large Chaplet 6s. 3d. Small Chaplet 3s. 3d.' There were twenty-six copies – enough to go round a combined house and dinner party if Frank Murray lived in style at 'Leidernot'. Once again there is a charming Frontispiece of a naked small boy. He stands in some bushes playing a pan pipe, his loins artfully concealed by a spray of leaves. But even in Arcadia there is jealousy, as we discover in some verses to 'my Prince'. Imprisoned in his lime-tree bower, the poet observes his rival:

Reasoning with myself in shady seat
   Shall no man's arm, forsooth, except your own,
   About your Prince's shoulder e'er be thrown?
I said, and watched them basking in the heat.
Rising, they sought the arbour's cool retreat,
   Their voices fallen to an undertone,
   Yet, till the maddening bees buzzed on alone,
I cried, O *leave them to their whisperings sweet!*

At this point any similarities to Coleridge's meditation abruptly
cease. Here we are certainly not dealing with a poet who believes
that:

> 'Tis well to be bereft of promised good,
>   That we may lift the soul, and contemplate
>   With lively joy the joys we cannot share.

Nor was this poet immobilized at the time like poor Coleridge,
whose wife had accidentally emptied a skillet of boiling milk over
his foot, to the discomfort of her husband but to the great benefit of
English poetry. Nicholson is considerably more a man of action,
and the poem's mood changes from Coleridgean to Byronic in one
of those deft switches which bring the reader suddenly and violently into collision with reality:

> But *then* – remembering what had once occurred
>   Within that very bower (ah, memory fair!)
>   I found his silence more than I could bear;
> Resistless jealousy within me stirred,
>   I muttered savagely, *the eternal third!*
>   Flung reason to the winds and joined them there!

After the poet's 'prince' deserts him, which unfortunately happens early on in the volume, his wandering eye lights on a number
of seductive youngsters – a hiker, a bandsman (the attraction here
seems to be the uniform), a centre forward, a goalkeeper, a runner,
a skater and the ubiquitous nude boy bathers. One of the bathing
poems is a skittish recollection of a bathing-machine idyll:

A Knight of the Garter

> When we were dressing in the bathing van
>   My lover's eyes, for ever on the alert,
>   Noticed while he was struggling with his shirt,
> That round his leg a broad red circle ran:
> I feigned despair, and then, as he began
>   *The garter's tight – that's all; it doesn't hurt,*
>   Authority I hastened to assert,
> And said, *I'll fix that stocking please, young man!*

289

Forthwith I bent down at his feet; and he,
   Because he knew I love to bully thus,
   Submitted without any further fuss.
I thought he'd change it when I didn't see.
But as we sat at dinner, one bare knee
   Peeped forth and brought the comedy back to us.

The atmosphere of Nicholson's verse surges unpredictably between the fun and fresh air of Greyfriars on the one hand, and a steamy longing for pure young flesh on the other. One moment he is the schoolmaster, posing as a benevolent father-figure who just happens to be inspecting the dorm:

Discovered in a night-shirt dance
   He cried, without a trace of sorrow,
Oh, do you think, Sir there's a chance
   Of a whole holiday to-morrow?

. . . the next he is on the verge of orgasm:

A very flower of youth in languid pose
   The charms of Summer centre all in him
Asleep with sun-kissed body and naked limb,
For Nature here her full perfection shows –
A dream of Beauty that with gazing grows
   Until the raptured senses reel and swim.

Schoolmastering must have been a frustrating profession for Nicholson, though perhaps not quite as frustrating as, in the best of all possible worlds, it should have been. Did the parents notice anything, one wonders? Perhaps they only saw those verses that seemed to betray no more than the arrested development sometimes observable in schoolmasters:

The Footer-Bunny I would sing –
His shots, his rushes down the wing . . .

The Cricket Bunny must not be
Unnoticed in my elegy . . .

(This of a boy killed in the First World War.) But what might have been their reaction if an ill wind had blown a leaf of some little triolet or rondeau in praise of Ernest, Alec or Victor their way? The middle-class parent of a public schoolboy is not necessarily a discriminating judge of verse, so perhaps he would have taken in his stride such lines as:

> . . . Ah, love, your sweet face flushes,
> You tell it to the thrushes,
> While all the tall bulrushes
> Bend down to hear you speak!

On the other hand, perhaps he would have removed his son from the school.

Twenty-One

THE REVEREND
EDWIN EMMANUEL BRADFORD
1860–1944

An innocent admirer of youth

His book is a feat of serene wisdom served in a silver spoon – silver, for there is no mistaking the value of the verse form.

The Glasgow Herald *reviewing* The Tree of Knowledge

> Eros is up and away, away!
> Eros is up and away! . . .
> Strong, self-controlled, erect and free,
> He is marching along today!

from: *The Call*

> If he loved, he'd love a lad,
>   So he says.
> Not a chap as old as dad,
>   So he says.
> But often after saying this,
> He gives me just a little kiss:
> So after all the question is
>   Does Davie tell the truth?

from: *Does Davie Tell The Truth?*

A breezy vigour inspires these poems, making them pleasant to turn to after the whimperings of much modern poetry.

The Evening Standard

BETWEEN 1908 AND 1930 THE REV. E.E. BRADFORD published some eleven volumes of verse in praise of adolescents and young men, each of which received respectful, if occasionally guarded, notices from the national and provincial press. Dr Bradford was, I suspect, a uniquely English phenomenon, in that not only had he managed to convince himself that courting adolescent boys was the purest activity known to man (much purer than pursuing women, for example), but he succeeded in getting the press to enter into a conspiracy of polite silence as to the obvious tendency of his verses. 'His books were widely reviewed and widely praised, never, as far as I can judge, with the slightest hint of irony', writes Jonathan Gathorne-Hardy.'Here is *The Westminster Review*, but it is absolutely typical, on *Passing the Love of Women*: "Friendship between man and man, and even more, the friendship between man and youth form the theme of many of Dr Bradford's poems. He is as alive to the beauty of unsullied youth as was Plato."

'Plato is the clue. There was a pretence that all this love was really the love of the classics, and that when it was pure it was a marvellous thing. The point is, of course, that the love of the classics wasn't pure in the least; classical literature is the most lascivious and openly erotic homosexual literature in the world. Knowing this, Bradford "purifies" it with the same fresh air that whips round Sedburgh and Rugby.'[1]

As a clergyman, E.E. Bradford was treated as though he were above the baser sort of suspicion in a way that he certainly would not be nowadays. The reviewers maintained – in the teeth of considerable evidence – that he hymned only 'Platonic' love, by which

1. Jonathan Gathorne-Hardy, *The Public School Phenomenon*, Hodder & Stoughton, 1977, p. 215.

The *Literary World*'s critic remarked of Bradford's work: 'He is sometimes lacking in the odour of sanctity, but then he makes up with fresh air.'

they meant the 'non-physical' kind. For example, Bradford published *In Quest of Love* in 1914, which opens with an observation that sets the tone for the whole poem:

> A lover of women must learn to be
>   Content with one and leave the rest;
> But a lover of lads can do like me –
> Make love to a hundred equally
>   And still love one the best.

There follows a sort of Cook's tour of Europe, the Near East, and North Africa, in which the poet picks up or salivates over boys at every port of call. The *Times Literary Supplement* described all this as 'an eloquent disquisition on love of different kinds and among different nations'. The various reviews, which are reprinted at the end of each successive volume of Bradfordiana, are all similarly tactful, and often make highly entertaining reading. The *Oxford Magazine* described Bradford's *Lays of Love and Life* as a call to the young men of England to 'turn away from the wench with her powder and paint', and recommended that the book should be read by 'all earnest schoolmasters'. 'He is afraid neither of the facts of life nor of their implications', reported the *Cambridge Review* solemnly; and *The Commonwealth* described the atmosphere of one poem as 'healthy and vigorous', adding that it showed that the author had 'not only an intimate acquaintance with the ways of boys, but also sound knowledge of how to meet and deal with the minor vices of boyhood'.

It is rather difficult to reconcile these bland judgements with the poems themselves. *Fomes Peccati* contains the classic Bradford ingredients: 'pure' love between boys, an equivocal schoolmasterly observer, and the intrusion of sinful female sexuality into this masculine arcadia. The poem begins with a lyrical description of two boys lying on the beach. The one is 'bright-haired with beryl-coloured eyes' whose 'slender naked form' lies 'bleak and bare' on the sand; the other is distinctly earthy:

> Close by his side a lusty lad lay prone,
>   With brawny back, broad loins and swelling thighs
> All dimpled o'er with muscle, thew and bone:

His curly head half-raised was turned slantwise
Propt on one arm, to let his thoughtful eyes
    Drink in the radiant beauty of the boy
Who, though his gaze was fixed upon the skies,
    Perceived and thrilled with shy and modest joy –
The bliss of friendship pure – a bliss without alloy.

That, at any rate, is their story. But they are not alone:

And I who passed, with well-approving eye
    In silence watched . . .

In the next cove two ragged girls are playing. At sunset the two boys
set off for home and encounter the girls. The elder boy is already, as
the poet regretfully notes, entering the danger zone of heterosexual
attractions:

The timid child, distressed,
Flushed as she caught the elder youth's dark eye
Fixed on her own. The taller lass, less shy,
Leered at the lad; who, troubled in his turn,
Blushed hotly; yet half-impudent, half-sly,
Strove with an air of manly unconcern
To meet her bold black eyes, that seemed to glow and
    burn.

Things go from bad to worse; lust consumes the young Apollo:

His gaze intense
Pierced through her rags, and where her tattered dress
    Yawned wide and left her breast without defence
He gloated on its beauty – none the less
Because he saw her shame and maidenly distress.

It looks very much as if there will be a disagreeable incident; but the
girl is (literally) saved by the bell:

Her pain
Was almost physical, when sweet and strong
Tolled out a deep church bell for daily evensong.

This brings the boys to their senses, and they go on their way, leaving the poet to ponder on:

> . . . that perfect life where will
> Be neither sex nor marriage, and where Love,
>   Having no carnal office to fulfil,
> Will soar aloft on pinions of the dove,
> Leaving his lower half, to seek his spouse above.

The Rev. Bradford's innocence imbues his verses with a distinctive charm, which is not to be found, for instance, in the knowing cynicism of John Gambril Nicholson's (q.v.) poems. Bradford would not have considered publishing his work privately – there was no need to, since it contained nothing in the least offensive to conventional morality, and was larded with exhortations to pursue 'ideal' love and worship 'purity'. Gathorne-Hardy describes the poet as a 'small, innocent, apple-faced man who kept pennies for when the boys came to see him'[1]; his physical yearnings were so well repressed that they float through his poems like the tips of icebergs. He is probably one of the very few writers of whom a Freudian analysis would provide a complete description:

Alexander Fergusson

> Why, what a name it is!
> A mouthful for a bigger one,
>   I'll warrant you, than his;
> For his is such a little one –
>   About the size of this.
> But though it *is* a little one
>   It's big enough to kiss.

Were those the sort of thoughts, one wonders, that ran through his mind as he handed out his pennies? Sometimes he does seem to be aware that 'the classics' provide insufficient cover for all the implications of 'boy-love', and stirs in a little Christianity as well. It is obviously much more romantic to interfere with choirboys by the

1. Jonathan Gathorne-Hardy, op. cit., p. 214.

rays of a dim religious light, than to hand out one's pennies to the
swarthy young gigolos of the Mediterranean:

> Is Boy-Love Greek? Far off across the seas
> The warm desire of Southern men may be:
> But passion freshened by a Northern breeze
> Gains in male vigour and in purity.
> Our yearning tenderness for boys like these
> Has more in it of Christ than Socrates.

Of course, the ideal of 'boy-love' does not allow much in the way
of competition. The reverse side of Rev. Bradford's penny is a
healthy suspicion of womanhood, which he does not hesitate to
develop into an ideology that would be unlikely to please the
tougher sort of feminist:

Woman

> We will not worship woman nor contemn her,
>   She's part of Nature's plan.
> Besides, we damn ourselves if we condemn her,
>   She is but meaner man.
>
> To love-sick lads her merits seem amazing
>   But 'twere a curious question,
> If calf-love be not much like crystal-gazing –
>   A case of self-suggestion!
>
> Man's tool or toy ten thousand generations,
>   She lived linked to his side:
> Her chiefest charm lay in her limitations –
>   Her folly fed his pride!
>
> If now she will be wise and work together
>   With man for some high end,
> She has our welcome and good wishes, whether
>   She come as foe or friend.
>
> But if she live by lust, and barter beauty
>   For the foul hire of whore,
> Alluring lads from the stern path of Duty,
>   She shall be slave once more!

Bradford well expresses the terror of women to be found in male chauvinists with suppressed homosexual impulses. The church was for a long time a convenient refuge for such uncertain souls, and, even today, one or two of the speeches concerning the ordination of women at the recent Anglican Synod make one wonder if that is not still the case. In Bradford's long poem *The True Aristocracy*, the hero realizes as an adolescent that he is 'different', becomes a curate when adult, and falls in love with a choirboy. His conflicting feelings as a boy are described with the Reverend's usual guileless candour:

> Awake lay Edward in the dark,
> 'I'm not like others I can see:
> And simply by one stray remark
> I made it plain. What can it be?
> I think it's called misogyny.
> But 'tisn't Woman that I hate.
> I love my Mother. It's in *me*
> The thing that I abominate –
> And girls who put me in that state.'

For the most part, Bradford sticks to his lathe – which is glamorous adolescent boys. His ventures further afield are rare, and do not exhibit his genius at its best. Theology is dealt with sporadically, but the reader can see that it lies outside the vicar's main field of interest, and the poems concerned are perfunctory, to say the least:

> Some fancy man must be God's favourite:
> I hold we all are equal in His sight,
> When Christian martyrs were by lions bit,
> God gave these courage and those appetite.

And church architecture also gets a mention in lines that unexpectedly reveal Dr Bradford as a precursor of Betjeman and Pevsner:

> Her spacious Church is picturesque
> Built not in one style but in all:
> The nave is Norman Romanesque,
> The later choir, transitional:

The tower's a stunted nondescript:
In Cromwell's time, 'tis said, 'twas stript
Of parapet and pinnacles;
But still it serves to hold the bells.

But these are isolated islands in the great sea of 'boy-love'. This, so to speak, was his natural bent; for he only had a third class degree in Theology from Exeter, and his ecclesiastical career, though blameless, was not distinguished. He was Assistant Chaplain at St Petersburg 1887–9, and Chaplain to the English Church in Paris between 1880 and 1899. From 1899–1905 he was resident in some clerical capacity at Eton, but not, as far as one can tell from the Eton Register, at the school itself. Nevertheless, the propinquity of boys must have had something to do with the flood of verses about schoolboys and the romantic school stories that flowed from his pen from 1908 onwards. The last of these, *Boyhood and Other Poems*, seems to have appeared in 1930, by which time the seventy-year-old lyricist was enjoying a well-earned retirement in East Anglia. By then, his relentless production was earning him reviews in *The Times*, *The Times Literary Supplement* and *The New Age*. In the last named journal one encounters with a shock of pleasurable surprise a glowing review of Bradford's *The Kingdom Within You* by Hugh McDiarmid. Is this, one wonders, really the same person as the noted author of *A Drunk Man Looks at the Thistle* and of the *First* and *Second Hymns to Lenin*? Anyway, he is in no doubt about the qualities of Bradford: 'His work is full of direct grappling with the problems of the age,' he writes, 'hard thinking, common sense, plain statement, no flowers, and no monkey tricks; virile useful work . . . Many of our "leading poets" would be greatly astonished if they could foresee how small they will look in comparison to Dr Bradford yet.' I fear that 'our leading poets' have yet to be astonished; but Rev. Bradford did not go entirely unappreciated by them. W.H. Auden was an enormous fan of his work, and used to give spontaneous after-dinner recitations of the poems which, it is said, frequently brought the house down.

Twenty-Two

WILLIAM NATHAN STEDMAN
floruit 1900–16

Fire, brimstone and unrequited love

The mongrel has the snarling sauce to sneer
His 'own idears' [*sic*] 'gainst Truth: the gas to rear
Big pronoun talk, so full of 'I's that he
Seems like a bad potato, which can't see
    That 'I's are no eyes when bunged up with 'me'.

from: *Stedman's Sonnets: Lays and Lyrics* (1911)
(It is not clear from the context who the 'mongrel' is. The Pope, perhaps.)

To tea! And Tête-a-tête! The Snowdrop white
With Mephistopheles just face to face!
. . . O it was marvellous! Comparison
Doth please my dext'rous mind, my poet's wit.
He and She! He – a Corpse – in unison
With 'fame' and 'tea', – just She and he and 'it'
    I stay to think, to frown at him – and SPIT.

(This poem appears to be about Jack the Ripper and one of his victims, but it may be about Marie Corelli and Gladstone. It is not always easy to tell in Stedman's work.)

The Bell! Ah, yes, the bell.
What fate may it foretell?
Birth, death, marriage, dinner,
News – for saint or sinner:
Visitors, – railway train:
FIRE – dustmen round again.
From start to finish life is
Largely hung with bells . . .

from: *What Might Have Been*

IN THE PRELIMINARY PAGES of his 1912 volume *What Might Have Been*, Stedman tells us that Lord Salisbury had described him as 'a genius, a gentleman and a hero'. This was certainly a weighty recommendation from the man who was soon to establish his reputation as a connoisseur of poetry by appointing Alfred Austin to the laureateship. However, Prime Ministers are two a penny and all publishers know that a royal endorsement sells books, whereas a politician's puff may repel as many as it attracts. Accordingly, we are further informed that Queen Alexandra described either Stedman or his work (it is not clear which) as 'fragrant and beautiful' in 1905.

'Fragrant and beautiful' are not the words that spring to mind as one leafs through Stedman's verses, to describe which 'violent', 'erratic' and 'unhinged' might seem more appropriate. Like so many poetasters, he has his obsessions, in this case Marie Corelli[1] and the Church of Rome. The Frontispiece of *What Might Have Been* introduces the reader at once to these two recurrent features of the Stedman oeuvre. On the left there is a photographic portrait of the author, a dapper-looking figure with a large buttonhole – the source of his fragrance, perhaps. Underneath runs the inscription: 'William Nathan Stedman, The Man of God.' On the facing page is a picture of Marie Corelli, looking bosomy and spiritual, with the caption: 'Marie Corelli, His Bride Elect.' These striking portraits are surmounted by a headline: 'The King and Queen of Pen. Two Great Champions of Protestantism.'

Stedman was clearly not a man to do things by halves; although he seems never to have met Marie Corelli, he appointed himself her

---

1. Marie Corelli (1855–1924), author of *The Sorrows of Satan* and other supposedly daring novels. She became so enraged at the mockery of the critics that she eventually refused to have copies of her novels sent out for review.

White Knight and rode out to meet the enemy – those 'white-livered parsons', 'hatchet-faced scribblers', 'grub-street lepers', 'bottle-nosed editors', 'pawnshop reviewers', 'syphilis-veined crit-ics' and 'bull-browed bastards', as he so elegantly described her detractors. 'My lance against the world for its Greatest Lady', he announces at the beginning of *Lays and Lyrics Addressed to Queen Marie* (1911), 'Any Man, Beast or Buffoon want SMASHING?' It seems that he does not intend to limit himself to corrective meas-ures of a purely literary nature, for elsewhere he writes: 'I have no literary language pungent enough to express my Unfathomable Disgust, but if any future attack is intended upon THIS LADY, and the writer or speaker will master sufficient temerity to send me his name and abode, one of my 7-foot Zulus (Faithful Fellows) will promptly attend – distance and expense immaterial – with his sjambok and FULL INSTRUCTIONS WHAT TO DO." Nor are the Lays in defence of Queen Marie any less robust:

> I've heard men say – one said it to my face –
>   'Think what she knows, and what she writes about'
> I laughed aloud, at merry gleesome pace,
>   Which made him stare, and then retorted, 'Lout
>   Wouldst measure wit with her? Heyday!
> As well compare thy dullard self and mind
>   Against the sun . . .

Stedman also points out in a note that 'none of you scrofulous swine-hounds' [her critics] 'could compose a page of Any of the books written by your Queen' – an accusation that is probably justified.

The logical conclusion of Stedman's gallantry on behalf of Marie Corelli (of which, so far as I know, she was totally unaware), is an offer of marriage. He already claims to be her husband in spirit (and in this capacity threatens to 'slog, slosh and SCRABB' the opposi-tion), but in one of his most passionate lays he actually proposes. Not the least weighty of the arguments advanced in support of his suit is the fact that God had clearly intended such an alliance in the interests of the Protestant cause; for Stedman is no ordinary mortal:

> Perchance within my countenance thou'lt see
> The shade of Him, The Man of Galilee . . .

Stedman's awareness of himself as among the few who are chosen is constantly surfacing in the truculent prefatory matter to his various books. *The Master's Foreword* to his *Sonnets: Lays And Lyrics* (Sydney, 1911) contains some of his most original observations in this vein, together with an extensive excoriation of Gladstone and the evangelist R. J. Campbell. Nor does the Laureate, Alfred Austin, escape what must be the only known example of unreasonable criticism of him: 'The beautiful gift of poetical genius', writes the Man of God, 'was ever intended for the service of God and not for prostitution to mammon, not for the antics of a court-paid wee-piping buffoon; (an office which I refused after Tennyson's death, though made with the offer of a premier's daughter and £30,000); nor to drag the prophet's mantle through the mud of party politics. How many puny little poetasters will sneer when they read this?[1] Hundreds, maybe thousands . . . but the Poet can neither be bought nor sold . . . so scoffer, cut your tongue out.' After some further vilification of these unnamed talentless scribblers ('I know that I have MORE clean sound sense in my backside than is in all the squirming lot of these Foul Slugs'), Stedman moves into overdrive when dealing with Gladstone. He points out that the numerical calculations made in certain passages of *The Revelation of St John the Divine* force us to the inescapable conclusion that Gladstone is the Man-Beast-666. In case of scepticism on this point, he silences the opposition with the following crushing observation: 'If Almighty God can be capable of making any mistake in His Holy Revelation, then I am a Fool; but YOU are a silly hump-backed, boss-eyed, slobbering and ghastly IDIOT. So how do we stand?' Having thus flattered his readers into acquiescence, Stedman proceeds to lambast Gladstone, two of his more picturesque epithets being: 'a DIRTY OLD DEVIL' and 'a protoplasm from the abyss of nowhere'. It seems that Gladstone had conspired with the Reverend Campbell ('moo-cow kid-gloved Campbell')[2], and others, to undermine the true religion (i.e., fanatical Protestantism). 'There is no sane manliness in bishops' aprons, wide beavers, bandy gaiters, and bloated paunches' says Stedman. 'National Protestantism' is the creed of the

1. Alfred Austin was exactly five feet tall.
2. Reginald John Campbell (1867–1956) was Congregationalist pastor of the City Temple in London (1903–15) and in 1907 published his *New Theology*, which was too 'advanced' for conservative tastes.

righteous, and 'the cesspool of Rome' that of the damned. All this is but a warm-up for some ranting verses that remind one of the Reverend Ian Paisley's speeches:

> I've read the histories of all mankind,
> Yet do I swear that I could never find
> Such guilty guilt as stinks in gilded Rome:
> Nor crafty craft as creeps beneath her dome.
> I've travelled earth and sea, yet never seen
> Such crimson sin as 'Her who sits a Queen.'
> The brain of man can not conceive a sin
> Which SHE's not done, abroad, without, within, –
> Still reeling DRUNK – SHE's 'ready to begin'

As with some medieval disputants, the obscurity of some of Stedman's insults occasionally blunts their effect. This is even more true of his prose tirade *Antichrist And The Man of Sin* (1909), which shares the eccentricity and generally opaque quality of many such works and is, indeed, more cracked than most. It is littered with sentences like: 'Never yet reigned ANY king but who was not more or less a selfish worldly PIG, David, the sweet Psalmist king, was a murderer and adulterer. Solomon, the wisest king, a spectacle of debauched PIG.' And so on right down to Teddy Guelph, 'the present FOND FRIEND of Antichrist . . . who has for upwards of fifteen years PIGGISHLY PREVENTED this holy Revelation [i.e. Stedman's], although fully cognizant of its FACTS.' While the book as a whole is an exercise in the demasking of the enemies of Protestantism in general, and of Stedman in particular, Chapter 9 presents an interesting comparison between Jesus and Gladstone, in which we are not surprised to see Gladstone come off worst. 'The character of Jesus', we are told, 'was All Sweetness, Lovable Kindness and Merciful; Heroically Patient and Stamped with Grace. Gladstone's with bitterness, hateful strife, and angry assertion, and smelling of satanic gloze.

'Jesus was a Golden Example of Open Honesty and Truth. Gladstone a Fraud and Lying Humbug, doing all things with craft, conceiving and breeding policies in darkness.' And so on, through a whole litany of hatred for 'the Inhuman Hog of Greedy Ambition'. One can only suppose that all this ferocity has something to do with

Gladstone's Irish policies, since only a measure as sane and just as Home Rule would be likely to provoke such mindless Protestant fury. At any rate, the tract ends with some thundering madness from the Book of Revelations, with additional material by Stedman, which has the flavour of a speech written by Enoch Powell and delivered by Denis Skinner.

Stedman's last work, *Sky Blue Ballads* (1916), contains only flashes of his old belligerence. He does say: 'the only way, and the best, sometimes, to convince a fool that the power of God is in you is to knock him down first and reason with him afterwards'; but this is merely a candid exposition of the theory which many Christians have previously put into practice. Somehow, the fire seems to have gone out of the old warrior, and we notice the absence of baroque insult and wild accusation. Perhaps his return from Australia had something to do with it (the book is published in Finchley), or perhaps he had simply been having treatment. Is there, for instance, a fleeting glimpse of self-knowledge in his latest assertion of his 'divine afflatus' when he remarks: 'a heifer cannot shoulder a rifle any more than a swine can play the bagpipes; and any man falsely assuming the prophet's mantle makes a mock of himself and is the derision of the sane'? As for *la grande passion* that too seems a pale shadow of the past. Could it be that someone had informed Marie Corelli of what was being addressed to her, and to her enemies on her behalf, by the furioso of Sydney; and that she had put a stop to it? Whatever the reason, we are left with only a sad little echo of *What Might Have Been*:

> For what to me a marble heart?
> Or soul cold as a stone?
> I loved her in the single art
> Of calling her my own.

Twenty-Three

WILHELMINA STITCH
died 1936
Thought for the day

'Chipsee, wee, wee, wee, wee!' 'Husband, how you
   chatter!
Twe, twe, what's the matter?' 'Chipsee, wee, wee, wee,
   wee!'
sang Mr Tomtit. 'Come, wife, look at it. A house and to
   let.
Nailed tight to a tree. A thatched roof, my pet a real
   luxury!
   'The entrance is small, so we needn't fear the
   sparrows
will call – they're common my dear. Chipsee, wee,
   wee, wee, wee!'

from: *House-Hunting* in *Out of Doors* (1934)

Now this is in praise of Nannie, no matter where
she may be; attached to a city baby or a dumpling by
the sea . . .

from: *To Nannies Everywhere* in *A Heap o' Folk* (1934)

He'd spent his life with clocks, he said. There wasn't
much he didn't know about their moods, some fast,
   some slow.
He smiled and slowly shook his head, then looked
   defiantly at me: 'They're just like women – clocks,'
said he.

from: *The Clockmaker's Philosophy* in *A Heap o'Folk* (1934)

WILHELMINA STITCH, PATIENCE STRONG, Helen Steiner Rice – the names are reassuringly awkward, like Rover cars in the fifties or late Victorian furniture. People with names like these must surely possess several pairs of 'sensible' shoes, and probably live in Hove. The names, of course, are pen names, carefully chosen to evoke the characters of the poetesses and of their work; their resonance is powerful and persistent, triggering a vision of a world flooded with beautiful thoughts, and of people confronting life with stiff upper lips and unflagging optimism:

> Up to its neck in water, boiling water too. Yet the kettle
> keeps on singing – that's what we ought to do!

So wrote the celebrated purveyor of *The Fragrant Minute* which from 1924 until 1936, appeared every day in the *Daily Sketch* and other newspapers. A cosy thought over the cornflakes, a tender tip at teatime – these were the stock-in-trade of Wilhelmina Stitch, pioneer of the prose poem for the mass audience.

She was born Ruth Collie, but we do not know when, for it is undignified for ladies to exhibit their age to all and sundry in *Who's Who*. The north seems to have been her base – at any rate the *Daily Despatch* of Manchester and the *North Mail* of Newcastle were for many years favoured with her 'Fragrant Minutes' on a daily basis. Before that she was a journalist in Winnipeg from 1913 to 1923, and sometime Literary Editor of the *Western Home Monthly* based in that city. The winter months were usually spent travelling around lecturing, and she also tells us that 'she responded to many requests to take pulpits in various churches'. Apart from the fact that she was an 'honorary member of the magicians club', we are vouchsafed no further information.

The content of her 'poetry' is in the tradition of the 'domestic bards', of which Ella Wheeler Wilcox was the most expressive modern representative, and which television soap operas and allied forms of pre-packaged consolation have all but extinguished. Only Patience Strong's mournful comfort is still on tap, accessible from over sixty books with encouraging titles like *Every Common Bush*, *Golden Rain*, *Crumbs of Comfort*, *Silver Linings* and *Sunny Byways*. The public for these anaemic lay sermons was Stitch's public too; homely thoughts, a 'smilin' through' philosophy, and themes of unabashed sentimentality are the bedrock of her appeal. This is 'uplift' with a vengeance, a bromide for the troubled soul, an anaesthetic for the intellect. Thus, *The Bright Side* begins:

> Pretty nice world if we take it all round, and this
> after all is the common sense way . . .

and *Wings of Faith* reassures the troubled swimmer:

> Doubting heart, worried heart, breasting life's high seas,
> it's water-wings you're needing, then you'll swim with ease.

Sitting at home in Winnipeg, or points east, the poetess fixed her formidable attention on the most mundane aspects of the most mundane lives, and then apostrophized them in an excruciating hybrid of prose and verse:

> The gateway to adventure, the door to the unknown, oft
> ruler of our destinies, such is the telephone. I always feel
> excited (though I hide my feelings well!) when silences are
> broken by the telephone's loud bell.
>
> That ring! What does it herald, an invite out to tea? Or a
> friend whom I love dearly has important news for me?
> Sometimes there's disappointment – 'wrong number, five
> not eight'. Sometimes 'tis husband calling, 'A meeting, I'll
> be late'.
>
> It's somewhat of a let-down when a charming voice says:
> 'Please, I wish to come to demonstrate how carpets clean
> with ease.' But it's always an adventure when the bell rings
> loud and clear, and we lift up the receiver – just wondering
> what we'll hear.

Wilhelmina's achievement is to have established, through her verse, a purely phatic communication with her audience. They know she's there prattling away about telephones and bathtubs, knitting and recipes; the sound of it is vaguely consoling, like *Songs of Praise*, or David Jacobs on Saturday mornings. She tells them what they want to hear, and what they know already – that every cloud has a silver lining, and the meek shall inherit the earth; that husbands should be indulged like children and flattered like emperors; that women and wives make all the sacrifices, but sometimes have their moods; that babies are little bundles of bliss and parents are besotted with them. This last theme is dealt with in one of Wilhelmina's most delightful poems entitled *Legs and Arms*:

> A CURIOUS thing, but a fact all the same, some
> friends of mine (never mind what name) thought
> of nothing but a William and Mary chair they'd bought
> and also a table, a tallboy, a chest, with which they
> had furnished the room for a guest. Whenever I visited
> just for a span, 'twas 'William and Mary' or good
> 'Queen Anne'. 'Twas 'Hepplewhite' this and
> 'Chippendale' that. I soon had the periods learnt
> off pat. They looked at a leg, 'cup-turned',
> they said, and bade me observe their Sheraton
> bed. But now all's changed and the reason's this.
> There's a little curved leg they love to kiss; there's
> a dimpled arm so smooth and white,
> its graceful contour gives delight. And as for
> the chest, it gives much joy, says Daddy,
> 'Just look at this fine tallboy!' Of Seventeenth
> Century they don't speak. Everything dates from
> just last week. For period furniture lost
> its hold – since they have acquired a one-week old.

These lines, with their charmingly turned conceits, exhibit Wilhelmina at her most beguilingly playful. They also remind us of the residual middle-class element which is to be found in all but her most populist work. Antique-furniture collectors cannot have been very numerous amongst *Daily Sketch* readers, nor can many of them have felt quite the same way as Wilhelmina about a boy's first dinner jacket. (In her poem *The Day of Days* she describes how he spends all of it ecstatically in his room, occasionally opening the cupboard to gaze at the garment.) Sometimes, indeed, her attitude to the lower orders verges on the insulting, as in her *Thoughts Before Shopping*. Referring to the shop assistants, she writes:

> Let me not be impatient if they're slow. Of all their private
> sorrows naught I know. I must remember they have
> feelings, too . . .

Like dogs, in fact. Yet Wilhelmina is always genuinely concerned about the people she encounters, as we learn from her booklet *A Heap o' Folk* (Methuen, 1934), which consists of tributes to life's unsung heroes – nannies, doctors, plumbers, firemen, nurses, lifeboat-men, window-cleaners – all the caring professions. One hesitates over the inclusion amongst all this of a ringing tribute to Robbie Burns, until one realizes that he is probably there in his capacity as a ploughman. It is of the nature of Wilhelmina's genius to make manifest, what is not always apparent to the untutored eye; namely that each and every one of these characters, from the railway porter to the muffin-man, is a paragon of patience and civility. Many of us will even view the London bus conductor in a different light after reading her moving description of him:

> A steadying hand, a cheerful grin, 'Hold tight',
> he cries, and helps us in.

All the greatest poets have the power to make us share their experiences, however alien they may seem to our own. With Wilhelmina, one sometimes has the uncanny feeling that the reverse process is taking place and that she is simply sharing *our* experiences. How does she manage, we wonder, to reproduce so accurately the tedious woolgathering and half-witted philosophizing that fill our waking hours:

> . . . Your digestion gives way, when thoughts are all wrong.
> Though someone may say the tea was too strong. More
> often it's hate that makes you feel ill. When in this sad state
> – take a Good Humour pill.

310

To thousands of her readers Wilhelmina Stitch was herself a 'good humour' pill; and by courtesy of the *Daily Sketch*, the pill was available every morning. '"Blessed are they"' she sang, 'who are pleasant to live with, "Blessed are they who sing in the morning" '; and again: 'Sing a song of Spring-cleaning! Polish up the mind . . ' A merry Martha of the Muses, she spread her sweetness and light across the land. When she described 'August', the *Enchantress of the Year*, she could almost have been describing herself:

. . . Lovely woman thou with buoyant gait walking the earth. Green apples fall from startled bough shaken by thy full-throated mirth . . .

And this even despite the distressing ubiquity of dilatory shop assistants.

APPENDIX

Passages for Recitation

The following poems, or extracts from poems, are reprinted as being suitable for recitation, since live performance will undoubtedly bring out their many hidden riches.

1. *George Meredith* (1828–1909) the erratic Victorian genius, wrote with great distinction, and even greater obscurity. The passage below is hypnotically compelling, although completely incomprehensible without the notes supplied in the *Collected Poems*. It comes from *The Empty Purse*, subtitled *A Sermon to our Later Prodigal Son* (1892). The description is of a curious custom of the people of Marseilles, as noted by a Roman scholar; they fattened a sacrificial victim for a whole year (paid for out of public funds), so that his eventual murder by the populace should relieve the city of the plague. When the year was up, he was led through the streets, while the people reviled him, and finally pushed off a cliff. The poem contains many delightful lines such as:

> We follow no longer a trumpet-snout
> At a trot where the hog is tracked,
> Nor wriggle the way of the worm.

But the murder itself is a *tour de force*:

> He cancelled the ravaging Plague
> With the roll of his fat off the cliff.
> Do thou, with thy lean as the weapon of ink,
> Though they call thee an angler who fishes the vague
> And catches the none too pink,
> Attack one as murderous, knowing thy cause
> Is the cause of community. Iterate

312

Iterate, iterate, harp on the trite:
Our preacher to win is the supple in stiff:
Yet always in measure with bearing polite:

2. *William Wordsworth* (1770–1850) was, of all the really great poets, the most determined not to be diverted from his purpose by the mere intrusion of bathos. *While Anna's peers and early playmates tread* (1827) is justly celebrated as an example of his unrepentant boldness in this respect. A captivating image from it was borrowed by D.B. Wyndham Lewis and Charles Lee for the title of their anthology of bad verse. A note in the *Collected Poems* tells us that: 'This [poem] is taken from the account given by Miss Jewsbury of the pleasure she derived, when long confined to her bed by sickness, from the inanimate object on which this sonnet turns.'

> While Anna's peers and early playmates tread,
> In freedom, mountain-turf and river's marge;
> Or float with music in the festal barge;
> Rein the proud steed, or through the dance are led;
> Her doom it is to press a weary bed –
> Till oft her guardian Angel, to some charge
> More urgent called, will stretch his wings at large,
> And friends too rarely prop the languid head.
> Yet, helped by Genius – untired comforter,
> The presence even of a stuffed Owl for her
> Can cheat the time; sending her fancy out
> To ivied castles and to moonlight skies,
> Though he can neither stir a plume, nor shout,
> Nor veil, with restless film, his staring eyes.

The first five lines of *Oxford, May 30th, 1820*, are also well worth committing to memory, in case one is ever invited to High Table:

> Ye sacred Nurseries of blooming Youth!
> In whose collegiate shelter England's Flowers
> Expand, enjoying through their vernal hours
> The air of liberty, the light of truth;
> Much have ye suffered from Time's gnawing tooth . . .

A number of Wordsworth's *Lyrical Ballads* benefit from a reading aloud, too, most notably *The Thorn* ('I've measured it from side to side;/'Tis three feet long, and two feet wide . . .'), *Simon Lee* ('"Give me your tool,' to him I said"') and *We Are Seven*. The ballad most guaranteed to keep an audience in thrall, however, must surely be *Peter Bell*, which is full of unexpected felicities:

> All, all is silent – rocks and woods,
> All still and silent – far and near!
> Only the Ass, with motion dull,
> Upon the pivot of his skull
> Turns round his long left ear.

> Thought Peter, What can mean all this?
> Some ugly witchcraft must be here!
> – Once more the Ass, with motion dull,
> Upon the pivot of his skull
> Turned round his long left ear.

3. The sentimental and patriotic verses of *Eliza Cook* (1818–89) were popular with the Victorian public, her greatest hit being *The Old Arm-Chair*:

> I love it! I love it! And who shall dare
> To chide me for loving that old arm-chair?
> I've treasured it long as a sainted prize;
> I've bedewed it with tears, and embalmed it with sighs . . .

The Lansdowne Poets edition of her *Complete Poems* (Frederick Warne & Co., 1869) contains 624 pages of stirring and/or pathetic verses. A speaker with presence and a taste for rodomontade could doubtless make much of her poem entitled: *I Laughed At The Storm*, which ends:

> The groaning blast that levelled the mast
> > Was pleasing music to me;
> I dared to rave at the giant wave,
> > Though that wave my shroud might be.

> Though I heard the yell of a last farewell
>   In a messmate's gurgling cry;
> Yet I firmly stood 'mid the lightnings and flood
>   To laugh at the storm, or to die.

The subject of death stimulates Eliza to some of her happiest flights of fancy; the funereal knell and the clink of the spade in the churchyard are music to her ears. *The Song of the Worm* is a typically cheery reminder of Keynes' observation that, in the long run, we are all dead:

> Daughters of earth, if I happen to meet
> Your bloom-plucking fingers and sod-treading feet –
> Oh! turn not away with the shriek of disgust
> From the thing you must mate with in darkness and dust.
> Your eyes may be flashing in pleasure and pride,
> 'Neath the crown of a Queen or the wreath of a bride;
> Your lips may be fresh and your cheeks may be fair –
> Let a few years pass over, and I shall be there.

4. *Adam Lindsay Gordon* (1833–70) was described as Australia's national poet after his death by suicide in 1870, although he only spent the second half of his life in that country. His two great passions – horse-riding and versifying – were combined in the series of betting tips which appeared as poems about imaginary horse races in *Bell's Life* under the title of *Hippodromania*. In 1865 he was elected to the South Australian House of Assembly; 'as a politician', observes his biographer drily, 'he could not see clearly beyond the ears of his horse, but it suited his restless temperament.'[1] Happily, the extremely light burden of parliamentary duties left him plenty of time for poetry. Four lines of his have achieved a certain permanence and were engraved on his memorial:

> Life is mostly froth and bubble,
>   Two things stand like stone
> *Kindness* in another's trouble,
>   *Courage* in your own.

1. *Adam Lindsay Gordon – The Man and the Myth*, Geoffrey Hutton, Faber, 1978.

Unfortunately, Gordon decided to attempt something much more ambitious than *Ye Wearie Wayfarer, Hys Ballad In Eight Fyttes*, from which those charmingly inoffensive lines are taken. This was *Ashtaroth*, an extraordinary tale of Europe in the Middle Ages, which the author himself described as mostly 'bosh'. The drama concerns Hugo, a Norman baron, who is trying to find the secret of life through astronomy; and Agatha, to whom he was pledged, but who once ran off with a handsome Dane called Harold, later killed by Hugo. The Crusader Baldwin is Agatha's father and has sent a letter from his deathbed asking Hugo to accompany his daughter to the Convent of Englemehr. Hugo's secretary is a man called Orion, who is an evil spirit in earthly disguise. When his terrestrial companions are looking the other way, he holds philosophical discussions with his dubious cronies in the ether:

> Man lingers through toils unavailing
> For blessings that baffle his grasp;
> To his cradle he comes with a wailing
> He goes to his grave with a gasp.

There is much wandering around in what is now West Germany. Eric, an old friend of Hugo, who seems to have been spending a long weekend with his mother, suddenly turns up at a farmhouse on the Rhine where Hugo is lodging:

> What, Hugo, still at the Rhine! I thought
> You were home. You have travelled by stages short,

(he remarks). During their conversation Hugo makes the unforgettable observation:

> Fighting is all a mistake, friend Eric,
> And has been so since the age Homeric . . .

Although Hugo succeeds in delivering a somewhat reluctant Agatha to the convent, he soon has to rescue her again, because some dastardly Teutons attack the retreat in order to relieve the monks and nuns of their cash hoard. The preparations for battle produce some striking speeches, such as Hugo's address to his horse:

Ha! Rollo, thou champest
Thy bridle and stampest,
For the rush of the tempest
    Dost long?
Ho! the kites will grow fatter
On the corpses we scatter,
In the parks where we shatter
    Their throng:

Where Oscric, the craven,
Hath reared the black raven
'Gainst monks that are shaven
    And cowl'd;
Where Teuton and Hun sit
In the track of our onset,
Will the wolves, ere the sunset,
    Have howl'd.

. . . Birds of prey they have been
And of carrion unclean
And their own nests (I ween)
    They have foul'd etc. . . .

In the bloody siege that follows there is some memorable dialogue between Hugo's victorious officers, Eustace and Thurston, and the Abbess Ursula. It would sound well in an after-dinner salon performance, providing a respectable amount of wine has already been consumed:

Thurston:	. . . Where's Ethelwolf?
Eustace:	Dying.
Thurston:	And Reginald?
Eustace:	Dead.
	And Ralph is disabled, and Rudolph is sped.
	He may last till midnight – not longer. Nor Tyrrel,
	Nor Brian, will ever see sunrise.
Thurston:	That Cyril,
	The monk, is a very respectable fighter.
Eustace:	Not bad for a monk. Yet our loss had been lighter,

Had he and his fellows thrown open the gate
A little more quickly. And now, spite of fate,
With thirty picked soldiers their siege we might
    weather,
But the Abbess is worth all the rest put together.
    [Enter Ursula.]

Thurston: Here she comes.

Ursula: Can I speak with your Lord?

Eustace: 'Tis too late,
He was dead when we carried him in at the gate.

Thurston: Nay, he spoke after that, for I heard him myself;
But he won't speak again, he must lie on his shelf.

Ursula: Alas! he is dead then?

Thurston: As dead as St Paul.
And what then? to-morrow we, too, one and all
Die, to fatten these ravenous carrion birds,
I knelt down by Hugo and heard his last words:
'How heavy the night hangs – how wild the waves
    dash!
Say a mass for my soul – and give Rollo a mash.'

Ursula: Nay, Thurston thou jestest.

Thurston: Ask Eric . . .

    The story is rounded off with a lament for Hugo and a rather self-righteous dirge from the monks. Admirers of Gordon, and indeed of horses, will relish the hero's dying words, which could almost have been the poet's own. *Ashtaroth* itself is perhaps not very suitable for stage production, but a 'reading' by dedicated Gordon fans could produce many enjoyable surprises.

5.   *J. Gordon Coogler* (1865–1901) (q.v.) is also a suitable poet for recitation, because of the way he slowly works up to his best effects:

Isn't This Bliss

O'er against the garden wall, thrice kissed by wayward lips
    She stood pondering and weeping
O'er that momentary bliss known to all fair maidens –
    A stolen kiss.

With ruby lips, bright eyes gazing upward in his face,
　　She stood delighted, yet angry;
Till strong arms embraced her, and forgetting all she sighed,
　　'Isn't this bliss?'

A Sweet Object

It lay on the back of the bench
　　In its magic beauty
　　A jewel rich and fair;
And as my thoughts enlarged
　　How I fondly gazed
　　On the sweet thing lying there.

It lay on the back of the bench,
　　A mysterious object
　　I could not understand;
Yet I loved its angel-shape,
　　As my passionate gaze
　　Sunk to her matchless hand.

God Correctly Understood

The man who thinks God is too kind
To punish actions vile,
Is bad at heart, of unsound mind
Or very juvenile.

6. *Mrs Julia A. Moore* (1847–1920) (q.v.) used to give performances of her own poems, much to the delight of the citizens of Grand Rapids, Michigan. In the chapter on Mrs Moore I have quoted a couple of stanzas from her *Sketch of Lord Byron's Life*, the whole of which is reproduced below. It has many of the poetess' most inimitable touches, and the suggested model for delivery is Lord Clark doing one of his pithy television lectures on 'Civilization':

'Lord Byron' was an Englishman
　　A poet I believe,
His first works in old England
　　Was poorly received.

Perhaps it was 'Lord Byron's' fault
   And perhaps it was not.
His life was full of misfortunes
   Ah, strange was his lot.

The character of 'Lord Byron'
   Was of a low degree,
Caused by his reckless conduct,
   And bad company.
He sprung from an ancient house,
   Noble, but poor, indeed.
His career on earth, was marred
   By his own misdeeds.

Generous and tender hearted,
   Affectionate by extreme,
In temper he was wayward,
   A poor 'Lord' without means;
Ah, he was a handsome fellow
   With great poetic skill,
His great intellectual powers
   He could use at his will.

He was a sad child of nature,
   Of fortune and of fame;
Also a sad child to society,
   For nothing did he gain
But slander and ridicule,
   Throughout his native land.
Thus the 'poet of the passions,'
   Lived, unappreciated, man.

Yet at the age of 24,
   'Lord Byron' then had gained
The highest, highest pinacle [sic]
   Of literary fame.
Ah, he had such violent passions
   They was beyond his control,
Yet the public with its justice,
   Sometimes would him extol.

Sometimes again 'Lord Byron'
    Was censured by the press,
Such obloquy, he could not endure,
    So he done what was the best.
He left his native country,
    This great unhappy man;
The only wish he had, ''tis said,'
    He might die, sword in hand.

He had joined the Grecian army;
    This man of delicate frame,
And there he died in a distant land,
    And left on earth his fame.
'Lord Byron's' age was 36 years,
    Then closed the sad career,
Of the most celebrated 'Englishman'
    Of the nineteenth century.

7.   *William McGonagall* (1825?–1902) (q.v.) was, of course, a performer-poet *par excellence*. Any of his poems may be read out loud with a devastating effect on the audience. Some of his better known pieces, such as *The Famous Tay Whale*, or *The Burial of the Rev. George Gilfillan*, have found their way into anthologies, so I have chosen a less hackneyed piece, which has the added advantage of a 'Chorus' so that the whole party can join in. It is entitled, quite simply, *Glasgow*, and seldom have the tourist attractions of that most noble city been so ably depicted in verse; or indeed prose:

Beautiful city of Glasgow, with your streets so neat and clean,
Your stately mansions, and beautiful Green!
Likewise your beautiful bridges across the river Clyde,
And on your bonnie banks I would like to reside.

Chorus
Then away to the West – to the beautiful West!
To the fair city of Glasgow that I like the best,
Where the river Clyde rolls on to the sea,
And the lark and the blackbird whistle with glee.

'Tis beautiful to see ships passing to and fro,
Laden with goods for the high and the low,

So let the beautiful city of Glasgow flourish,
And may the inhabitants always find food their bodies to nourish.
Chorus

The statue of the prince of Orange is very grand,
Looking terror to the foe, with a truncheon in his hand,
And well mounted on a noble steed, which stands in Trongate,
And holding up its foreleg, I'm sure it looks first-rate.
Chorus

Then there's the Duke of Wellington's statue in Royal Exchange
    Square –
It is a beautiful statue I without fear declare,
Besides inspiring and most magnificent to view,
Because he made the French fly at the battle of Waterloo.
Chorus

And as for the statue of Sir Walter Scott that stands in George
    Square,
It is a handsome statue – few can with it compare,
And most elegant to be seen,
And close beside it stands the statue of Her Majesty the Queen.
Chorus

Then there's the statue of Robert Burns in George Square,
And the treatment he received when living was very unfair;
Now when he's dead, Scotland's sons for him do mourn,
But, alas! unto them he can never return.
Chorus

Then as for Kelvin Grove, it is most lovely to be seen
With its beautiful flowers and trees so green,
And a magnificent water-fountain spouting up very high,
Where the people can quench their thirst when they feel dry.
Chorus

Beautiful city of Glasgow, I now conclude my muse,
And to write in praise of thee my pen does not refuse;
And, without fear of contradiction, I will venture to say
You are the second grandest city in Scotland at the present day!
Chorus

8. *John Gambril Nicholson* (q.v.) (*floruit* 1890–1930) is one of the few
    bad poets to have produced a parody of another poet not quite as
    bad as himself, but still capable of engendering dismay and hilarity
    in his readers. His pastiche *The New Prospect* is annotated with the
    words: 'Mode of Isaac Watts D.D.' and irreverently reproduces the
    rhythms of the good doctor's famous hymn. The content, however,
    is startlingly different:

> There is a Pond of pure delight
>   The paidophil [*sic*] adores,
> Where boys undress in open sight
>   And bathers banish drawers.
>
> There youth may flaunt its naked pride
>   Unscathed by withering Powers –
> Conventions narrow laws divide
>   That swimming-bath from ours.
>
> And prudish pedagogues still shrink
>   To bid this garb be gone,
> With horror shivering as they think
>   Of boys 'with nothing on!'

9. *The Rev. E.E. Bradford* (1860–1944) (q.v.) has attracted so distin-
    guished a reciter as W.H. Auden, and certainly his poems would
    make for a lively performance. In his long poem *The Tree of Know-
    ledge* (1925), he deals forcefully with such matters as sin, faith, doubt
    – and, most particularly, with the role of women. Canto XI, 'Equal-
    ity', is the Reverend's answer to the 'new woman', and it is a pretty
    crushing one:

> I
>
> In a sense a bee may be
>   Equal to an elephant,
> Seeing she can certainly
>   Do a score of things he can't:
> All the same the fact remains
>   She has not his force or brains.

II

That evening when the girls and Ray
Resumed their regulated play,
The lusty lad, more lightly dressed
Rolled up his sleeves and bared his chest.
A sister served: the boy returned.
A ball came bounding back and burned,
As if red-hot, her dainty cheek.
She cried and raved. Ray did not speak,
But let the girls, like angry bees,
Swarm round and sting him at their ease;
And when they all had said their say,
He simply bowed, and strolled away.

III

'I can sting; you can't'
The bee said, 'and I'll do it.'
She stung the elephant.
He never even knew it!
But soon by chance the burly brute
In passing crushed her with his foot.

10.   *Ella Wheeler Wilcox* (1850–1919) (q.v.) wrote hardly a poem that
lacks dramatic potential. She herself read her work to the soldiers at
the Western front during the First World War, and one can imagine
she made quite an impact with her *Song of the Allies*, and especially
Come Back Clean:

This is the song for a soldier
To sing as he rides from home
To the fields afar where the battles are
Or over the ocean's foam:
'Whatever the dangers waiting
In the lands I have not seen,
If I do not fall – if I come back at all,
Then I will come back clean.

'I may lie in the mud of the trenches,
I may reek with blood and mire,
But I will control, by the God in my soul,
The might of my man's desire.
I will fight my foe in the open,
But my sword shall be sharp and keen
For the foe within who would lure me to sin,
And I will come back clean.'

11. No recitation of the verse equivalents of analgesics would be complete without a contribution from the *Rev. Cornelius Whur* (1782–1853) (q.v.). His verse was rediscovered in the 1920s by E.V. Lucas, and celebrated by Sir John Squire in his essay on *The Beauties of Badness*. The following poem is printed in *The Stuffed Owl*, but I make no apology for making it available once more to a new generation of readers:

The Female Friend

In this imperfect, gloomy scene
   Of complicated ill,
How rarely is a day serene,
   The throbbing bosom still!
Will not a beauteous landscape bright,
   Or music's soothing sound,
Console the heart, afford delight,
   And throw sweet peace around?
They may, but never comfort lend
Like an accomplished female friend!

With such a friend, the social hour
   In sweetest pleasure glides;
There is in female charms a power
   Which lastingly abides –
The fragrance of the blushing rose,
   Its tints and splendid hue,
Will with the season decompose,
   And pass as flitting dew;
On firmer ties his joys depend
Who has a polished female friend!

The pleasures which from thence arise
  Surpass the blooming flower,
For though it opens to the skies,
  It closes in an hour!
Its sweetness is of transient date,
  Its varied beauties cease –
They can no lasting joys create,
  Impart no lasting peace;
While both arise, and duly blend
In an accomplished female friend!

As orbs revolve and years recede,
  As seasons onward roll,
The fancy may on beauties feed,
  With discontented soul!
A thousand objects bright and fair
  May for a moment shine,
Yet many a sigh and many a tear
  But mark their swift decline;
While lasting joys the man attend
Who has a faithful female friend!

SELECT BIBLIOGRAPHY

PART I: *Varieties of Badness*

Chapter 1 · OUR UNFORTUNATE ENGLISH HEROES

Most of the poems referred to in this chapter are unreliable as history and unreadable as poetry. This applies to *Boadicea: A Tragedy* by Sir Coutts Lindsay (Bt.) (London, 1857), and the following efforts by Sir Richard Blackmore, the eccentric physician: *Prince Arthur – An Heroick Poem – In Ten Books* (London, 1696), *Eliza – An Epick Poem – In Ten Books* (London, 1705) and *Alfred – An Epick Poem – In Twelve Books* (London, 1723). Of the poetical rehashes of the life of Alfred, the most satisfyingly bad are: *Alfred – An Epic Poem In Six Books* by Henry James Pye (London, 1801), and *England's Darling* by Alfred Austin (London, 1896). Another poem on Alfred is a literary curiosity, the longest poem in the language, and also the one most superfluous to requirements. This is *King Alfred – A Poem* by John Fitchett, edited by Robert Roscoe, printed in London, Vols I & II in 1841, Vols III & IV in 1842.

Chapter 2 · LIMPING LAUREATES

Every thirty years or so a new book on the Poets Laureate appears. Most of these mix scholarly accounts of the origin and development of the office of Laureate with incredulous comments on the output of the incumbents. Three relatively recent books are all entertaining in their way, and do their best to maintain an air of academic decorum despite having to discuss such poets as Eusden, Pye and Austin. In order of publication they are: *The Laureateship* by Edmund K. Broadus (Oxford, 1921), *The Poets Laureate* by Kenneth Hopkins (London, 1954) and *Poets By Appointment* by Nick Russell (Blandford, 1981). So far as I am aware, no publisher has been reckless enough to undertake an anthology of laureate productions.

Chapter 3 · OLEAGINOUS ODES AND ECCENTRIC ELEGIES

Connoisseurs of sycophancy will not want to miss William Watson's poem *The Three Alfreds*, nor his eponymous puffery of Lloyd George in his volume *The Man Who Saw* (London, 1917). A biography of the poet came out in 1982 (*I Was An English Poet: A Biography of Sir William Watson* by Jean Moorcroft Wilson). 'The oddest puzzle presented by this book', said Marghanita Laski in *The Spectator*, 'is why Jean Wilson . . . chose this subject for what is apparently her first work. It is not as if Watson was, apart from his poetry, a likeable or even an interesting man.'

Kennedy ephemera is hard to come by, but an acerbic account of it will be found in Malcolm Muggeridge's *Tread Softly, For You Tread On My Jokes* (London, 1966). It is well worth tracking down *¡Viva Che! Contributions in tribute to Ernesto 'Che' Guevara* edited by Marianne Alexandre (London, 1968); each contribution mingles bathos with cant in about equal proportions. The assiduous collector of awful tributes will also want to have *Lilibet* by *A Loyal Subject of Her Majesty, An account in verse of the early years of the Queen until the time of her accession* (London, 1984); and *Victoria The Good* by Christopher Tower (London, 1982). Sir John Squire has a genial study of the art of writing undeserved eulogy in his 'Charles II in English Verse' (*Life At The Mermaid and other Essays*, Glasgow, 1927).

Inept elegies are, of course, a recurring phenomenon of the literary scene. Christopher Adams has been assiduous in collecting spectacularly grotesque ones in *The Worst English Poets* (London, 1958). Wordsworth and Dr Isaac Watts have made some memorable contributions to the genre, but the most persistent elegy monger is surely Marion Albina Bigelow, whose collection of graveside platitudes *The Northern Harp* was published in New York in 1853.

Chapter 4 · THE DIDACTIC MUSE

Joshua Sylvester's *Tobacco Battered and The Pipes Shattered (About the Ears, that idl'y Idolize so base and barbarous a Weed or at least-wise over-love so loathsome Vanity)* (London, 1672) makes lively reading, and so, in parts, does *Syphilis or A Poetical History of the French Disease Written in Latin by Fracastorius and now attempted in English by N. Tate* (London, 1686). A modern translation with an informative introduction is *Fracastor – Syphilis or the French Disease – A Poem in Latin Hex-*

ameters by Girolamo Fracastoro, with Translation, Notes and Appendix by Heneage Wynne-Finch (London, 1935). John Armstrong's *The Art of Preserving Health* (London, 1774) is a sort of Gayelord Hauser tract, but lacking that gentleman's *joie de vivre*; Armstrong's exhortations have more to do with enduring life than enjoying it. The physician poet expected little in the way of literary recognition, and his pessimism proved to be amply justified. Probably the most eccentric, and certain the most engaging, didactic poem in English is Solyman Brown's *Dentologia – A Poem On The Diseases of the Teeth And Their Proper Remedies with Notes, practical, historical, illustrative and explanatory by Eleazar Parmly*, Dentist (New York, 1833). Anyone who neglected cleaning their teeth before reading this would be unlikely to do so afterwards. Brown is also the author of *Dental Hygeia – A Poem* (1838) which is dedicated, perhaps significantly, to his brother, and *Cholera King* (1842) which suggests a marked broadening of his literary and medical interests.

James Grainger's *The Sugar Cane* (1764) contains moments of unalloyed bliss, when the author warbles elegantly about muckspreading; but for the most part it is impenetrable to the modern reader, as indeed it was to Grainger's contemporaries. Grainger described himself quaintly as 'a ruptured poet lost in holy trance', but although one may feel sympathetic towards the poet's ailments, it is hardly a justification for inflicting *The Sugar Cane* on the public.

The steam-engine caused such widespread and justified wonder when it was first introduced that naturally the poets were infected with the general enthusiasm. The resultant poetry, while it contributes nothing to either literature or science, may well please those with a taste for the grotesque. Anna Seward dealt with the subject in her inimitably uninspired way, and Dr Erasmus Darwin was early apprised of the poetic potential of steam, with what results may be seen from *The Economy of Vegetation* (Lichfield, 1792). The Laureate of steam is of course Thomas Baker, whose *The Steam Engine – or the Powers of Flame – An Original Poem in Ten Cantos* appeared in 1857 in London.

There was a lot of temperance poetry, especially in America, in the nineteenth century. Apart from Ella Wheeler Wilcox's *Drops of Water* (London, 1874), which was wholly devoted to the theme, many other poets included a token temperance tract in their collections. Some of these are justly famous, like *The Lips That Touch*

Liquor shall never Touch Mine by Harriet A. Glazebrook, or the Great
McGonagall's castigation of *The Demon Drink* (in his *Last Poetic
Gems*, Dundee 1902). *The Poems of M'Donald Clarke* (New York,
1836) contain blasts against alcohol, and Roswell Rice, 'The American Orator and Poet', in his *Collection of Poems and Acrostics* uses the
drink theme to attack some editor who was unaccountably indifferent to the poet's literary achievements:

> . . . Nature's own dwarf, seeking a poet's crown
> Whose eyes are bloodshot with the sparkling glass . . .

Chapter 5 · RHYMING RELIGION AND HUMOROUS HYMNOLOGY

Apart from various charming examples of over-enthusiasm
recorded in *The Stuffed Owl* by D.B. Wyndham Lewis and Charles
Lee (London, 1930), the interested reader is referred to *The Poetical
Works of Isaac Watts D.D. Collated with the best editions by Thomas Park
Esq., F.S.A. In two volumes* (London, 1807). Dr Watts seems aware
that hymns are sometimes considered the poor relations of poetry
(and of music, for that matter) when he writes plaintively:

> Why should the trumpet's brazen voice,
> Or oaten reed, awake my joys,
> And yet my heart so stupid lie, when sacred hymns begin?

But he did his best to remedy the situation. In common with other
religious poetasters, he exploited the doctrinal potential of death at
every opportunity:

> Swift as the sun revolves the day,
> We hasten to the dead;
> Slaves to the wind we puff away,
> And to the ground we tread.
> 'Tis air that lends us life, when first
> The vital bellows heave . . .

The Rev. Patrick Brontë's effort, *The Phenomenon or An Account
In Verse of the Extraordinary Disruption of a Bog which took place in the
Moors of Haworth, 12th September, 1824* (Bradford, 1824), may be
skipped by all except the most diligent collectors of disingenuous

banalities, and his other poems may be encountered in some of the earlier editions of the Brontës' works. Robert Montgomery's *The Omnipresence of the Deity* (1828) is not half as entertaining as Macaulay's lambasting of it in *The Edinburgh Review* of April 1830. (See any edition of the *Essays* of Thomas Babington Macaulay.)

The aggressive side of religious writing is most apparent in the seventeenth century – not surprisingly for a period of such political and religious turmoil. Nicholas Brady and Nahum Tate did *An Essay of a New Version of the Psalms* (London, 1696) which is lively in parts, as is also the oeuvre of George Wither, particularly *Hallelujah, or Britain's Second Remembrancer* (London, 1641). *The Minor Poems of Joseph Beaumont D.D. 1616–1699 Edited from an autograph Ms. by Eloise Robinson* (London, 1914) contains some passages where the opposition is heavily shelled, e.g. in *Unreasonable Reason*. In *Books in General* (Second Series) (London, N/D) Sir John Squire has some interesting examples of Delphic utterances from Joanna Southcott and others (in his essay *Humorous Hymnology*). A not untypical quotation is:

> And so the bread is on the waters cast
> And like thy uncle now the Jews will burst.

Chapter 6 · EROS AND BATHOS

Mr Craig Raine's poem on his friend's arsehole was published in *The New Statesman* in the second week of April 1983. Readers interested in other poems about arseholes could do worse than consult *The Penguin Book of Homosexual Verse* edited by Stephen Coote (London, 1983). 'Stephen Coote', remarked Peter Levi reviewing the book in *The Spectator*, 'must be a pseudonym, surely a don; he has so little sense of good and bad in poetry, he is probably an English don.' The collection as a whole he described trenchantly as 'the most vulgar sentimentality, interspersed with the dribble of lechery'.

There is a good deal of information about Edward Jerningham in *The Stuffed Owl*. He was apparently very prolific and very unsuccessful. Stanley Savill's *Songs By The Way* was published in 1891, and remained justifiably unremarked until Mr Adams resurrected it for his anthology. Thomas Holley Chivers' description of budding and blossoming breasts may be found in *Virginalia, or Songs of my Summer Nights, A Gift of Love for the Beautiful* (Philadelphia, 1853). Alfred Lord Tennyson's peep down the décolletage of Rose occurs in *The Gardener's Daughter* written between 1832 and 1834 and published in the *Poems* of 1842. Alfred Austin's notably unmoving *The Human Tragedy* was published in 1862. George Meredith's *With the Persuader* can be enjoyed in the collected *Poems of George Meredith*, edited by Phyllis B. Bartlett (2 vols, London, 1977).

There are many volumes of astonishing verse by Francis Saltus Saltus. *Dolce Far Niente* comes from *Dreams After Sunset* (Buffalo, 1890). The first-mentioned volume has perhaps the greater number of arresting lines, e.g.:

> Her laugh is like sunshine, full of glee,
> And her sweet breath smells like fresh-made tea.

John Gray is best known for the exquisitely produced *Silverpoints* (London, 1893) containing twenty-nine poems between green and powdered gold covers. He was surely a better poet than his nineties confrere Richard Le Gallienne, who mocked Gray in his review of the curious little volume. Le Gallienne's own *Beauty Accurst* would make a marvellous recitation piece – it should be read with a completely straight face to an audience not previously prepared for it – and appears in his *English Poems* (London, 1900). His staggering larks and flowers with bodices occur in a poem entitled *An Impression* in the volume *R.L.S. An Elegy* (1895).

There are, of course, numerous editions of Tennyson's *The Idylls of the King*, but a little more energy is required to hunt down Coventry Patmore's *The Angel In The House* (1854–62), whose tepid piety is just the tonic required for a damp and dreary Sunday afternoon in winter. *The Promise of May*, Tennyson's shocking exposé of passion and betrayal apparently set in Ambridge, was produced in 1882 and appeared in *Locksley Hall Sixty Years After* (1886). A complete edition of *The Poems*, edited by Christopher Ricks, appeared in 1969. *Jane Hollybrand and Other Original Poems by Edward Edwin Foot (Edited and Illustrated by James Thorpe)* appeared in 1932, and is well worth acquiring. The illustrations exactly capture the poem's atmosphere of prim romance and unctuous snobbery. Percy Goddard Stone's *Cupid and Euphrosyne* appears in a highly enjoyable *Anthology of Vectensian Poets* (Newport, 1922). An unexpected bonus of this collection are the photographic portraits of the authors opposite their work. Percy is a handsome fellow wearing a trilby, who looks as if he has just come in from a day's racing. Perhaps he does not strike us as so poetical in aspect as his fellow Vectensian Mary Gleed Tuttlet, but he is better looking than Percy Scott-Jackson, who has eyes like Boris Karloff and an alarming sneer. It is astonishing that such a small area as the Isle of Wight should have produced such a quantity of irredeemably bad poetry, and we must all feel ourselves in debt to the editor, Charles Arnell, for diligently collecting so much of it.

Chapter 7 · IF NO TALENT, JOIN A MOVEMENT

For a dry-eyed account of the lachrymose Della Cruscans see John Mark Longaker – *The Della Cruscans and William Gifford – The History of a Minor Movement in an Age of Literary Transition* (Philadelphia, 1924). *The British Album* Vols I and II (London, 1790) contains the most comprehensive selection of their effusions, and it certainly does not repay study. Gifford's *The Baviad* (London, 1794) and *The Maeviad* (London, 1795) are, at this distance, not too entertaining, since his targets were so pathetically insubstantial. The assiduous reader will, however, find the occasional brilliant example of Gifford's aptly named 'sledge-hammer style' in them.

The Spasmodics are excellently covered in Mark A. Weinstein's *William Edmonstoune Aytoun and the Spasmodic Controversy* (New Haven and London, 1968) in which an unwise British attempt at *Sturm und Drang* is handled with exquisite tact. *Festus – A Poem* by Philip James Bailey was published in a Fiftieth Anniversary Edition (40,000 lines, 785 pages) by Routledge in 1889. Sydney Dobell's *Balder* (Part the First) appeared in 1854; Part the Second was never written and readers will not feel the lack of it. *Firmilian or the Student of Badajoz* (1854) was a spoof by William Aytoun. At the end of a truculent Preface Jones (the supposed author) makes a remark in keeping with Spasmodic pretensions: 'I am not arrogant enough to assert that this is the finest poem which the age has produced; but I shall be very much obliged to any gentleman who can make me acquainted with a better.'

THE JOY OF BAD VERSE

Chapter 8 · A NOTE ON NOMENCLATURE

Browsers in *The Collected Poems of Wordsworth*, Edited by John Hayden (2 vols, London, 1977) will find various examples of the bard's uncompromising attitude towards nomenclature in his poetry. The *Poems On Various Subjects, Entertaining, Elegiac and Religious* by Miss Jane Cave were published by subscription at Winchester in 1783. These ponderous and singularly inappropriate tributes strike me as irredeemably authentic, but she was evidently accused of favouring the Princess Michael approach to literary composition. At any rate one is surprised to stumble upon an indignant *Poem Occasioned by A Lady's Doubting Whether The Author Composed an Elegy to which her Name is Affix'd*. I have not studied the whole oeuvre of the 'Poet Close', which would be an imposition greater than the human frame can stand, but readers interested in him will find that he is knowledgeably dealt with in *The Stuffed Owl* by D.B. Wyndham Lewis and Charles Lee.

Of our two German swans, the Silesian one is written up in *Frederike Kempner, der schlesische Schwan, herausgegeben mit einem Essay von. C.H. Mostar* (1953, 1974); and the other one has been featured in several volumes, one of which is her incredible *Tagebuch*. Some of her most fatuous addresses may be found in *Wenn ich liebe seh ich Sterne − Gedichte der Julie Schrader* (Munich, 1971). For details of Mary Robinson readers are again referred to *The Stuffed Owl*, and for details of American sobriquets to *The Almanac of American Letters* by Randy F. Nelson (Los Altos, 1981). The hidden penchant of Eugene Field for off-colour literary production is revealed in *The Erotic in Literature* by David Loth (London, 1962). A delightful book by Rayner Unwin *The Rural Muse* (London, 1954) deals with such literary phenomena as Stephen Duck, 'The Thresher Poet', Henry Jones, 'The Bricklayer Poet' and others of the same kidney. The most enterprising seems to have been John Taylor, 'The Water Poet', who attempted to sail down the Thames in a paper boat with two dried fish fastened to canes in place of oars. This was certainly an original feat, but one wonders if it was worth doing in an age that had not yet invented *The Guinness Book of Records*.

The Autumn Anthology (London, 1930) appears to have been a vanity publication, drawing material from as far afield as the Argentine, India, and the Isle of Man. It describes itself as 'A compilation of representative verse from the world's living poets'. I cannot speak for the one poem printed in Swedish, but if this is a representative sample of the world's living poets, then poetry in 1930 was at a pretty low ebb.

PART II: *The Best of the Worst*

Chapter 9 · MARGARET CAVENDISH, DUCHESS OF NEWCASTLE

The general flavour of her work is provided by her *Poems and Fancies* (with the emphasis on 'fancies') written by the *Rt. Hon. The Lady Newcastle* (London, 1653). Horace Walpole has some amusing things to say about her in *Royal and Noble Authors* (London, 1758). 'One of her poems,' says *Everyman's Dictionary of Literary Biography*, '*The Pastimes and Recreations of the Queen of Fairies in Fairyland*, has some good lines.'

Chapter 10 · THE REVEREND CORNELIUS WHUR

A trip to the British Museum is required for the perusal of the works of Cornelius Whur. His perfect assimilation of platitude and thorough distillation of moral complacency are exhibited in the two volumes he gave to the world: *Village Musings – On Moral and Religious Subjects* (Norwich, 1837) and *Gratitude's Offering, Being Original Productions On A Variety of Subjects* (Norwich, 1845).

Chapter 11 · MARTIN TUPPER

There were four series of Tupper's dreadful *Proverbial Philosophy* published in 1838, 1842, 1867 and 1876. This work is written, as Dr Brewer's Dictionary puts it, in 'a sort of verse'. In 1850 Tupper contributed his mite to the persecution of King Alfred by the poetasters with his translation of Alfred's poems into modern English. And in 1858 he followed up with a drama entitled *Alfred: A Patriotic Play In Five Acts*. His compilation of themes for books he did not have time to write appeared in 1841 as *An Author's Mind*; and *My Life As An Author* was offered to a by now less infatuated public in 1886.

There is a cheerfully rude study of Tupper by Patrick Scott in Volume 32 of *The Dictionary of Literary Biography – Victorian Poets Before 1850*, edited by William E. Fredeman and Ira B. Nadel

(Detroit, 1984). He gives the biographical background and the genesis of *Proverbial Philosophy* very well, and adds some irresistible quotations, e.g.:

> . . . the wearied spirit lieth as a fainting maiden
> Captive and borne away on the warrior's foam-covered
>   steed
> And sinketh down wounded as a gladiator on the sand,
> While the keen falchion [*sic*] of Intellect is cutting through
>   the scabbard of the brain.

Various writers have dealt with Tupper as an expression of Victorian middle-class culture, of which the most specialized is Ralf Buchman's *Martin F. Tupper and the Victorian Middle Class Mind* (Bern, 1941). Derek Hudson is the author of a biography entitled *Martin Tupper: His Rise and Fall* (London, 1949). It is really surprising that there is so much literature on Tupper, since all the books seem to agree that he was an unimaginable bore as a man and worthless as a writer. For these two qualities is he famous.

Chapter 12 · WILLIAM McGONAGALL

McGonagall – A Library Omnibus (London, 1980) contains all the known poems of 'The Scottish Homer'. However, an added bonus of some of the earlier editions, e.g. *Poetic Gems Selected From The Works of William McGonagall, Poet and Tragedian* (Dundee and London, 1934) are the extended reminiscences, the recommendations, and the 'tribute to Mr M'Gonagall from Three Students at Glasgow University'. The students sent him a questionnaire which included such innocent enquiries as: 'Is the most intellectual benefit to be derived from a study of the M'Gonagallian or Shakespearian school of poetry?'; and: 'What chances do you consider we have in knocking out Tennyson as Poet Laureate?'; and: 'If we should resolve going to Balmoral (to visit the Queen as a patron of poetry), which route would you recommend? Also, name any "models" that may be known to you in that direction; stating landlady's name, and if married or single.'

Chapter 13 · JOSEPH GWYER

The first collection issued by the inimitable Gwyer seems to be the undated *Sketches of the Life of Joseph Gwyer (Potato Salesman) With His Poems (Commended by Royalty). Published by the Author J. Gwyer, Ivy Cottage, Penge, and can be had of all booksellers.* A bumper edition of Gwyeriana was issued in London in 1895: *Poems And Prose by Joseph Gwyer with a short Autobiography and Anecdotes of and Personal Interviews with the Late Rev. C.H. Spurgeon and others.* The binding is gold-stamped with the legend 'Commended by Royalty'. This is a handsome volume and contains a photographic portrait of the author revealing him as an innocent-looking bald-headed gentleman with a dense beard. There are seventy-two pages of advertisements at the end of the book, including some for Temperance Hotels and one for Kops Non-Alcoholic Ale and Stout. This is described as the 'finest non-intoxicant in the world'. These advertisements no doubt helped to defray the costs of publication.

Chapter 14 · ALFRED AUSTIN

Austin's output was substantial but nobody has ever seen the need for a 'Collected Edition'. His terrible verse dramas are probably the most entertaining part of his oeuvre, and if anyone should ever hold a season of unactable plays, Austin's work should come into its own. His play about King Alfred has already been mentioned; but *Fortunatus The Pessimist* (London, 1892), *The Tower of Babel* (London, 1890) and *Prince Lucifer* (London, 1887) are good examples of Austin doing his best to load every rift with dross.

In 1911 the poet issued his *Autobiography*, which brought new refinements to the art of self-esteem. There is an excellent critical biography by Norton B. Crowell – *Alfred Austin – Victorian* (Albuquerque, 1953) which is more merciful than the pontifical little egoist had any right to expect.

Chapter 15 · JOAQUIN MILLER

The Poetical Works of Joaquin Miller (New York and London, 1923) is edited by Stuart P. Sherman. Miller wrote several autobiographical books in the manner of Lillian Hellman, i.e. with the facts embellished to show him in a suitably heroic light. Read simply as adventure stories, these are entertaining, particularly *Memorie and Rime* (1884) which describes his visits to England.

There is a thorough literary biography by Martin Severin Peterson – *Joaquin Miller, Literary Frontiersman* (Stanford and Oxford, 1937) and a genial exposé by M.M. Marberry – *Splendid Poseur – The Story of a Fabulous Humbug* (London, 1954). Mr Marberry remarks in a characteristic aside that Miller's 'Autobiography' is indexed in many American libraries under 'fiction'. Also that the only favourable review of Miller's novel, *The One Fair Woman*, appeared pseudonymously in the Providence *Press* – necessarily so, for it was written by Miller himself.

Chapter 16 · JULIA A. MOORE

Mrs Moore's second selection is the one to go for, as it contains a generous quantity of the reviews of her first volume. It is a moot point whether these reviews are not more entertaining than the poems themselves, for Julia had a knack of provoking her critics to their highest flights of rhetoric. 'The cover of this first volume from Julia's pen,' writes the *Rome Sentinel*, 'is ornamented with a picture of her lovely face. The lineaments are those of a well balanced person, and the possessor of strength of great resources. Greatly as Julia would shine in the social circle, the grandeur of her character, we think, would be best appreciated by those who could behold her as the shades of night gather on, in the sanctity of her own woodshed, with dull but tried and faithful ax attacking the unregenerate hemlock slab, and shattering the stubborn knot into kindling wood.' This, and other eloquent tributes, may be found in *The Sweet Singer of Michigan – Later Poems of Julia A. Moore, together with Reviews, Commendatory Notices Etc., Etc., of her Sentimental Song Book* (Grand Rapids, 1878). There is a later edition of *Poems by Mrs Julia A. Moore, Edited and with an Introduction by Walter Blair* (Chicago, 1928). Mark Twain's comments about her occur in Chapters VIII and XXXVI of *Following The Equator*. He describes how a shipboard companion who wrote lyrics about kangaroos put him in mind of the Michigan poetess.

Chapter 17 · ELLA WHEELER WILCOX

An act of homage to the poetess was carried out by the London publisher who produced in 1971 *The Best of Ella Wheeler Wilcox, Edited by Lalique, Lady L'Endell.* It contains her best-known and most punchy poems such as *Come Back Clean* and *Settle The Question Right.* Her temperance propaganda is to be found in *Drops of Water* (London, 1874). Enthusiasts may want to seek out *The Collected Poems of Ella Wheeler Wilcox* (3 vols, London, 1917).

In her capacity as self-appointed and much respected agony aunt she published *A Woman of the World – An American Woman's Counsel to Other People's Sons and Daughters* (London, 1905), which exhibits her personality at its most trenchant and uncompromising. Her own life is covered in *The Story of a Literary Career* (Massachusetts, 1905) which was written in deference to the demands of her fans. There is a very penetrating study of her by Naomi Lewis in *A Visit to Mrs Wilcox and Other Essays* (London, 1957). She concludes: 'If we find her at her best when she is at her worst, this is the inevitable fate of a bard of Mrs Wilcox's capacity, unhaunted by the sad anxieties of taste, the pains of critical doubt.'

Chapter 18 · AMANDA McKITTRICK ROS

Her two slim volumes of verse are *Poems of Puncture* (Belfast, 1932) and *Fumes of Formation* (Belfast, 1933). Her opinions of the critics are collected in *Bayonets of Bastard Sheen* (London, privately printed, 1949). These opinions are not flattering.

An amusing biography was written by Jack Loudan, *O Rare Amanda! The Life of Amanda McKittrick Ros* (London, 1954). Aldous Huxley's study, *Euphues Redivivus*, which also deals with her incredible novels, appeared in *On The Margin* (London, 1923). He hails her as a latter day 'Euphuist', disastrously seduced by the sounds of words, and enthralled by her own entirely erroneous notions about the nature of 'art'. Her self-confidence, like her ignorance, was invincible.

Chapter 19 · J. GORDON COOGLER

There is a photographic reproduction of the bard's *Purely Original Verse with Original Reviews and a Biographical Sketch* (Columbia, 1974) edited by Claude Henry Neuffer and Rene La Borde. This was originally published and printed by Coogler himself in 1897. Coogler, together with Julia A. Moore and other literary outsiders, are discussed in Edmund Pearson's *Queer Books* (London, 1929). He remarks percipiently that: 'To become famous for queer poetry it is necessary to have a combination of unusual qualities. There must be an absolute inability to know what is ridiculous; absence of the sense of humour must be congenital. Great seriousness of purpose must exist, together with a persistent itch for literary fame. But all these will avail nothing, unless the poet has, in addition, a diabolical aptitude for the wrong word in the wrong place at the wrong time.'

Chapter 20 · JOHN GAMBRIL NICHOLSON

The curious volumes of Nicholson's homoerotic verse were mostly published privately, except for *Love In Earnest* (London, 1892) where the general tendency of the verses is suitably camouflaged. Then came *A Chaplet of Southernwood* – a Limited Edition issued by Harpur and Murray of the Moray Press, Derby 'from Plants grown by John Gambril Nicholson and offered to Collectors by Frank Murray at his Country House "Leidernot", Ashover, Derbyshire on May Day 1896. Large Chaplet 6s 3d, Small Chaplet 3s 3d.' *A Garland of Ladslove*, the most frank of his productions, appeared in 1911 and records a lengthy love affair with the irresistible 'Victor'.

Nicholson's schoolboy novel, *The Romance of a Choirboy*, innocuous despite its title, was privately printed in London in 1916; and another novel, *In Carrington's Duty-Week – A Private School Episode* found a commercial London publisher in 1892. This is a curious hybrid of a book combining elements of Ian Hay and Frank Richards. The later novel retains these hearty schoolboy ingredients but adds a good deal of pseudo-erotic heart-flutter.

Chapter 21 · THE REVEREND EDWIN EMMANUEL BRADFORD

So far as the Rev. Bradford's output is concerned, there is an embarrassment of riches to choose from. Almost all of his fifteen or so volumes printed between 1907 and 1930 yield nuggets of pure gold. *The Tree of Knowledge* (London, 1925) is perhaps especially up to date, as it deals with feminism in the Reverend's usual no-nonsense manner. *Passing The Love of Women* (London, 1913) contains many of his most infectiously enthusiastic celebrations of handsome boys, while *In Quest of Love and Other Poems* (London, 1914) shows us the poet at his most uninhibitedly sensual.

The Nicholson–Bradford–Tuke proclivities, and indeed the whole topic of suppressed homosexuality in our great public schools, is dealt with amusingly in Jonathan Gathorne-Hardy's *The Public School Phenomenon* (London, 1977). 'I sometimes think', remarks the author, 'that the very siting of their public schools had something to do with Victorian sex panic. At Roedean you're blown flat on your face . . .'

Chapter 22 · WILLIAM NATHAN STEDMAN

Stedman's Sonnets: Lays and Lyrics (Sydney, 1911) is a crackerjack collection with an extravagant dedication to 'Queen Marie' (Corelli) and a supporting quote from one of the author's mad sonnets:

> To thee my love alone, my song is sung,
> Which makes it sacred on the world's long tongue . . .

1912 saw the publication of *What Might Have Been – Ballads and Poems for Reading and Reciting*, also published in Sydney. This selection, so the author tells us, comprises those items that have 'gone well' in his own renditions, and he thoughtfully appends some advice for tyro performers on how to get the best out of them. 1916 saw the poet back in the country of his birth, and *Sky Blue Ballads* were first exposed to the public in Finchley; it is intimated that the educated inhabitants of Mrs Thatcher's future constituency received them well.

By far the most violent of Stedman's productions is his *Lays and Lyrics Addressed to Queen Marie* (Sydney, 1911) with a subtitle: *My Lance against the World for its Greatest Lady. Any Man, Beast or Buffoon Want SMASHING?* From first to last these poems, interspersed with maniacal threats and denunciations, are completely unhinged.

Chapter 23 · WILHELMINA STITCH

Typical of the Stitch genre is *Garnered Gleanings* (London, 1933) which contains such uplifting verses as *Don't Fret, Indigestion*, and *Thoughts Before Shopping*. There are several other volumes in much the same mode. For those who could not be without their Stitches wherever they were, Messrs Methuen and Co. produced in 1934 the *Wilhelmina Stitch Booklets*, six in all, with titles like *A Heap o' Folk*, *Friendly Things*, and *Beacons In The Night*. In 1933 also appeared the wittily titled *A Triple Stitch* consisting of *Silken Threads*, *Silver Linings*, and *The Gold Web*. 'Start the Day with Stitch' would be a good publisher's slogan. Bleary-eyed and hung over, one's whole mood could be transformed if one began reading over the bacon and eggs such lines as: 'Blessed are they who are pleasant to live with. Blessed are they who sing in the morning, whose faces have smiles for their early adorning.'

GENERAL WORKS AND ANTHOLOGIES

There are all too few studies in depth of the worst poetry ever written, and far too many studies of the best. One of the first category that is both entertaining and useful is *By-Ways Round Helicon* by Lolo Williams (London, 1922), though perhaps not all the verse quoted is absolutely as bad as it should be. I owe to Mr Williams the information that the Rev. Samuel Wesley produced his *Maggots, or Poems on Several Subjects never before Handled* in 1685. 'Those that allow of no second-rate in that Art (of Poetry), have endeavoured to lessen his reputation', said Mr Dunton, Wesley's publisher, but goes on to say that he was also much celebrated. So he should have been, if only for his heroism in tackling such subjects, in his inimitably jocular manner, as *A Cow's Tail* or *Three Skipps of a Louse*. There is much similarly fascinating material in Mr Williams' book.

A very thorough coverage of American late nineteenth-century poetasters is C.T. Kindilien's *American Poetry in the Eighteen-Nineties* (Providence, Rhode Island, 1956). Drawing on the enormous Brown University collection of amateur authors' slim volumes, Kindilien illuminates the poets and their subject matter, casting a suitably cold eye upon their endeavours. He assembles a typical volume in terms of the obligatory themes and predictable titles. Above all, he demonstrates that these writers were no shrinking violets; as he remarks: 'Now flippant, and defiant, again humble and sincere – always ambitious – the typical versifier of the Nineties approached his work with manifold attitudes. Poetry for these bankers and farmers and physicians was no mysterious goddess to be worshipped from afar. While many of them conventionally disparaged their efforts in launching a new 'bark upon the sea of literature' (how often this phrase begins a preface), few had any doubts that their contributions were important.

There are two anthologies dedicated solely to bad verse. The first of these is *The Worst English Poets* by Christopher Adams (London, 1958), who confines himself to the unknown eccentrics. The selection is coruscating and Mr Adams' notes on the poets are models of editorial restraint. The second is something of a cult book and has been in print for over half a century – *The Stuffed Owl – An Anthology of Bad Verse* by D.B. Wyndham Lewis and Charles Lee (London, 1978). This is a conscientious record of the very best bad verse by the very best practitioners of it. Although it is perhaps not an anthology that the featured authors would have struggled to get into, their shades may be grateful that the book has assured them of immortality.

Lovers of Victorian kitsch will also want to have on their shelves Michael Turner's *Parlour Poetry – 101 Improving Gems* (London, 1967), an unputdownable selection of such immortal and educative verses as Rose Hartwick Thorpe's *Curfew Must Not Ring Tonight*, Lydia Howard Sigourney's *The Mother's Sacrifice*, Mrs Hemans' *Casabianca*, and Thomas Haynes Bayly's *Oh No! We Never Mention Her*. This is the kind of book for which many of us have a secret passion; when the cultural snobs have left, we remove the Shostakovich from the record-player and put on the Tammy Wynette; then we slip the latest Bruce Chatwin and John Ashbery's poems back into the bookshelf, and settle down with Eliza Cook, Sir Henry Newbolt and Ethel Lynn Beers.

NAME INDEX